KATHARINA SCHLEGL-KOFLER

The Complete Guide to
DOG TRAINING

► User-friendly, authoritative reference work
► Field-tested training sytems and activities
► Instant answers: Quickfinder from A to Z

BARRON'S

KATHARINA SCHLEGL-KOFLER

The Complete Guide to

DOG TRAINING

Photos by Christine Steimer

Contents

1 The Basics of Dog Training

2 On Familiar Terms with Your Dog

Basic Training—Learning for Life

3

Training with "Advanced" Dogs

4

5 Out in Public with Your Dog

6 Meaningful Play and Activity

Solving Problems, Mastering Specific Situations

Dog Information from A to Z

Foreword

Dogs are born to be friends with humans— enjoy this gift!

Dear Readers,

As is generally known, the dog is considered man's best friend, and for this reason is one of the most popular pets in the world. Nearly four in ten households in the United States own at least one dog, and there are good reasons for this. We value the dog's positive qualities, such as loyalty and an unfailingly good mood. Our four-legged friend is simply a beloved and versatile companion. Whether serving as a faithful playmate, a comforter in many life situations, or a fitness coach—a dog's presence is always beneficial and enriches our lives in multiple ways. The positive effect of a dog on body and soul has now been scientifically proven.

Human and dog—the two have worked together as a good team for a long time. The dog is a pack animal requiring more than daily meals and a place to sleep for happiness. The dog needs to keep body and mind occupied, and needs a role model to lead the way. This position, which an owner fills for a pet, is more important today than ever before. Big city noise, crowds of people, showing good manners in the park or dog run, riding in an elevator—a dog has to cope with all these sets of circumstances. Not an easy challenge! So it is crucial to make your pet familiar with these situations and demonstrate how to behave. Dealing with everyday life together as successfully as possible is the goal of your dog's training. Doing so will make life easier both for you and your four-legged friend.

Intense involvement with your dog should begin even before the day of purchase. Each breed has its own special traits and quirks—will the dog you want fit in with your lifestyle? Once the dog finally is yours, the training process begins the day he or she joins your household. Now it is important to know something about theory. How does a dog actually learn? What kinds of commands does he or she react to? What roles do word choice, tone of voice, and body language play in this? How can I understand my dog better? It's time to find a common language, so that mutual trust can develop quickly, building the basis for the life you share. Then, living with your four-legged friend will bring you great enjoyment and happiness.

I wish you great success in the training process and a wonderful time with your dog!

Katharina Schlegl-Kofler

The Basics of Dog Training

▶ Training a dog—it sounds quite easy, really. But before you begin, there are a number of questions you need to ask. What kind of dog fits into my life? Where do I find the right dog? How does a dog "think" and learn, and what are the stages in its development? It's crucial for you to become familiar with your dog's developmental phases, since puppyhood is a good time to steer many things in the right direction. This chapter will tell you everything you need to know about your new companion's development and training. Equipped with this know-how, you and your dog can easily become a dream team.

1

Dream Team:
Dog and Human

The dog has always been a valuable partner for humans, guarding the farmyard, assisting with hunting, controlling flocks and herds, and even carrying loads.

AT FIRST, DOGS were bred to be especially well suited for a certain purpose. Gradually, appearance also came to play a role in breeding. Breed standards were established, and breed and kennel clubs founded worldwide. As a result, there are about 400 dog breeds in existence today.

Over time, the dog became an "unemployed" companion for humans. This category was once restricted to the smaller toy breeds such as the Maltese, Pekingese, and Havanese, but today, at least in our culture, most breeds serve exclusively as companion dogs—regardless of whether they are suited for this use.

Why Training Is Important

Today's dogs serve principally as companions in our daily life and recreational activities and share their lives closely with humans. There is really no other pet that forms such a close bond with a human, sees him or her as a true social partner, and can adapt to all possible circumstances of human life. In their ability to communicate with humans, dogs are undoubtedly superior to all other household pets.

Though very distinct differences developed between wolves and dogs in the course of the ● DOMESTICATION process (page 262), their behaviors still show many similarities. For starters, both wolves and dogs are oriented toward life in a social unit. It is this characteristic that makes the close association between a dog and a human possible. A wolf pack is not an unorganized "cluster," but a unit usually under the leadership of two dominant animals, an experienced mated pair. Intense loyalties among the pack members, strict rules of coexistence, and teaching of the juveniles by the experienced older individuals contribute heavily toward ensuring the pack's survival.

In many ways, our domestic dog behaves throughout his life like a young wolf. In part, this why he displays constant affability and a great willingness to fit into the human "pack." But the dog needs an "alpha leader" to show him, in an appropriate way, what rules apply to their life together.

Unlike most other domestic animals and pets, the dog does not live in a cage, but is free to accompany us almost everywhere. Thus, it is quite clear that a dog must learn not to walk on tables and seats, not to help himself to our food, and not to misuse rugs, furniture, and the like as chew toys. In addition, he must not go out and about on his own, jump up on everybody he meets, or regard every stranger as an "enemy." A dog that is well integrated into the pack can stay alone for several hours without summoning the entire neighborhood with his howling, or tearing the house apart. Moreover, he will obey certain commands—and not only when he happens to be in the mood.

Problem-free coexistence is possible only when these and many other things, which I address in the section starting on page 72, are under control. Since your four-legged friend, as you now know, has a natural willingness to accept rules, training represents nothing negative or even contrary to canine nature, but really seems quite normal to the dog. In fact, it's

1

▶ INFO

Educational Counseling for Dogs

If you need help with the training process, you can get in touch with dog training schools or clubs. "Titles" such as trainer, dog whisperer, and pet psychologist tell you little, however, since there is no officially recognized professional education in this field.

important and necessary, since a rule that provides guidance will give your pet a sense of security and confidence. Species-appropriate training, however, also means never forgetting that your dog is a dog. Viewing your canine as a child or partner substitute, or as a "cuddly toy" can lead to problems in training, since the dog's interpretation of many things differs from ours.

How Much Obedience Do You Need?

Here people's opinions frequently differ. One reason for this could be that everybody interprets "obedience" differently. Many people

▷

Once you've trained your four-legged companion systematically and thoroughly and familiarized it with environmental stimuli, the dog can easily go with you anywhere, even in busier areas. This dog is heeling properly, even in a crowded pedestrian zone.

associate the drills of the barrack-yard type at dog training grounds with obedience and quite rightly reject such a way of handling their pet. Others, however, think a dog is "badly" treated if restrictions are imposed, and often look pityingly at dogs that are obeying nicely, while they themselves continue to struggle with their own four-legged pet, now accustomed to "freedom."

Recently, at a family celebration, I witnessed a conversation between two dog owners. They were discussing pros and cons of dog training. One woman had two very well-trained dogs with her, lying obediently under and next to the table. The other person told this woman that he was opposed to "functioning" dogs like these and to any systematic training. Things could be done differently, he said. All the while his dog, tied somewhere off to one side, barked and howled to the guests' "delight" and pulled at his leash, while his owner kept standing up and going over to calm him—unsuccessfully, of course.

How much obedience and training are required depends in part on where the dog generally spends its time. Little, if any, training is needed by a guard dog restricted to a

kennel on a piece of property or standing sentinel over the farmyard. But a dog that lives with his human family, accompanies them in their daily lives, and is out in public absolutely must have systematic training so that he doesn't bother or endanger others. The better trained a dog is, the more liberties he can ultimately enjoy. For example, a well-trained dog can be allowed off leash much more often than one that can't be counted on to come when called. An untrained dog also quickly becomes a burden to his owner. You may find yourself forced to stop doing one thing or another, for example, because your pet won't stay alone or "misbehaves" so badly outside his home territory that you can hardly take him along.

Moreover, the answer to the question "How much obedience do you need?" depends on your own requirements. Some people may not mind giving an audible signal umpteen times before the dog finally obeys it, or possibly waiting half an hour when they meet other dogs before their pet is finally tired of playing. Others, fortunately, see the need to train their pet to obey reliably and to adapt well to a great variety of situations. Such human-and-dog teams can do a lot to restore the badly marred image of dog owners in the public eye. For more on this topic, see page 153.

There's No One Way to Train a Dog

In recent years, luckily, methods of dog training have come a long way. The extensive studies done on wolves by behavioral researchers have contributed substantially to that. Many of their findings are now being incorporated into dog training programs and are making them far more species-appropriate and understandable for dogs—in contrast to previous approaches, still based chiefly on "drilling" with ⊙ STRONG-ARM METHODS (page 273).

Which of Today's Methods Is the Right One?

This question can't be answered definitively, because there's no "one best" method, just as there's no "one best" dog. It is clear, however, that training by use of overt physical force is just as poorly suited to the dog's nature, as is the anti-authoritarian approach. Today, we have various training methods available, some of them even patented. By no means, however, does that mean that they are suitable for all dogs. Dogs are just as variable in their temperament as they are in their outward appearance. Along with very headstrong individuals, there are also "model students" self-motivated to do everything correctly. Some dogs are very independent types, while others are easily distracted by everything, and still others inherently have a strong inclination to follow their owner's lead. Many can be successfully motivated with food; others are more influenced by toys and a wish to play; some are generally difficult to get excited about anything. While some bubble over with high spirits, others tend to be more easy-going. And the strength of the hunting instinct, too, varies from dog to dog.

Every canine makes different demands on his two-legged friend's qualities as a leader and a trainer. Here's my practical guidance:

Always attune the training to your dog's temperament—and to your own as well. What seems logical to you, what can you implement successfully? Only if you're behind it all the way will you seem convincing to your pet.

Certain principles of training are always valid, of course, as you'll read in the section starting on page 83. Look at different methods and professional trainers and then make your own decision about what best suits your dog and you. Different elements of various methods can certainly be combined without concern. In any event, a professional trainer should be able to respond to the individual differences in dogs as well as to the human-dog team.

1

Whether you use training or correction to solve problems—such as stealing shoes—the method should always be adapted to suit each individual human-dog team.
▽

Bonding and Building Trust

Your best-case scenario: Human and dog form a real team, in which the human is the higher-ranking partner. To make you and your dog into such a dream team, a strong bond and mutual trust are crucial. For owner and pet, this is one of the most important foundations for living together in harmony.

Here too, study of wolves' behavior has yielded valuable information for dog owners. In a wolf pack, there are a great many behavior patterns that promote attachment among the wolves (→ page 38). Close contact between the animals—in your case, between human and dog—is most certainly a part of this. Let me give two examples as illustrations:
▷ A dog living alone in a kennel usually can't form such a bond, since it doesn't share in any of the events in its pack. Such a dog may be a good worker, because after hours of contact deprivation it is enormously happy that somebody is bothering with it at last, but a real, genuine bond can hardly be the result.
▷ On the other hand, you won't form an authentic bond by just coddling the dog all day. This is too much for the animal, and the attention loses its appeal and becomes bothersome.

Creating the Human-Dog Bond

"Creating a bond" means that you make a point of engaging in activities with your four-legged friend. This is accomplished through joint adventures, playing together, training, and physical contact, but also by setting limits for your dog, showing that you're the boss, and exuding an inner authority. These three aspects, in addition, are a prerequisite for getting the dog to acknowledge you as the higher-ranking partner and thus to develop the willingness to follow your lead. Moreover, recognizing these "leader attributes" in the owner gives the dog a sense of security and trust. Only in this way will your dog feel safe and secure in his "pack."

Another part of developing a bond is good communication with your pet. Your dog has to understand what you want of him, how it should be done, and what is off limits. In addition, you supply the dog's food, which further cements the relationship between owner and pet.

These things need to be consistent, so that your dog can rely on them. That also applies to your behavior. Irascibility, moodiness, or abrasiveness in dealing with the dog will have an adverse affect, making it difficult for your

INFO

How to Develop a Bond

Not every puppy displays equal readiness to bond. Some stick like glue; many enter into a normal, trusting relationship without surrendering themselves. And then, there are even more independent puppies. To develop a healthy degree of attachment, you must be responsive to your puppy's temperament.

pet to size you up properly. But if your behavior is clear, firm, fair, and consistent, the dog will always know where he stands and will develop trust in you. If not, the dog will do as he likes or be anxious or bewildered.

Another major bonding factor is purposeful engagement with, or systematic training of, the dog in a way that suits his individual abilities—all in a species-appropriate way, of course.

How Much Contact Is Good Contact?

As you now know, the dog is a pack animal in need of companionship. Canines are not like parakeets or guinea pigs. For them, being the only dog in the household is anything but species-appropriate, since a human can't take the place of an animal partner. For a domestic dog, the human is not a substitute for another dog, but a real social partner, with whom the animal communicates and forges a close, lifelong relationship.

Dogs are extremely adaptable with regard to living with humans. Through domestication, they have developed the ability to interpret the facial expressions, body language, and speech of their two-legged friends quite successfully. Nevertheless, they need contact with other members of their species in order to acquire their traditional behaviors from one another and be able to employ them. If a dog lacks that opportunity, misunderstandings and problems can easily arise when he encounters other dogs.

Experience shows, however, that dogs often are more likely to have too much contact with other dogs, or that dog owners unconsciously arrange these contacts in such a way that the bond with the human is adversely affected. By this, I mean that a dog easily becomes too fixated on other members of its species—for example, when the human-dog bond, along with obedience, is not firmly established; when your pet is allowed on principle to make contact with every other dog; or when playing with other dogs is the only real pursuit it enjoys. An extremely strong bond with other dogs can also result, from frequently taking your pet for walks in fairly large groups, so that it finds its pleasure chiefly in playing with other dogs, rather than walking with you. I have found that many dog owners often virtually stop playing with their dog once puppyhood ends.

When this occurs, the sight of other dogs signals to your four-legged companion, "Yaaaay, some real fun at last!" And off he runs. He no longer cares about his two-legged companion, because there is fun to be had without him. I

△

Everything a four-legged companion enjoys should be experienced with you, if possible. This strengthens the bond of the human-dog team, which has a positive effect on the life they share.

often hear dog owners say, "I wonder what's wrong with my dog. He behaves fine when we're alone, but as soon as another dog appears on the horizon, he forgets everything."

Choosing and Buying the Right Dog

You want to acquire a dog. I applaud this decision. But the purchase has to be carefully considered, because it is an important step on the road to creating a human-dog relationship that is as uncomplicated as possible. Unfortunately, many future dog owners are unaware of this. They don't realize that buying a dog is not altogether simple. Which breed, and ultimately, which individual, should you choose from the great variety of dogs beaming at you from breeders' Web sites or offered for sale in newspaper and dog magazine ads? You can't always tell what is really behind these offers.

It Depends on the Breeder

A major criterion in making your choice is the ○ TEMPERAMENT (page 274) of a dog. This is made up of both inherited traits and acquired experiences. The breeder and the parent animals are responsible for the dog's genotype; his experiences are the responsibility of the breeder and the owner, since the dog will live in your home.

Genes also play an important part in the dog's health, but the kind of rearing provided in the first few weeks also counts. Here again, the breeder is responsible. The eight weeks the puppy spends with the breeder are part of a very sensitive developmental phase, in which many things can be favorably influenced, or go completely wrong. Choose a breeder who doesn't raise the puppies in a stall or the like and who gives the little creatures an opportunity to come into contact with various people and explore their surroundings. Such a puppy has a good start in life, and the positive effect of that will sometimes last a lifetime.

Both health and temperament will develop in the best possible way only if the breeder consciously attaches importance to these factors—that is, if the dam and sire are completely healthy and have good temperaments of their own. If you have your eye on a certain breed because of its character traits, take special care in choosing the breeder—even if you don't plan to take the dog to trials or shows.

Even the most conscientious breeder can't guarantee that a dog will be healthy in every respect. But the stricter the supervision, the better are your chances of getting the kind of four-legged friend you wish.

Where to Learn about Breeders

The first place I recommend contacting is the American Kennel Club (AKC), with which special purebred dog clubs are affiliated. These specialize in one breed or several related breeds. The members of these organizations are predominantly hobby breeders, who are required to adhere to strict breeding regulations, however. Depending on the breed, there are ○ TEMPERAMENT TESTS (page 274) for breed-specific and ordinary, practical attributes, various tests for ○ HEREDITARY DISEASES (page 265), working tests or ○ TRIALS (page 276), and so forth. Only when a dog has successfully gone through all the stages of the approval process can the breeder use it as a breeding animal. In addition, there are regulations for raising puppies, as well as age and litter limitations and much more. This prevents females from being misused as "breeding machines."

As is true everywhere, the AKC also has its share of black sheep, and for this reason I suggest that you visit several breeders and become well informed about the breed in advance. Purebred dog clubs can refer you to members with the proper expertise. Ask to see the documents certifying the parents' pedigrees, which should always contain, along with the logo of a recognized kennel club or shelter, the AKC acronym (page 258). Only if the puppies also receive a pedigree from the

AKC is the breeder really operating under the auspices of this umbrella organization.

Whether the AKC is involved or not, every breeder should meet certain criteria.

▷ **Number of dogs:** The breeder should keep only a few dogs and should not raise more than two litters simultaneously.

▷ **Breeds:** The breeder should breed no more than two breeds.

▷ **Bitches:** Pay close attention to the appearance of the female dogs (bitches). Are their teats hanging down almost to the ground? This indicates they've borne many litters and is not a good sign.

▷ **Dam:** Make sure you see the mother (dam) of your puppies. A reputable breeder will be willing to present her. How old is she, and how many litters has she had? According to AKC rules, a bitch must be at least 8 months and no more than 12 years old at the time of mating.

▷ **Dogs' living quarters:** Do the dogs live in close contact with the family, or in kennels, open runs, or barns? Choose only puppies that grow up with a family connection.

▷ **Sire:** Your puppy's father (sire) rarely lives with the breeder, because reputable breeders rarely use the same studs several times. Many take on long trips and high costs in order to have the bitch bred from the desired partner.

Before you acquire a dog, I suggest that you get as much information as possible about the breed you want and about breeding in general—only then can you ask the breeder meaningful questions and evaluate his or her answers.

1

Many hunting breeds are better off in hunters' hands. This Small Münsterländer is swiftly and enthusiastically retrieving a downed pheasant for its owner.

▽

▶ TEST

Do You Already Know Some of the Basics?

To avoid facing a mountain of theoretical knowledge when your new pet moves in, I suggest that you become somewhat acquainted with the subject of "dogs" before acquiring one, because there are certain things you need to know before you buy. Mark the correct answers below.

	Yes	No
1. Which prerequisite is important for living in harmony with a dog?		
a) The dog must be attractive.	○	○
b) Its traits have to suit my lifestyle.	○	○
c) I'll take the puppy that's the first to run toward me.	○	○
2. Which statement is correct?		
a) Dog breeds differ only in terms of how they look.	○	○
b) Every breed always has inherent specific traits.	○	○
c) A breed has the desired traits only if they are deliberately promoted by breeders.	○	○
3. In the human-dog relationship, it's important that...		
a) a reliable bond be created between the two.	○	○
b) the dog always have plenty of contact with other dogs.	○	○
c) the dog be kept in a kennel.	○	○

Answers:
1b) ⇦ Pages 18–20
2c) ⇦ Page 18
3a) ⇦ Page 16

What Breed Should I Choose?

Clarification of this matter is important, since not every breed fits into every environment. Write down the canine qualities that match up well with you and your family, your available free time, and your living environment, and those that don't. If you live in a densely built-up area or if a lot of people come and go at your house, a dog with a strong ▶ INSTINCT TO GUARD AND PROTECT (page 267) can become a problem. If you want a dog purely as a companion and don't plan to train him or use him for a specific purpose, you should avoid breeds that are bred primarily for performance, since hunting breeds and ▶ WORKING-DOG BREEDS (page 277) can quickly become a burden. Size, too, should enter into your considerations. If you live on the fifth floor and have no elevator, a big, heavy dog can present problems if he is ever injured and unable to walk. Small dogs, however, are not necessarily easier to keep than big ones. The somewhat trendy Jack Russell Terriers, for instance, usually demand quite a lot of consistency and stamina on their owners' part. In the case of mixed breeds, traits and size when fully grown can be roughly predicted only if both parents are known.

Choosing the Right Puppy

Once you've found your breeder, it's time to choose the right puppy. Rarely is it the one that is the first to run up to you. I advise first-time dog owners to pick neither the most self-confident puppy nor a nervous, fearful one. A good breeder knows his or her puppies' temperaments and will advise you on choosing the right pup.

When Children and Dogs Live Together

Many people buy a dog as a playmate for their children. And it is a proven fact that a good relationship between a child and a dog can have a very positive affect on the child's development. Children can learn to respect a living creature and to be considerate of its needs and characteristics. But that happens only if the parents can convey this to the child through their own behavior.

Most child dog relationships, luckily, are harmonious and unproblematic, yet time and again there are biting incidents—most involving the child's own dog or one that he or she knows.

If you acquire a dog for your child's sake, you need to keep these issues in mind: The dog will react quite differently than a guinea pig or parakeet, for example, and is not a cuddly toy or a plaything. A dog does not see a child as another member of the canine species or as a "puppy," and most definitely not as a person who commands respect.

Taking a dog into your home, then, makes sense only if you as parents completely support his or her acquisition and are willing to take responsibility for all of the pet's training and most of its feeding and care. A child is incapable of that. How old the child should be when the dog joins the household is impossible to say across the board. I suggest, however, that you postpone getting a dog until your children are past the toddler stage and thus are a little more mature.

Is There a Really Child-Friendly Dog?

There is no one ○ BREED (page 260) that is automatically "child-friendly," but there are certain characteristics that make one dog breed more suitable for a family with children than another. If there are children in the home, the dog should have a well-balanced, robust temperament and relate readily with humans. It should not be bothered by noise and excitement, nor should it have a strong hunting instinct or prey drive. Children, especially younger ones, often run around or move in a frantic way, yell, and fall down. These behaviors can trigger prey-capture behavior in a dog.

A pronounced instinct to guard and protect, too, can become a problem, if the dog makes a distinction between children in the family "pack" and those who are not. If the children and their playmates quarrel or engage in roughhousing, the dog may feel the need to take sides.

There are a great many situations that the dog could misunderstand. Children in

Whether your dog is "child-friendly" depends on its temperament, its living conditions, and its experiences: good, bad, or nonexistent

▽

1

the crawling stage, for example, tend to use the dog to pull themselves to a standing position or may startle a sleeping pet. Smaller dogs sometimes are more likely to feel threatened then than a big dog.

If, after careful deliberation, you've found your dream breed, with breed-specific attributes that suit your family with children, then the breeder re-enters the equation. As you've read by now, the temperament of a dog is made up of inherited characteristics and a large share of acquired experiences. Therefore, it is essential for a future ⊙ FAMILY DOG (page 263) to grow up in close contact with a family, to be socialized with children (and a wide variety of humans in general) in the first

 TIP

Reacting to Warning Signals

If you notice signs of trouble between your child and the dog—growling, for example, even if only a little—or aggressive play, you should seek professional help without delay. This is especially true if you are unsure about how to deal with the dog in such a situation.

eight weeks, and to have positive experiences. A puppy that learns about "family life" from the breeder thinks of children as something pleasant, and is accustomed to noises, including loud ones, will manage much more successfully later on than a puppy that is reared in isolation with few stimuli. Naturally, it's also important for the dog to have only good experiences with children later on as well.

A Puppy or a Full-Grown Dog?

Assuming he comes from a good breeding facility, you take on a puppy at a time when he

has experienced and learned a lot of positive things. Now he will be shaped by your life and surroundings and will grow up with children from an early age, so that both sides have a chance to grow accustomed to each other and adapt smoothly. If the children are somewhat shy, then they will do better with a puppy anyway, because of his size and appearance, than with a mature dog, which may even be only slightly smaller than they are. By the way, this is also true for many adults, especially novice dog owners, who first have to learn to feel at ease with a dog.

A full-grown dog may mean less work, since he is already housebroken and perhaps even already trained. However, a mature dog also has a certain amount of past history. Depending on the dog's origin, it often is hard to know for sure what experiences, especially negative ones, have molded the dog and what situations can potentially trigger problematic behavior. You don't always learn the real reason why a full-grown dog is being passed on to a new owner. In addition, problems can arise if the dog comes from a completely different environment—as a senior citizen's pet, for example—into a family with small children.

Rules Are Important

If you exercise some caution, nothing stands in the way of a harmonious life together for child and dog. That includes carefully training the dog, as well as establishing a clear hierarchy within the family. It's also important for all the family members to deal with the dog in the same way. Rule No. 1: Never let children, especially smaller ones, play unsupervised with the dog, and never entrust your canine companion with "babysitter tasks"—thinking, for example,—"It's okay for the children to play in the back yard alone; the dog's there and will watch out for them." Younger children in particular also like to experiment with the dog, with no bad intentions, of course. They just don't understand all these things yet. But most dogs are not happy about having their tail pulled or having fingers poked into their eyes and ears.

If your child is at an age when he or she can understand certain rules, make sure they are obeyed. Point out that the dog mustn't be bothered when eating or sleeping, and that it's never okay to take food, a chew bone, or the like away from the animal. If the dog retires from the scene because he's had enough of the activity at hand, the child should leave him alone.

Games for Children and Dogs

You must make it clear to your children that despite his cuddly looks a puppy is not a toy or a doll that can be carried around, laid in a toy stroller, dressed up, and so forth.

Understandably, children want to play with their four-legged companion. But here too, I advise all parents not to leave them alone. Children sometimes tend to "push" the dog so much that he gets overly boisterous. You need to apply the brakes in time. Games that involve a child running away from the dog, possibly even shouting, should be put to a stop immediately. It's better, for example, for the child to roll a ball to the dog—unless he is inclined to defend such things.

Many dogs love games that involve tugging, but these are suitable for children only if they are superior to the dog in terms of strength, and if the dog does not get in a fighting mood during games of this type. Somewhat older children, under their parents' guidance, can try a few fairly simple training exercises with the dog, such as "Sit" or "Down," and reward their pet with food or a toy. The extent to which children can train with the dog varies quite widely and depends both on the dog's temperament and on the child's level of maturity.

In conclusion, one other important concern: Again and again we see dog owners allowing their pet to be walked by their own

If the child and the dog follow certain rules, then both will enjoy playing together. You should always keep an eye on them, however, so that nothing gets out of hand.

children or a neighbor's children. I strongly advise against this, and with larger dogs in particular I consider this irresponsible behavior. A big dog is always superior to a child in terms of strength and can drag him or her, at the other end of the leash, across fields and roads if he has smelled or seen something interesting. Children do not have a dog under control in any situation. This can easily lead to serious incidents.

How Dogs Learn

Before we start discussing the practical aspects of training, you need to learn what developmental phases your puppy goes through as it grows and how a dog learns. Then you'll know what really matters.

ONLY WHEN YOU'VE understood the fundamentals of canine learning behavior can you get your ideas across to your pet, so that she always knows what you want of her. Once these basics are clear to you, there'll be plenty of "A-ha!" experiences, and many things about dog training will become relatively simple and logical. Often we humans see things in a much more complicated way than necessary.

Unfortunately, dog owners frequently let their emotions guide them, are not objective enough, and try to treat their dog like a human. These three facts, however, are not conducive to species-appropriate training. If you fall into this category, I seriously urge you to change and to view your dog as a dog. I can assure you that you have no need to fear— your four-legged friend will still like you, or rather, she will like you more than ever!

The Dog's Developmental Phases

Before a dog is grown, he or she passes through important developmental phases, especially in puppyhood.

The Neonatal Phase

The ○ NEONATAL PHASE (page 269) covers approximately the first two weeks of life. As members of an ○ ALTRICIAL SPECIES (page 258), puppies are born blind and deaf and are fully dependent on their mother's nursing and care. Nevertheless, ○ PUPPIES (page 271) already possess certain abilities essential to survival. Their sense of smell functions to some extent, they can sense heat and cold, and they can already "crawl" at a relatively good pace. These attributes enable them to find their mother's teats on their own, right after birth. If a puppy is hungry or is slightly separated from the rest of the litter, it needs no help to find its mother or get back to its littermates in the birthing box. These experiences are important for puppies. Even at this early stage, they have the experience of being able to achieve something through their own efforts. Therefore, there is no need for a breeder to supposedly "help out" in such situations.

The Socialization Phase Begins

The ○ SOCIALIZATION PHASE (page 273) is the decisive phase of development. It begins during the second or third weeks. Gradually the eyes open, and the other senses also begin to function more and more. As of now the puppy consciously observes its environment and starts to react to it. The puppies play together with increasing frequency and want to explore with more frequency. Now, if not sooner, a puppy needs lots of contact with humans.

Human contact is necessary because at this point the puppy is going through an ○ IMPRINTING-LIKE LEARNING PROCESS (page 267), acquiring lasting knowledge. At this time its image of the surrounding world is formed, and it learns the rules of living together and communicating with other dogs. Its willingness to learn and its receptivity are especially keen. In this limited time span, its brain is especially receptive to experiences and stimuli, and it stores everything—both positive and negative—in a lasting, permanent fashion. But nonexistent experiences, such as deficient ○ HUMAN CONTACT (page 266) or ○ INADEQUATE EARLY SOCIALIZATION (page 267) with no opportunity for exploration, also have permanent effects. As a result,

○ INFO

Constant Attachment Figure

During the socialization phase, if at all possible, never leave the puppy frequently or for an extended time in the care of a stranger—that is, of someone who does not live in your household. Having different caregivers impairs the development of the bond between you and your "canine child."

later on a dog may be fearful of people and of the surrounding world, or may have a limited capacity for learning.

The socialization phase reaches its peak in about the eighth week. It ends, depending on the breed and the individual, no later than the twentieth week.

The "Young Dog" Phase

Puppyhood is followed by the "young dog" phase, as the dog continues to learn and his or her interest in the surrounding world increases. The bond to its human caregiver must be repeatedly reinforced. For detailed information on puberty, see page 214.

How Does a Dog Learn?

Learning behavior in principle is quite a complex subject, on which much academic research continues to be done. In the following pages, I plan to outline the most important findings of these studies with regard to dogs. For recommended readings on this subject, see page 284.

Experts use the term ● CONDITIONING (page 261) to refer to the form of learning applied in training dogs. There are two types: operant conditioning, also called instrumental conditioning, and classical conditioning.

▷ **Operant conditioning** is the type most frequently used in dog training. This basic concept was developed by the American behavioral researcher and psychologist B. F. Skinner. With this form of conditioning, the dog learns through success or failure. ● POSITIVE REINFORCEMENT (page 270), such as praise, causes the dog to display a behavior more frequently. For example, if she gets a wonderful reward in return for coming when called, the incentive to come will be correspondingly great for the animal. Thus, the dog gladly does what yields a benefit for her. This can also be "soothing" stroking or coaxing, for example, when the dog growls at someone. Therefore, you need to pay attention to what you're really "praising" your dog for. Learning from success also occurs when the dog exhibits a behavior in order to suppress a negative reinforcement (→ page 30). If a behavior is not worthwhile because it results in a negative impact on the dog, the animal will exhibit it less often or discontinue it altogether. For example, if the dog leaves the *sit* position without permission, light pressure on her rear end will serve as a corrective.

▷ **In classical conditioning**, a previously neutral stimulus becomes a so-called ● CONDITIONED STIMULUS (page 260). The best-known example of this type of conditioning is the experiments on dogs made by the Russian physiologist Ivan Pavlov. When the dog sees food (= ● UNCONDITIONED STIMULUS, page 276), she begins to salivate (= unconditioned reaction). If the appearance of the food is always combined with the sound of a bell (initially a neutral stimulus), after some time the sound of the bell alone (now a conditioned stimulus) will result in salivation.

Many dogs are allowed, for example, to lick out an almost-empty yogurt container. This too is an example of classical conditioning, since the dogs start salivating as soon as they hear the noise the spoon makes when the container is almost empty. That noise is the equivalent of the sound of the bell; that is, it is a conditioned stimulus. And if your dog does a dance of joy because you're putting on your "dog-walking jacket," then this type of learning is also involved.

Positive Motivation and Reinforcement

Modern methods of dog training now predominantly make use of positive ● MOTIVATION (page 268). That is, to teach a dog something new, you arrange the situation so that your canine friend is led by the expectation of a reward to do of its own accord exactly what you want. Previously, training was based primarily on ● AVOIDANCE BEHAVIOR (page 259), a kind of "negative motivation," such as a yank on the leash or pushing down on the dog's rear end. Let's examine learning through positive motivation by looking at the example of the "Sit" exercise (→ page 88). Here you hold a treat above the dog's head and wait for her to sit down on her own. Then you give her the reward. The dog has an attitude of happy expectation and learns without any negative stress. The reward, usually in the form of a snack or a toy, is the positive reinforcement.

Also important is the well-directed use of the reward. This example will serve as clarification:

Conditioning Response to the "Come" Whistle

If you want a dog to learn to come reliably in response to a whistle blow or a word, it must be systematically conditioned to do so. I did that with our litter of nine puppies, so that their future owners, who still had and have much to learn anyway, would at least have a little less work facing them.

When just four weeks old, the little pups were served their first meals of solid foods. Then I waited a few days until they had grown accustomed to the food and mealtimes had become a highlight for them, because that is indeed the prerequisite for attaching the right value to the whistle blow.

First I called the little creatures to dinner with our "normal" puppy call, from up close, since at that young age they still have trouble getting a fix on a noise from far away. At first they wandered around in response to the call, excited but still a bit aimless. Then, as soon as all nine, smacking and munching, were absorbed in their food, they heard two short whistle blows in succession—the life-long signal for them to come right away. For about a week, this was repeated at every meal, that is, four times a day.

Then came the next phase: The call was followed by a double whistle blow at the very moment the puppies reached me and I put their shared bowl on the floor. I kept this up for about a week as well. The puppies and their sensory abilities were continuing to develop, and they were getting a better and better overview of their environment.

As the next step in the conditioning process, for a week I blew the whistle every time the little rascals moved in response to the verbal summons, recognized me clearly, and headed in my direction. In this phase I

added a "second foreign language" as well: In addition to the double whistle blow, I called "Here." With their increasing ability to get their bearings, I produced the double whistle blow and the "Here" sooner and sooner, and

◁

This breeder is conditioning her puppies to come in response to a signal. At first the "Come" whistle signal is heard while the little pups are eating right beside the breeder. This helps them closely associate the sound of the whistle with their food right from the outset.

finally just after I got their attention with the initial call. In the last ten days, then, the whistle blow and "Here" came right before every meal. The nine little puppies came unerringly, no matter what they were doing at the time, whether they were playing together or sleeping, and raced to me at once, their tiny ears flying.

I gave the puppies' new owners a whistle with the same frequency and, of course, instructions on further reinforcement of the lesson. The "little ones" now are about a year old and come immediately in response to the whistle blow—they learned it during the socialization phase in an intense and systematic way, resembling imprinting.

1

If the puppy tends to sit up from the *down* position too soon, either stop rewarding the sit with a treat altogether, or at least stop rewarding the *sit* after the *down*—even if the dog executes it correctly in response to the audible signal. Then, you see, the dog would always have an incentive to sit too soon, which you actually would like to avoid here. Instead, increase her reward if she remains in the *down* position.

Negative Impact

In contrast to positive reinforcement, there is also ◉ NEGATIVE REINFORCEMENT (page 269). This means that the dog employs a certain behavior so that an unpleasant feeling will stop. Example: You want the dog to assume the *down* position. You shorten the leash and step on it, which creates a downward pull. The dog can counter this unpleasant influence only by lying down. Then she is also motivated to perform an exercise, because by doing so she can stop the unpleasant effect. But that is a "negative motivation." Such dogs can still work happily, because they ultimately are "happy" to get rid of the unpleasant influence.

Negative reinforcement can definitely be useful and effective on occasion, as a corrective for a stubborn dog that already knows what "Down" means. Personally, however, I would never teach a dog something new by using negative reinforcement.

In summary, we can say that dogs are happier learning through positive motivation and develop a better relationship of trust with their owner than when the learning is based on fear and avoidance behavior (→ page 259).

Teach new lessons through positive motivation. The treat is in the right position for teaching the "Heel" command—this way, the dog learns to walk at heel properly, without feeling any stress.
▽

Giving Rewards—But How?

If you want your dog to repeat a behavior willingly, you must practice the behavior relatively frequently and reward her each time for a certain length of time.

The Right Timing

The ◐ TIMING (page 275) is important, because a dog can associate the reward with the behavior only if it is produced immediately after the behavior or directly linked with it. If the dog is learning the *sit*, for example, reward her as soon as her rear end touches the ground and all four legs are on the ground. This means that you must always have the reward ready, without first having to dig it out of your pocket.

Exclusiveness of the Reward

If you want your dog to repeat a certain behavior readily, you have to work with a reward that truly appeals to her.
▷ **Edible treats** have to taste really good, and the dog has to be hungry. In addition, it's advisable to use little treats only during the training session, since if the dog gets a tidbit at other times possibly because she just looks so cute or for some other reason—then

her motivation to "earn" the tasty tidbits will not be very high.
▷ **Verbal praise, petting,** or rewarding with a toy: What I said above applies here as well. If the dog is "petted to death" or "serenaded with praise" all day long anyway, or if the toy used as a reward is always readily available, you can't expect to have any real impact on the learning process by using such things for the purpose of rewarding the animal.

How Long Do I Continue the Rewards?

You need not reward the dog all her life every time she exhibits a desired behavior that is already in place. Once a lesson has been mastered, you should use variable rewards. That means that sometimes the dog gets something, and sometimes she doesn't. For exceptional performance—for example, when your pet does an exercise despite exposure to distraction or does it especially well—you should occasionally give an extra-large helping of treats. Then the dog will remain highly motivated—much like a slot-machine player who keeps playing in the hope that the machine will eventually produce a jackpot.

"Dog-Appropriate" Reprimands— the Right Way to Correct

Puppies learn early on that some things are not allowed. For example, if they're clinging to mama's "milk bar" at closing time, or if they want to get hold of mama's chew stick, they get a real "chewing out." In dog language, this means that mama uses the muzzle grip (→ page 30) or nudges hard with her own muzzle, in case gentler forms of warning such as growling aren't sufficient. Under no circumstances does she distract the pups with little balls or the like.

Training a dog without any ◐ COERCION (page 260) or without correction, therefore, is neither possible nor species-appropriate. But it all depends on how you do it—and on the dog. There are dogs for which a stern look or an equivalent tone of voice is quite adequate. For many others, however, more is needed, and here you have to bring in the heavy artillery. An important request: If the undesirable behavior is fear-related, don't punish the dog under any circumstances. By doing so, you only reinforce her anxiety, making the situation worse.

There are various ways of putting a halt to undesirable behavior, and it's impossible to make an across-the-board judgment that one method is the "best." This ultimately depends on the dog and on the situation. The method you select, however, should be used judiciously. That is, it should be effective enough for the dog to stop the undesirable behavior at once, if at all possible, but it should not make too strong an impression. To assess this correctly, it is important that you know your dog very well.

Negative Reinforcement

A behavior can be stopped by depriving the dog of something pleasant—for example, by denying her the treat you've led her to expect or putting the toy back in your pocket. This is called "negative reinforcement." It sounds strange, but that's what it is. An example: The dog is allowed to chase a ball if she first obeys the command to sit. You have the ball in your hand and say "Sit," but the dog doesn't sit. Then you immediately put the ball back in your pocket. This works, however, only if the

△

The muzzle grip is widely used among dogs. It can be meant in a playful way, but frequently it serves as a reprimand.

ball is plainly the highlight for the dog, and your pet is not more interested in the mouse hole in the meadow.

Positive Reinforcement

By contrast, we use the term "positive reinforcement" when the undesirable behavior is interrupted by an unpleasant influence. Examples of this are the ⦿ MUZZLE GRIP (page 268), the grip on the back of the neck, an angry "No!" contact with an electric fence, and the like. For instance, the dog starts to chase some cows and in the process makes painful contact with the electric pasture fence. Now she will at least avoid these cows, and if you're lucky she will avoid all cows from now on. Or the dog may jump up on the kitchen chair to get a better view of the table. You immediately put her back on solid ground with one fell swoop, by taking hold of her nape or collar and growling "No!"

▷ **The muzzle grip** is a widely used "educational aid" among dogs and wolves. The prerequisite is that the dog must know the human's hand basically from petting, including stroking of the muzzle area, and from feeding, as something positive. Then, putting your hand around her muzzle more firmly or for a longer time, in combination with a stern "No," serves as an appropriate and understandable rebuke for the dog. But please don't use the muzzle grip for every little thing that comes along. It makes sense, for example, when the dog bites too hard while playing or chews on the carpet, and when your tone of voice alone is not enough. If the dog then licks your hand or changes her behavior without protesting (by snapping at you, for example), you have executed the muzzle grip correctly. If the dog snaps, the muzzle grip was unconvincing, too hasty, or usually too brief.

▷ **Correction during training:** The goal of training is for the dog to obey a command immediately, not only if she happens to feel so inclined, and also not until you've repeated it for the fifth time. Once the dog has learned and fully understood an exercise through positive motivation, one or two audible signals should suffice for the dog to carry it out. An example: Your canine trainee is refusing to sit (although she has mastered the exercise). Then you help by gently pressing down on her rear. Use this method of correction, however, only if you're sure that the dog has completely understood the exercise and the demands are not too great. If you're not certain of this, it's better to redo the lesson from the start or make it easier.

▷ **Timing:** What applies to correcting also holds true for giving rewards. The action must immediately follow the undesirable behavior or even begin during the behavior. If the dog is stealing food off the table, for example, the action is helpful only if it occurs before the dog has the food in her mouth. It is useless once she has started eating.

Ignoring

This means that you say nothing, have no eye contact with the dog, and also don't move in the dog's direction. This is important, since the slightest bit of attention could be interpreted by the dog as "praise" for what actually is undesirable behavior, even if it is "Don't do that!" or an angry "Stop that!" Ignoring is suitable for situations in which the dog wants to achieve a certain goal by means of a certain behavior and through you (or someone else). These behaviors include, for example, begging at the table or jumping up on people. By ignoring the dog, you teach her that the behavior she has exhibited accomplishes nothing. Finally, she will discontinue the behavior. How fast that happens depends on the individual animal.

Ignoring, however, is effective only if you persevere long enough. Giving in to the dog only reinforces her behavior; she learns that if

△
These puppies want to get mama's chew stick. She shows them beyond the shadow of a doubt what she thinks of that. The puppies try to placate her and crouch slightly.

she is recalcitrant enough, she will still get her way. Perseverance on your part is also called for when you want to get rid of an already established behavior. Since the dog's actions have already met with success, she first will increase the behavior in order to reach her goal. If you stay firm in ignoring her, she will gradually stop acting that way. So don't give up, and you'll be successful!

○ SELF-REWARDING BEHAVIORS (page 272) or actions by which the dog endangers itself or others, such as chewing on an electrical cable or a rug, must never be ignored, because the animal does this for pleasure and not to achieve an objective. This also applies to chasing, be it joggers, cats, or other things. Here, the pursuit itself is what the dog enjoys—whether she catches anything in the process or not.

10 Questions About Training

For family reasons, we can't bring our puppy home from the breeder until she is eleven weeks old. Is this a problem?

If the breeder provides good socialization and early training, it's okay, if there's no other option. But if the breeder keeps the puppy predominantly in a kennel, stall, or exclusively indoors and deprived of contact with other humans and the surrounding world, this will have an unfavorable influence on the puppy's development.

We still have fairly young children and would like a smaller dog. Recently we saw a Jack Russell Terrier, and we really like its looks and size. Would this breed be right for us?

This breed is currently in fashion, but the dogs are not always easy to live with. They are real bundles of energy, and sometimes they can be quite boisterous. This could be too much for children, and you yourself will need plenty of perseverance in the training process. Occasionally there are some quieter individuals as well. Don't buy one from a breeder who raises them for superior hunting abilities. Ideally, visit several breeders.

Won't using the muzzle grip make my dog, Tino, shy away from my hand?

Dogs communicate many things with their muzzle; we use our hand for this purpose. Among themselves, dogs don't become "muzzle-shy" when another dog seizes their muzzle as a form of reprimand. Since we otherwise use our hand in an exclusively positive way, the muzzle grip won't make your dog hand-shy. It is important, however, for you to react firmly and quickly, but without seeming frantic.

Next week we pick up our little puppy from the breeder. Could we just go ahead and take along a sibling as well?

I would advise against it. It would take far more effort to ensure that each of the two is more attached to you than to its sibling. Later, once the two are grown, there could be problems of hierarchy between them, which frequently are not easy to resolve.

Can I teach my dog, Ben, to recognize only a certain word as a term of praise?

Like a stop command, a term of praise also can be conditioned. For example, repeat the word "Good" about 15 times in succession and right after each "Good," give Ben a little treat. Do this twice in a day, and if necessary repeat the procedure again the next day. Then Ben will link the word "Good" with praise. The crux of the matter is that people usually talk to their dog too much anyway, so a single word doesn't stand out. Or someone else may happen to say this word to the dog. For these reasons, I suggest that you use a clicker (→ page 192).

▷

Jack Russell Terriers are active, usually very courageous and self-confident dogs, whose training requires great persistence and consistency. Their passion is hunting foxes, rats, and other vermin.

△

To make two puppies into well-trained dogs takes far more effort than training just one puppy.

Can I train my bitch, Kimba, exclusively through positive motivation?

This method reinforces only desirable behavior shown by the dog of its own accord, and ignores undesirable behavior. To train a dog by means of this method exclusively, the reinforcer (for example, food or a toy) must be what it clearly values most. This works with many play-loving animals, workaholics, or with dogs that are extremely greedy. But if the dog would rather chase rabbits than be rewarded for a *sit*, you will not succeed.

Does a dog interpret wearing its leash as something negative?

If you put the dog on leash whenever you're annoyed with it and fussing at it, or if your pet prefers to do something without you because there's no strong bond between you, it naturally will not exactly see the leash as positive. But if there's often something good (such as a game or a treat) happening after the leash is put on, then your dog will form a positive association with the leash.

Our children, ages 9 and 14, want a dog and would also like to train it themselves. Will that work?

That depends on both the child and the dog. A 9-year-old is still too young, but a 14-year-old may do very well. It's important, however, for the child to understand the context of the dog's training. If your pet belongs to an easily trainable breed and readily takes guidance from humans, this will have additional advantages. Nevertheless, you need to take responsibility for most of the training, because a child's interests can change over time. This means that the entire family has to want a dog.

In a few weeks, we're expecting a baby. Will this be a problem for our dog, Balou?

If he's been the "crown prince" until now, you should change the way you deal with the dog. Introduce any new rules—such as making the nursery off limits—before the baby arrives. When Balou is near, connect doing things with the baby—such as bathing it or going outdoors—with positive things for the dog. At the baby's bath time, make sure there's a chew bone for Balou, and an outing with the baby should mean a walk for him.

◁

In the canine world, gripping the muzzle serves an educational purpose, and the dog will interpret the grip the same way in the owner-dog relationship.

Is it true that collars are harmful for a dog and that it's better to use a harness?

A harness can be used for very small breeds. A normal collar is not harmful for a dog. If the dog is properly trained, it will not tug at the leash. Otherwise, a Halti head collar (→ page 223) can be helpful in addition. If the dog is not well trained, it will pull at a harness too. It will only make tugging more pleasant for the dog, giving it even more energy.

Ground Rules of Training

If you follow a few important fundamental rules in day-to-day dealings with your four-legged friend, then the training process will be smooth from now on.

THE BASIC RULES, which I want to introduce to you in the following section, are really not technically demanding and thus, are easy to implement in theory. But as Goethe so nicely put it, "All theory is gray." As a result of convenience, emotions, and "inner temptation," a good many dog owners again and again commit infractions when trying to apply the ground rules. If you think in human dimensions, you will often see your four-legged companion literally (and quite unnecessarily) as a "poor dog," and will not be doing either of you any favors.

Therefore, you need to pull yourself together and hang in there as best you can. I promise you that the following pointers will have a very positive effect both on you and on your dog and the life you share. Your pet will view you as his or her "idol."

Be Consistent

Consistency, that magic word, is very important in training your canine companion. It makes many aspects of coexistence easier and safer for both dog and owner. Being consistent means setting up rules that continue to be in force as fully as possible. This also means that the dog has to execute a command that he has already mastered whether he feels like doing so or not. If rules are always in effect and if the dog always has to obey signals (→ page 272) in the same way, lessons will be understandable, binding, and easier to learn. This can prove valuable in more dangerous situations as well. For example, if the dog has learned that the only response to "Sit" is really to sit immediately, he will be quite likely to do that even if he is just about to cross a cyclist's path. (The biker will be impressed.) And if your dog knows that, despite his pining look or his appearance of being about to die of hunger, he really won't get any food from the table, begging will stop.

The Consequences of Inconsistency

Woe to you if you weaken. If you don't stick to the rules you've introduced, if you're inconsistent, the dog will repeatedly put both you and the rules in effect to the test. Alternatively, he will tend to do whatever he believes to be right—that is, he will set up his own rules. Many dog owners think they're making their pet happy by not being such sticklers. Or they think the dog won't like them anymore if they're so "strict."

The tendency to anthropomorphize—to treat the dog like a human—crops up again here. But the truth is just the reverse. Unlike a child, a dog can't interpret exceptions differently. They are more apt to make the dog insecure or cause him, as mentioned earlier, to become overly independent. Clear guidelines, however, give the dog a sense of where he stands and a feeling of security. Therefore, even before starting the training process—better still, before the puppy or older dog joins your household—think about what you expect of your canine companion and decide what rules should be followed and what commands he should learn. Then, you must be consistent in carrying out your decisions.

Uniformity in Dealing with the Dog

The need for consistency applies not only to the dog's primary caregiver, but also to the entire family. Children are exempted here, because they shouldn't "train around" with the dog, and in addition, they also can't physically prevail against the animal.

Ideally, all family members should sit down and agree on what the dog can and can't do, which audible or visual signals will be used, and so forth. Success is attainable only if everyone deals with the dog in the same way. This is true when a puppy first moves in and later on as well, when he is fully grown.

In this situation you need to ignore the dog consistently, so that it will stop begging once and for all. Even brief visual contact or a hand movement in its direction can be interpreted by the dog as success.

The Question of Hierarchy

It should be clear to everyone that the human must be the higher-ranking, dominant partner in the human-dog team. But what constitutes a good higher-ranking partner?

Such a partner radiates an inner authority, behaves in a confident, intelligible way, and is stable, consistent, fair, and trustful. It is the human who generally takes the initiative with respect to playing together, petting the dog, opening the patio door, and the like. Certain areas, such as the bedroom, may be off limits for the dog. At the same time, however, you also provide his food and a sense of security. All these things cause you to have a "dominant" influence on your four-legged friend.

The dog will let you know whether you are behaving correctly, because he is trustfully ready to follow your lead, that is, to "subordinate" himself to you, instead of ignoring or resisting you. If the hierarchy is what it should be, the dog will not be constantly demanding something, for example, to be let out into the yard, to play with you, or to have you pet him. Moreover, he will not claim any

⬤ PRIVILEGES (page 271) for himself, such as the occasional use of the sofa, or seriously defend his toys and food.

With regard to hierarchy, however, you can't lump all dogs together. Some dogs fit into the ⬤ PACK (page 269) without a single hitch and are not quick to take advantage of weak points. Others, however, need very consistent leadership to prevent them from swiftly exploiting every tiny sign of slackness for their own benefit.

Here's an example from my classes: Recently, a dog owner asked me what she should do, as her male dog was leaving the property fairly frequently because a bitch was in heat somewhere. There was so much snow on the ground that the fence around the yard resembled a kind of low "edging" and thus presented no real obstacle for the dog. I advised her to simply leave the dog indoors. No, that wasn't possible, she said, because he so enjoyed being in the yard and whined and scratched at the door. But when the human decides the dog should stay inside, that's where it should stay. For more on this topic, reread the section on ignoring your pet, on page 31.

Indirect Assignment of Rank

If the dog is convinced by the qualities of his "lead human," generally he will see no reason to force through his own ideas over the long term. Then it won't matter, for example, if he is allowed to join you on the sofa on occasion or gets on it in your absence, thus enjoying a privilege of a superior—provided he gets off the sofa immediately and without protest when told to do so.

There are dogs, however, that are so submissive and ⬤ BIDDABLE (page 259) that they are reluctant—and made uneasy by conflicting impulses—when asked to cuddle next to their "boss" on the sofa or in his or her bed,

▷ *Don't react every time your canine companion thinks it has to go out in the yard—possibly because another dog is passing by. You are the one who decides when the dog can go out and when it can't. If it can go out, however, first ask it to sit as advance payment for your opening the door.*

though they fully enjoy the same activity on the floor. Don't force such a dog to overcome its distance from you as the "higher-ranking" partner. It is best to snuggle with your pet on neutral ground.

If the hierarchy is unclear, possibly because you simply can't act the way you need to, can't size up your dog, or because you've just acquired or adopted a dog, then I suggest that you grant the animal no privileges for the time being. Especially with dogs that have had another owner, it is hard at first to gauge what they have experienced and what ideas they have associated thus far, and as yet there exists no social hierarchy between you and the animal. For the time being, use ○ INDIRECT ASSIGNMENT OF RANK (page 267) as an aid, or institute certain rules.

These indirect ways of indicating rank include forbidding the dog to use elevated places for resting or to lie down at a strategically important place, such as in the entryway or next to a flight of stairs. In bottlenecks such as doorways, the human precedes the dog. To a great extent, you must ignore calls to play, demands for affection, and similar behaviors on the dog's part. They should originate mainly with you and also be ended by you. In addition, never feed the dog right before you eat, but afterwards, if necessary—because the "boss" eats first.

If your consistent behavior has brought you to your objective, this means:
▷ The hierarchy is clear.
▷ You have the requisite assurance in dealing with the dog.
▷ You radiate the authority of a "capable pack leader."

Only now can you ease up a bit on a few rules, if you are so inclined, but please don't toss them all overboard. Cuddling together on the sofa or in bed is more likely to be soothing for you than for the dog, since he really does

△
In prey games, you should be the "winner" most of the time. In response to your audible signal, the dog should immediately drop the object it's playing with—a rope, for example. Under no circumstances can the dog be allowed to defend the object.

not suffer from being kept off the couch or out of your bed. Apart from this, you also should consider the hygienic aspects, not to mention the problems of space that arise with dogs of a certain size.

If you grant the dog such privileges without having the kind of hierarchy you need, problems can result. For example, the dog may use unmistakable threats to determine who has access to the sofa or the bed. Then it can be quite difficult to come to grips with such problems once more.

Research & Practice

Findings of Wolf Studies

Observations of caged wolves and dogs by the Comparative Behavioral Research Group at the University of Kiel's Institute for Research on Domestication of Animals, and Günter Bloch's studies of wild wolves in Canada have great significance in our exploration of wolves' and dogs' behavior. Bloch succeeded in getting wolves used to the presence of his automobile, and thus he was able to follow their life throughout the year. Both types of research yield valuable information about wolves, dogs, and their needs.

▷

The wolf is the sole ancestor of our domestic dogs. The wolf population was stamped out for a long while, but for some years now there have been wild wolves living in parts of the United States.

In the following section, I would like to offer a brief digression on our present state of knowledge: A wolf pack usually consists of a family, including the parents and the young born during the past two or three years. The parents lead the family authoritatively, have a great deal of experience, and model for their offspring what is important and proper in

life. That alone makes their influence dominant. Depending on motivation, the father (for example, when danger threatens) or mother (looking for a safe den to give birth in) leads the group, but sometimes the young wolves also run out ahead. In a group hunt, however, it is usually the lead animals that ultimately "sound the attack."

In the first few weeks of life, the puppies enjoy "puppy license" within their family; that is, they are given free rein to do as they wish. That changes later on, however, and they learn what is or is not allowed. To put their beliefs into practice, the parents use three methods: ignoring, employing the muzzle grip, and forcing a pup to the ground, in that order of frequency. This applies to roughly the first eight weeks, and from then on a tougher driving style prevails. That is, the sequence of the parental methods changes: muzzle grip, forcing to the ground, ignoring.

Young wolves play quite a lot, but the parents also play with their offspring from time to time, depending on how much energy they need for hunting. The leaders sleep in more highly favored places (on which they also insist) and enjoy close physical contact with young pups and each other. The other group members, however, must maintain a certain individual distance from them, though occasionally there is also close physical contact with older offspring. If a sexually mature young male or female wolf places the social position of its father or mother in question it is forced to leave the pack.

When the pack goes hunting, a lower-ranking older sister babysits the little wolves, and during this period she may use the privileged sleeping places of the top-ranking wolves. Or she may "train" the pups. As soon as the elder wolves reappear, however, she quits the scene and leaves the pups alone.

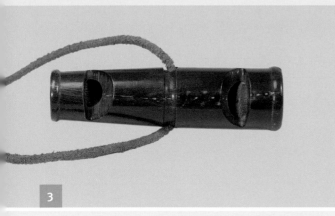

1 *The collar must not be too narrow and should fasten securely. Young dogs in particular need a collar that is expandable.*

2 *The leash should be stout, but not too heavy. A second spring clip can be used to vary its length.*

3 *Ideally, the whistle should be made of natural horn or sturdy plastic. Go ahead and buy two identical ones, so you'll have one in reserve.*

The Right Equipment

For training and schooling a dog, you need certain pieces of basic equipment.

▷ **The collar** should not be too narrow. Best for a puppy is one that can be expanded, so it doesn't outgrow it too quickly. After a few weeks, however, you'll need a bigger one. The material is a matter of taste, but you need a collar that fastens securely. The size has to be right as well. It mustn't be too tight, only tight enough that the dog can't slip out of it—you should be able to slip a finger between the dog's neck and the collar.

▷ **The leash** should be the type that can be lengthened by means of a second spring clip and several metal rings. Especially for a puppy, the leash should not be too heavy. Here too, there are different models, but sturdy spring clips that don't break if tugged on hard are always important. When the dog gets bigger, you'll need a new leash again.

▷ **A dog whistle** is useful in drilling and practicing. With the right training, you can teach the dog an unfailing "Come" signal. The emphasis here is on "training," since only if it has been correctly trained will the dog understand exactly what it should do in response to the whistle blow. Without systematic training, it will respond to the whistle only haphazardly, because it finds the noise interesting, and thus, won't come reliably. The strength of the ◐ DOG WHISTLE (page 262) is that the sound is an "exclusive" command—unlike the voice signal, which often is given unclearly and ambiguously. A long blow on the whistle is always a long blow on the whistle. On the other hand, the whistle is not so lavishly used as the voice.

Another plus is the whistle's greater range. At a distance, its sound is much more distinct than a spoken "Here." My tip: Choose a whistle that you can hear too. Then you know that it works.

▶ TEST: ALL ABOUT TRAINING

If you're in good shape as far as the basics of dog training are concerned, then common errors easily can be prevented.

1. What species-appropriate ways are there to influence undesirable behavior?

a) Lock the dog in the basement.
b) Ignore the dog.
c) Punish the dog by making it skip a meal.

2. What period of canine development is especially important for training?

a) The dog's entire life.
b) The first two years.
c) The third to sixteenth weeks of life.

3. Your pet will learn something new when you:

a) Give its leash a tug or do something similar to make it do what you want.
b) Set up the situation so that the dog has a positive motivation to do your bidding of its own accord.
c) Explain everything to it in as much detail as possible.

4. What is important for effective learning by a dog?

a) An atmosphere that's free of anxiety and negative stress.
b) Military-style drills.
c) Inconsistency.

5. Which of the following situations can you influence by ignoring your pet?

a) The dog stands at the fence and barks at people passing by.
b) The dog barks to get you to feed it.
c) It chews on valuable rugs.

6. How can a dog tell that you are the higher-ranking partner?

a) You intimidate it as often as possible and thus subordinate it.
b) Mostly, you let it do whatever it wants.
c) You behave in an authoritative, self-controlled way and insist on certain rules.

7. Your dog sits in a trance in front of you while you're eating a piece of cake. What's the right way to react?

a) Look right through the dog, ignoring it.
b) Give the dog some of the cake so it will leave you alone.
c) Reprimand the dog, using the muzzle grip.

8. You find a chewed-up shoe in the yard. What's the best way to react?

a) Show the shoe to the dog and scold it.
b) In the future, you put your shoes away, but you show no reaction right now.
c) Pick up the damaged shoe and give the dog a slap with it.

Answers:

1b) → Page 31   2c) → Page 25
3b) → Page 26   4a) → Pages 26, 35
5b) → Page 31   6c) → Page 36
7a) → Page 31   8b) → Pages 29–31

On Familiar Terms with Your Dog

You want to understand what your dog would like to tell you, for example, when he or she stands in front of you wagging its tail and barking loudly. Or when he immediately takes to his heels as soon as he sees the haughty dog from the neighborhood, whereas she gives strange dogs a thorough sniffing. Keep me company here as I take you on a short journey through the world of canine communication. But first we need to make a detour and take another look at the wolf, the dog's forebear, since this will help us understand the dog.

2

How Dogs
Communicate

Wolves communicate with each other through sounds and smells, but largely they employ a sophisticated body language with a wide range of means of expression.

AS THE WELL-KNOWN behavioral researcher Dr. Dorit Feddersen-Petersen writes, the wolf displays sixty different facial expressions alone, while the German Shepherd exhibits only twelve. Wolves make use of this highly differentiated "language" to regulate their social relations in the pack. They employ it, for example, to reinforce the bond between them, make their social status clear, "bring up" the pups, or keep things from coming to blows. The last-mentioned task is important for the survival of a pack, because injured members can't participate in getting food and thus, could endanger the success of the hunt for all concerned.

The Dog's Body Language

Over the course of its breeding history, the dog has lost some of the multifaceted ◗ EXPRESSIVE BEHAVIOR (page 263) displayed by the wolf (→ page 38), because in a life intimately associated with humans, this is no longer necessary to the same extent as in the case of a wild animal. When dogs meet, this oversimplification of the means of expression can have negative results at times. In addition to the loss of some behaviors, breeding also has resulted in many dog groups that no longer possess the physical prerequisites to express themselves as wolves do. Drooping ears, for example, or a shortened skull, impede communication. Facial wrinkles, very pronounced flews, tail positions resulting from breeding and unable to convey moods correctly, and long hair have the same disadvantageous effect. If the dog's long hair also hangs in its face, this makes communication twice as difficult: Not only can such a dog send out less expressive messages, but he also can hardly see the signals sent by other dogs. This promotes misunderstandings.

If a dog wants to understand a conspecific correctly, then (as is true of humans) he must always keep an eye on the other dog's overall body expression, because a message always contains several signals. Such signals are conveyed by the position of the ears and tail, the shape of the flews, the posture of the body, and the like. All the signals together produce, depending on the combination, a very specific message and cause the conspecific to react.

Neutral Mood and Attention

If a "station break" is in progress and nothing catches the dog's attention, he's in a neutral mood. You can recognize this by your pet's overall air of calm and serenity. The tail is in its default position (usually down, but this can vary depending on the breed), the face is relaxed, the ears likewise. The mouth may be slightly open. Perhaps the dog is even snoozing a little.

If something gets his attention, the tail lifts a little and the mouth closes. Then the dog alertly brings his ears forward into the "attention position." His entire body seems slightly tensed.

Display Behavior

This behavior can be easily observed when male dogs meet. Their bodies are tensed, and

◗ INFO

Wagging the Tail

Wagging is not only meant in a friendly way. Short strokes and a raised tail are often part of display behavior. Rapid wags and a lowered tail are frequently signs of submissiveness. Wide sideward movements are part of a friendly greeting. Slow wagging, side to side or up and down indicates an uncertain, temporizing attitude. Pay attention to the body language.

their movements are stiff and slow. Their tails are held fairly high, sometimes wagging slightly. In addition, they straighten their joints in order to look bigger. Their ears point slightly forward, and they avoid making eye contact with each other—after all, they don't want to start anything right away. At the same time they try to sniff each other's muzzle or rear end to collect more specific information about each other.

If the two dogs like each other, they may start to play. If neither is interested in the other, they'll be on their way again, perhaps still lifting a leg here and there to make it clear once more that they've passed through. To underscore this yet again, many dogs then scratch the ground more or less thoroughly.

Threatening Behavior

If there's no love lost between the parties, a fight usually does not start at once; instead, the dogs first threaten or menace each other. There are two different forms of threatening behavior. Depending on whether the dog thinks it is the stronger or the weaker, it will make either defensive or offensive threats.

▷ **Defensive threats:** This method is used by the weaker dog. It crouches, holding its head and neck low. At the same time, its tail is down or tucked between its legs, and its ears are laid against its head. The hair on its back may be standing up. It bares its teeth, turning the corners of its mouth slightly or distinctly downward to reveal the molars as well. If the dog feels really cornered and threatened, it may suddenly lunge and bite or it may run away.

▷ **Offensive threats:** This method is used by the stronger dog. Typically, it continues to stand tall, moving with its legs held stiffly. Its tail is straight up, and the hair on its back stands up. The corners of its mouth are taut and rounded, and only the front teeth are bared. It makes direct eye contact with its opponent.

▷ **Combinations of both categories:** These behaviors are used if neither one of the dogs is clearly inferior or superior, or if the tide turns during the encounter. The outcome ultimately depends on several factors, including the owner's reaction and the specific behavior of the dogs. In the wild, threatening behavior serves to prevent altercations involving "roughness." Its success is harder to predict with domesticated dogs, since their temperament and

This bitch is showing submission but remains relaxed, since the other dog is not threatening her. Her tail is not tucked between her legs, and she is looking at the other dog.
▽

socialization also play a role. Some ultimately are more inclined to fight. Occasionally there are even dogs that can no longer control their threatening behavior and bite without any warning.

Passive Subjugation

If things go no farther than the threat ritual during the encounter, the weaker dog may plainly adopt a submissive posture. Usually he will lie on its back and refuse to look at his opponent, while tucking his tail firmly between his legs. His mouth is shut, his lips are narrowed and pulled back, and his ears are flattened against his head. The entire face looks smooth. If the "winner" is satisfied with that, he goes on his way, and the weaker dog can get back on his feet.

Active Subjugation

Dogs exhibit this behavior, for example, when greeting a higher-ranking canine or a familiar human, in an attempt to put the other dog or the person in a friendly mood.

A dog that is actively submitting seems playful and friendly. He crouches slightly and waves his tail invitingly, holding it "at half mast." His ears are laid back, his eyes are narrowed, and he licks the other dog's muzzle or even nudges the other dog's muzzle with his own. Often he lifts a paw in the air as well. If the behavior is really pronounced, puppies and young dogs in particular also release some urine at this time.

Communicating by Body Contact

Dogs, like humans, touch each other as a sign that they belong together. They strengthen their common bond by touching, and this is especially common within a pack. Nibbling each other's coat, taking another dog's muzzle in their mouth, nudging, licking ears and muzzle—all these emphasize the sense of togetherness.

 The practice of SNUGGLING (page 273), in which dogs lie close together to sleep or nap, is also common. This is another way of reinforcing the feeling of belonging together.

Body contact can also be used in a "negative" sense. For example, when a dog lays his head on another dog's back and uses correspondingly dominant body language, this is a DOMINANCE GESTURE (page 263). Pushing and jostling are also meant in a negative way. These behaviors are exhibited predominantly when dogs have a run-in.

In rearing puppies, gripping the muzzle somewhat more forcefully functions as a type of reprimand, as does taking a firm grip on a puppy's nape or pushing it down on the floor.

▷ TIP

Brimming Over with Exuberance

Some young dogs behave quite disrespectfully and urge every other member of their species to romp—regardless of whether it wants to or not. If the other dog's signals of unwillingness are ignored, a stern admonishment can easily result. Keep an eye on the situation, and call the young whippersnapper to order in good time.

How Dogs "Talk"

Dogs use a sophisticated system of vocalizations to communicate. It is not equally well developed in all dogs, however, but depends on temperament and breed. There are "more talkative" and "more silent" types.

Barking

Wolves scarcely bark at all, but dogs use a broad spectrum of barking sounds. Basically, barking means that the dog is excited. The more rapid the barking; the more agitated the animal. Most often, it is the instinct to guard that causes dogs to bark—they want to report that an "intruder" is approaching their territory. Dogs may also bark to issue an invitation to play, to indicate uncertainty, to express a greeting, or to show excitement before a walk or at mealtime. The body language (→ page 45) your dog uses will tell you how to interpret its barking in each specific case.

Some dogs howl when they hear sirens or other high-pitched or loud noise. Unfortunately, we have no idea why this is so.

▷

Growling

Serious growling is always a warning and is used in both offensive and defensive threats. It may also be combined with barking. Some dogs also growl playfully, but in a way that sounds less threatening. To interpret growling correctly, you or the other dog, as the case may be, have to pay attention to the overall body posture and the situation. For example, if your dog growls playfully during a game that involves tugging, this sound is not intended to be threatening.

Some dogs "grunt" when they greet the humans they are fond of. This often is misinterpreted as growling.

Whimpering and Whining

Whimpering may express joy, stress, impatience, boredom, or even pain. Males often whimper or whine for days at a time when there is a bitch in heat nearby. The tendency to whimper varies widely among dogs.

Whining is to a certain extent an escalation of whimpering. It too can be triggered by pain, as well as by boredom, separation anxiety, demanding behavior, and the like. To the neighbors' "delight," dogs that have a problem staying alone frequently whine to indicate their unease.

Howling

Howling is a vocalization that wolves have mastered. It serves to keep the pack together. Domesticated dogs seldom howl, though Nordic breeds, such as the Siberian Husky or the Alaskan Malamute, still exhibit this legacy from their ancestors. In many dogs, however, howling is provoked by certain acoustic stimuli, such as church bells or sirens.

Using Scents to Send Messages

Scents, too, are used by dogs as a means of communication. Since we humans have far less sensitive noses than dogs, we lack the ability to understand the full range of this type of communication.

At various places on its body, a dog has scent glands whose secretions it can use to send olfactory messages. These pieces of information are "read" when dogs sniff each other's face and anal region. In addition, feces and urine play an important role, since secretions from glands in the anal area are deposited along with these waste products.

Scent Messages

Unlike body language, a dog does not need a direct partner in communication to interpret olfactory messages—he or she can read the message even if its sender has long since gone elsewhere. And the recipient's own response, of course, can still be read even after they have returned home. Such a "canine instant messages" can provide dogs with a great deal of information. For example, they can ascertain the other dog's gender, the hormonal condition of a bitch, the social status of the message's originator, and also determine whether the scent was left by a puppy or a full-grown dog, or by a friend, enemy, or stranger.

If the dog leaves a scent message in liquid form, this is called "marking." When marking, a male lifts his leg at every possible spot and releases a little urine. Unlike a female, he does not empty his bladder all at once, but in many small amounts. He not only informs other dogs about himself in this way, but also "writes over" another dog's urine mark and designates his territory. The more pronounced a dog's marking behavior and the higher he lifts his leg, the more self-confident he is. There are even some bitches that lift their legs.

A typical canine encounter—each dog sniffs at the other, concentrating its attention on the rear end. In this way they try to get as much precise information as possible about each other.

Self-confident males often scratch vigorously at the ground after relieving themselves, sending clumps of grass flying—after all, they want to broadcast their message as widely as possible.

Bitches that are about to go into ◐ HEAT (page 265) also mark with urine more frequently. They use this trace of scent to inform as many potential "suitors" as possible of their condition and hope for appropriate callers at the right time.

How Your Dog Understands You

Do you want your pet to understand your words and gestures correctly? Then you need to know how your four-legged companion interprets your signals. In other words, learn "dog talk!"

THROUGH DOMESTICATION, dogs have developed a special ability to interpret our behavior. They interpret everything from the canine viewpoint, however, and react to it correspondingly.

The messages we send our pet consist of our posture, movements, facial expressions, and voice. To ensure that the dog actually understands all the things we're trying to convey, these elements must be combined in the right way. You need to consider this and "translate" it before you begin to send out a message. First, think about exactly what you want to accomplish.

Talking with Your Body

Dogs can recognize the slightest nuances of our body language. He or she can tell exactly whether you are radiating a sense of security and authority, or are hesitant and uncertain. They notice if you're in a bad mood, under stress, nervous, or irritable. Just as accurately, of course, they can recognize your good mood and tell whether you're focused on the matter at hand or are only half-hearted about it. They will take you correspondingly seriously—or not. This is my advice: Take a proactive approach and use your body language consciously; then your dog will react to it.

The correct dosage required depends on your dog's nature. If your pet is inclined to be easy-going, then you need to motivate her a little more forcefully, to get her started. Go about it calmly, however, if you want your pet's behavior to be calm. On the other hand, a high-spirited or even nervous dog needs no great motivation to get going. But if calm behavior is what you're after, you need to convey a strong sense of calm. Don't let yourself be influenced by the dog's mood.

The intensity of body language required also depends on how sensitive, thick-skinned, or strong-willed the dog is. Your body language must be clear, but should not make the animal uneasy.

Using Facial Expressions Correctly
Staring straight at a dog with a serious or angry look on your face is just as threatening as it would be to a human. Depending on your pet's temperament, you definitely can use such an expression, perhaps in combination with clearing your throat, to get her to stop doing something you disapprove of. If you stare at a strange dog the same way, however, she may feel threatened. A friendly face, on the other hand, will have a positive effect on a strange dog

Posture and Movements
These means can also be used to successfully influence your dog to do something, to stop doing it, or to do it differently. If you walk right up to your pet more or less briskly, that will inhibit her and cause her, depending on how crisp your manner is, to stop or to move back or to one side. By the same token, your dog will not come cheerfully when called if you approach her in a threatening way. If you walk in the opposite direction, however, this will encourage her to follow. The faster you

> ## INFO
>
> ### Helping Your Dog Understand
>
> Adapt your body language to your dog's temperament. With many dogs, subtle signals are sufficient. Others, however, need more expressive gestures, and then the owner has to really put some effort into it. This doesn't come easy to everybody. Just try out various kinds of body language in private, when you're alone with your pet.

move away, the more decisively and quickly the dog will follow. Equally inhibiting or threatening is leaning over your dog and then "popping up," that is, standing up suddenly. These signals also will cause your pet to keep her distance or to try to evade you. Squatting down, thus, making yourself seem smaller, is very welcoming, especially for puppies and young dogs, and they will come racing up with their little ears flapping.

If you want the dog to come to you, for example, you should always walk away from her. Then she is more likely to make an effort

Here's the right way to approach strange dogs: While looking away from the dog, turn your body toward it, holding out your hand in its direction. Then you won't seem threatening. Make sure to watch the dog out of the corner of your eye.

Really energetic movement is also called for when you want your dog to come quickly.

▷ **Even completely neutral behavior** can act as a signal for your dog. Imagine this situation: You're out walking your dog. Along the way her attention is attracted by a visual stimulus, such as a fluttering piece of foil or a colorfully dressed person, and she briefly wonders whether anything here is worth getting excited about. If you stay calm and don't react to the flashy object, then you give the dog a signal: "There's no reason to get excited." The prerequisite, of course, is the existence of the right bond between you and your four-legged friend. In addition, staying calm will not work if the dog is inherently anxious or mistrustful.

Body language also plays a role when you use hand signals or other visual signals. An upward motion causes the dog to look up, while her rear end almost automatically goes down: she sits. A clear downward motion encourages the dog to lie down. For more on this, see the section beginning on page 106.

to maintain contact than if you simply wait for her or even run after her.

Depending on the intensity of your movements, you can express either calm or energetic action.

▷ **When you want your dog to behave calmly,** you need to convey this through the way you move. For example, if you are still training your dog and you want her to lie quietly where she is, don't start jumping around her excitedly; that will only make her imitate you and enjoy the fantastic game. If you want your dog to be calm and quiet, you need to be the very embodiment of tranquility yourself.

▷ **When you want your dog to be active and energetic,** you need to model this behavior for her. If you want your pet to *heel* cheerfully, then you have to radiate enthusiasm, decisiveness, and energy. That will give a signal: "Hey, something's going on, and I want to be part of it." On the other hand, simply ambling along in a bored way will cause the dog to lose interest as well or to give her attention to more interesting things along the way, like scents on the ground or other members of her species.

Touching

Touching is very important, not only among dogs, but also in the relationship between owner and pet. Stroking your dog's head and body, brushing her coat, or snuggling (→ page 273) are ways of touching that promote a sense of togetherness. This is especially critical for a puppy or a young dog, because physical contact strengthens her bond with you as her caregiver.

As I have explained, touch can also be employed in a negative way, and this is equally true for the relationship between human and dog. For example, you can correct your dog by pushing her away (from a strategically important napping spot, for instance), jostling her (if the dog is oblivious and inattentive), gripping her muzzle firmly, with an appropriate audible signal, or restraining the dog.

Using Your Voice Correctly

The voice is also a very important means of communication. Since tone of voice and speech are the means of communication *par excellence* for us humans, we often tend to use them too lavishly and too indiscriminately with dogs.

A dog, however, does not understand the words. She is guided by the sound and by the tone of voice and can read various signals from them. Explanations, angry tirades, and lengthy outpourings of praise mean nothing to your four-legged friend. She will simply tune out, and over time she will no longer react well to your voice. For these reasons, you need to talk to your dog as thoughtfully and as purposefully as possible.

Give Clear Signals

The clearer and more unambiguous the ● SIGNAL (page 272) you give, the easier it is for the dog to learn. For each exercise, choose a specific audible signal that distinctly differs from the others. When you give your four-legged friend an audible signal, then use only the one you've chosen —for example, a friendly, authoritative "Sit"—without any embellishments like "Come on, be a good girl and sit."

The voice command "Come" is used by many dog owners when they want the dog to come to them. But this word is common in daily usage as well, so the dog hears it repeatedly without associating it with anything meaningful. Often "Come" is also used unconsciously as a filler word in other voice commands, such as "Come on, down," or "Come on, heel," and so forth. The dog is irritated by such a command, because she doesn't know whether she should come or assume the *down* position. As a result, she is likely to obey inconsistently and sporadically.

Find the Right Tone of Voice

Your tone of voice tells the dog whether you're talking to her in a friendly way, are angry, or are delighted because she has done something well. Therefore you need to choose your tone very deliberately. The range of tones you need to master depends once again on the dog. Her reactions will tell you whether you've gotten it right. You should be able to see your pet's joy when you praise her, for example.

Pleasure, too, is something you can express either calmly or exuberantly—depending on whether you're praising the dog for sitting quietly or for racing up to you at top speed when called away from a game with other dogs. On the other hand, "No" and "Bad dog" must sound appropriately stern, so that the dog can interpret them correctly.

Incidentally, there's no need to use a loud voice with dogs. They hear better than we do.

All ears? A dog can get a lot of information from the sound of our voices, providing that we use them consciously and deliberately.

▷

53

Combining the Signals Correctly

If you want the message you send your pet to be deciphered unambiguously, you have to combine the separate elements of communication in an appropriate way. This means that you have to match your body language to your voice.

Adapting Your Voice

You may want, for example, to practice getting your dog to lie down in a certain place and stay there. To achieve that, you give the voice command "Stay" quite calmly and walk away, remaining cool and collected. But if you were to say "Stay, stay, stay" in a tense voice and walk off in a flurry, your pet would certainly stand up and come to you, because you would be unmistakably giving her a signal that you're upset. Similarly, when you practice *heeling* with your dog, an encouraging audible signal should accompany your act of stepping forward—otherwise, your dog may not even notice that something is going on.

Another example: You want to take something away from your dog, such as a child's toy or a bone she's been gnawing. To do so, you quietly and firmly give the voice command "Out" and just as quietly and firmly take the object from your pet. If you only say the audible signal correctly but lack the confidence to take something away from the dog and thus, act hesitant and uncertain, you won't have a convincing effect on your four-legged friend. As a consequence, she is more apt to run off with the toy to keep it safe.

And one final example: You want your young dog, which is just sniffing at a scent mark, to come when you call her. You walk away from her correctly, but use a stern tone of voice for the command "Here." In this fairly unappealing situation, the dog is hardly likely to run after you. But if you move off in the opposite direction and call out in a tantalizing, interest-arousing voice, she will come at once, because that gives the dog (if her bond with you is good) a signal: "I'd better go there, or I'll miss something really good." And she will be right, too, because a tasty treat will be waiting for her!

In conclusion, some advice: Work on your voice and manner, so that you can convey information clearly enough to your dog. In my classes, I've observed that men often have a harder time praising a dog lavishly or getting her attention with an inviting tone of voice. Women, on the other hand, usually have a different problem: They have trouble exuding the necessary air of authority, which men often find easier because of their voices alone.

Combining Scent Messages with Your Voice

Scents also play a role in the human-dog relationship, but they are difficult for us to use consciously. A dog can learn a lot from our body odor, however; among other things, our pet can tell whether we are stressed out or anxious. This can lead to problematic situations, for example, when you're trying to use relaxed body language and the appropriate tone of voice, but a cold sweat has broken out on your forehead. That's not the way to seem convincing and authoritative to your dog.

An example: You're quite afraid of large dogs, but want to tell your canine companion that she need not be afraid of the big dog approaching you just ahead. You're not likely to succeed convincingly, since your pet can tell you're afraid by the way you smell. In addition, even the slightest nuances of your body language will betray your discomfort at the sight of the big animal.

The Human as "Pack Leader"

On page 36, I introduced the topic of the pack leader and the assignment of rank. In the chapter on communication, I want to go back to that subject and urge you really to be the "leader of the pack," so that you can control your dog. Every dog that lives in a family or goes out in "public" in any way needs that kind of control.

What Makes a Pack Leader

Ultimately your body language and voice are the means you use to radiate aplomb and authority. It's all right to seem a little "overbearing" to your pet. Part of this overbearing attitude entails ignoring your dog. This means, as pointed out on page 36, not responding in the affirmative every time your pet issues an invitation to play or cuddle. It also means ignoring your dog when she barks or stares hypnotically at you while insistently reminding you that it's time for a walk or a meal.

In the latter situation, if you jump up with a guilty conscience, apologize by petting the dog profusely, and rush into the kitchen to get the food into the bowl quickly, then you're more likely to seem "submissive" than "dominant." But if you pay no attention to the dog until she stops her demanding behavior, you'll seem just as masterful as the lead wolf, the only difference being that the wolf, of course, doesn't fix any meals.

Since my younger son occasionally gives our bitch some food from the table, despite the ban on this practice, she sometimes tests him by sitting discreetly, but with an unmistakably pleading look in her eye, next to the

▶ WHAT DO I DO IF . . .

... my dog is not interested in me?

Are you always there for your pet, and do you rarely pass by without talking to her or petting her? Then make a conscious effort to pay less attention to her; instead, deliberately set aside certain times to devote yourself to your pet. For example, play with her at least once a day, and show her plenty of attention when you're out walking together in particular. This is also important if you have the feeling that the bond between you is not strong enough.

What is the dog's daily routine? Is something always going on? Do the children play with it all day long? Then the dog lacks peace and quiet and is so "wiped out" by all the action that she no longer has any incentive or any energy to focus on you. If this is the case, make sure that your pet's life is calmer. Don't leave her in the yard all day to play with the children; instead, keep her indoors. If necessary, you can give her some fresh air while she stays in her pet crate (→ page 75). If your four-legged friend is an independent-minded type by nature, food often serves as a motivator to remind her of your importance. Take a careful look at the hierarchy that's been established, and if necessary, change the way you relate with the dog.

table. Then all it takes is a stern glance from me as "pack leader," accompanied by a gently growled "No" or a growling noise, to get her to lie down immediately under the table, her eyes averted, or to go to her bed and nap. If you constantly try to please your dog, you'll lose your standing in her eyes. You'll only teach your pet that it can manipulate you, and she will do just as she likes. If need be, she will even emphatically demand what it wants.

But dogs don't act this way out of malice; it is simply part of their nature. They can't behave any differently.

A Few Words about Dominance

● DOMINANCE (page 262) does not mean being aggressive or demonstrating physical strength. Anyone who is dominant has no need to be aggressive, but demonstrates superiority by the behavior described above, and also by setting limits and claiming privileges. On the other hand, being dominant also means that the "boss" takes care of the others and protects them from danger. Therefore, the human, not the dog, answers the door and sees who's there. Or another example: My four-year-old bitch (she usually is submissive) recently was seriously threatened by a one-year-old Rhodesian Ridgeback. My bitch did return the threat, but also wanted to appease the other animal and avoid conflict. But after the other bitch used more threatening body language and gave no sign of relenting, I assumed the role of "boss" and stepped in to make the opponent back off.

Putting a paw up on her owner's leg means expressing a demand in this case. Nevertheless, there's no evidence that the dog is trying to dominate. Presumably, this is a long-standing way of getting her owner's attention.
▽

How to Deal with Strange Dogs

You've trained your dog to deal with all possible situations in an uncomplicated, trusting way. You can consider yourself lucky, since not all dogs are like that. Children who grow up with a four-legged companion often go up to strange dogs in a relatively naive way. This can be problematic if the dog reacts differently from the child's own pet. Your dog too, may respond to strangers differently than to his or her own family.

If you want to establish contact with a dog that is unfamiliar to you, you should always ask the owner first whether he or she has any objection.

Signals That Seem "Threatening"

Human beings engage in some behaviors that a dog may dislike or find threatening—especially if she is fearful or frightened or thinks her owner is being threatened. Most people bend over a dog when they want to make contact with it, but not all dogs like that. Having their head stroked from above is something that some dogs find unpleasant. If you speak to a dog in a loud voice, walk right up to her, or make frantic movements, she may also feel threatened. The same thing is true if you try to make direct eye contact with a dog.

If you don't know a dog, don't squat down right next to her. If you crowd a dog that way, she can easily feel that you're pressing too hard, and under some circumstances she may react by biting.

A dog with a pronounced instinct to protect may even misinterpret an enthusiastic greeting of his or her owner—possibly including a hug or a pat on the shoulder—as an attack, and react in defense. This can also result if the dog is startled, perhaps by being touched from behind or jostled.

The Right Way to Approach

If you've asked the dog's owner whether it's all right to pet him or her, then you should say the animal's name in a calm, friendly way. Move toward it slowly, but without making direct eye contact. If the dog seems interested, let it sniff your hand. Don't bend over the dog, however (→ photo, page 52). At this point its body language will tell you how it feels, and you should gauge your further actions accordingly.

If the dog is uninterested, moves away, or growls, then you should leave it alone.

If you want to give a strange dog a treat, I also recommend asking the owner beforehand for permission, even if it's only a very tiny one. Not all people want their dog to be fed by strangers, because many dogs then will really start thrusting their nose into jacket pockets and insisting on a treat come hell or high water. And not all passersby will be amused by a pushy dog and a saliva-covered jacket.

Hey, There's a Dog Loose!

If you're out with your dog and come across another free-running dog with no owner in sight, your behavior should be guided by the situation (→ also page 69):

If the other dog gives you an uncomfortable feeling, change direction promptly and avoid making direct contact.

If the strange dog seems okay, but your dog is on leash, then unleash it (→ page 168). There is no one best reaction, however, so you need to decide on the basis of the particular situation.

How Dogs Talk to Humans

Your pet's tail is tucked under, or he or she is pawing you affectionately, and you don't know what it all means? Here you'll learn to understand your dog's behavior. Make yourself into a dog interpreter!

AS WITH OTHER MEMBERS OF THE SPECIES, dogs use their "language" to signal their moods and feelings to us humans, whether they are stressed out or afraid, want something from you, or want to show that they belong to you. Dogs can convey all these things to us.

Approaching problems, too, can be recognized in time if you know how to read the signs correctly and take them seriously. At first, it may not be so easy to understand your pet, but if you watch its behavior closely, you'll soon be able to interpret your dog's language correctly.

How to Recognize Trust and Fear

In an optimal human-dog team, the four-legged member has a good bond with and confidence in the human member and enjoys being around him or her. The dog always looks to the human for guidance, because his life centers around this person. More evidence of this is given by the dog's tendency, when outdoors, to voluntarily stay near his two-legged partner and to keep checking to see whether the human is still there—with no need for the latter to try hard to attract attention.

Such dogs frequently enjoy close physical contact. When snoozing, they like to rest their head or paw on their owner's feet. Should you lie down on the rug, the dog will crawl up close to take a little nap within touching distance—if possible, with their head resting on some part of your body. That happened to me when I was lying facedown on the rug, trying to do a few exercises for my back. My bitch pressed herself close and put her head on my back to snooze—and a dog's head can get quite heavy in the long run!

How a Dog Shows Trust

If a dog greets his owner trustingly, he wags his ⬤ TAIL (page 274) so sweepingly that his entire rear end often swings back and forth at the same time, while the tail is held in a horizontal position or slightly lowered. The dog will avoid direct eye contact by ducking his head slightly or partly closing his eyes and squinting, with his ears laid back. Some dogs also "shake hands" by raising a front paw. If the human squats down, the dog may try to lick the corners of his or her mouth, behaving as it would with other dogs.

If the dog is very submissive, he will hold his tail quite low when wagging it, seem more restrained in general, and hunch to look smaller. Puppies and young dogs may release a small amount of urine when greeting

strangers in particular. This behavior is meant to appease, so please don't fuss at your dog because of it. Ideally, you should take no notice of your pet at all and make sure that the dog gets only a restrained greeting or is first ignored and then quietly greeted after a few minutes. This is sure to be difficult for many visitors, because puppies are simply very appealing, but they may accept it if you explain the background to them.

How Fear Is Expressed

The transition from submissiveness to uncertainty, the stage preceding fear, is fluid. An uncertain dog often seems servile, and his tail is more or less tucked. If a dog greets his owner or people in general with his tail tucked between his legs, his level of trust is very low. This can result from bad experiences or from being raised in isolation, but the cause may also be a certain natural inclination. Depending on the extent of these influences, it may be that the dog even more or less avoids all contact with human beings.

Real fear is expressed by a lowered stance and by looking away or gazing into the distance, not focusing on anything. A dog that is fearful lowers his head and tucks his tail tightly between his legs. In addition, he may tremble

◁

His tail is tucked under, and the dog's overall bearing seems uneasy—this animal is feeling very insecure. He may have seen something that is frightening and appears to be deliberating whether to flee or to wait and see what happens.

This dog has a submissive, slightly fearful facial expression. His ears are flopped and laid back; his face is impassive, but seems tense. His pupils look small.

or pant. If such a dog feels cornered, he may engage in fear-related aggression. Be careful—such an animal may bite without warning, so don't get too close.

Insecurity and fear related to people, objects, and noises or to certain situations can be a real problem, depending on how pronounced the symptoms are. For example, if the dog panics in response to noises or visual stimuli and flees headlong, is scared to walk on slippery floors, feels uncomfortable around people, and so forth, this can lead to irksome as well as dangerous situations in daily life. The dog will also suffer in the process, because he

will frequently be exposed to great stress. To read more on this subject, see pages 242–243.

How to Deal with a Fearful Dog

Depending on the origin and extent of the problem, fear often can be assuaged by specific kinds of training. If there is only a slight uncertainty, a confident pack leader whose "aura" alone conveys a sense of security and safety can be helpful. However, I strongly advise against trying to "console" or "commiserate with" an insecure or fearful dog. If you pet him comfortingly or talk to him consolingly and try to get him away from the "dangerous" object quickly, in order to keep your pet from seeing it, then you are only validating the dog's behavior by providing this type of attention. Hence, you ultimately reinforce his insecurity and fear instead of alleviating them.

Instead, encourage your pet in a lively, friendly voice to investigate the object of his fear along with you, and touch the object yourself. Alternatively, distract the dog with a game or a toy, depending on the situation. Make sure your own behavior is composed and calm; this will signal your dog that there is no reason to get upset.

For more serious problems of this kind— for example, if no attempts to alleviate his fear seem to work—it is best to seek the help of a professional with special training in dealing with behavioral problems, or of a dog training professional.

Reacting Correctly to Demands

Dogs really know how to "train" their humans with looks and other body language so that they attain their goals sooner or later. Wait, shouldn't that be the other way around? Yes, it should. And in this section you'll find some examples of ways of making demands, so that you can tell when your pet is wrapping you around his or her little finger again. Remember this: the one making demands and taking action is the real "boss."

When the Dog Makes Demands— Examples from Everyday Life

I'm hungry! Mealtime is approaching, and your dog is following you like a shadow. Or he suddenly is sitting right in front of you like a statue and giving you a hypnotic, piercing look. Many dogs also try to take their owners by the arm and lead them into the kitchen, or bark. If your pet demands dinner in this way, the right reaction is to ignore him until he stops his efforts and behaves normally again. You need to persevere, even if it takes a while; your dog won't starve! Only then should you seize the initiative and fix your pet's meal.

Please play with me or pet me! If the dog brings his toy and lays it at your feet, barks at you, or nips at your pant leg, he is clearly inviting you to play. To get attention and be petted, a dog will nudge his owner or push his head under his or her arm. Some canines will do that mainly when you're busy doing something else, such as having a nice conversation and holding a full coffee cup in one hand.

Of course, it is important to play with your dog and to pet him as well. Not all the time or only when the dog wishes, however, but primarily when you feel like doing so. Make it a habit to ignore his attempts frequently.

Dogs: Great Beggars

Many canines have perfectly mastered the art of begging. The dog will sit next to the table or lay his paw or head in a person's lap. In the "advanced stage" he may bark at the same time, to lend emphasis to his demand. If you want to keep the begging from getting worse, then you should never give in to the dog's endeavors. This means that you have to be absolutely firm in ignoring your pet. If he has already been trained, have him lie down in his place during your mealtimes.

Other Ways of Being Demanding

Some dogs get carried away when the time for a walk is approaching, and they become pushy, urging their owner to hurry up and get ready. Or they may keep asking to be let out the patio door or another door and then back in again, getting your attention by scratching, barking, or whining.

You need to be firm and consistent. The time for the walk is always your decision. Don't get ready until the dog has stopped his demanding behavior. You also decide whether

◁

One paw on his owner's arm, his gaze presumably fixed on a toy or on his owner's sandwich—this is an unmistakable demand, expressed in canine terms. If you usually respond to him, the dog will learn that you can be manipulated in this way.

2

the dog absolutely has to chase the bird in the yard right now or not. If you want to let him out, then wait until he first sits down quietly, for example. If you happen to be resting comfortably on the sofa and don't feel like getting up to open the door, while the dog thinks it's time to leave the living room and go back into the hallway, he will just have to stay in the living room.

In everyday life, pay conscious attention to the times when your pet demands something of you. You'll be surprised how often he tries to get his way. If the dog's efforts usually succeed, he will reinforce them if the human fails to "obey" immediately, and will extend them to other areas as well. Over time, then, your four-legged friend may become too much for you to handle.

Signals of Conflict and Appeasement

In dealing with a human, a dog may occasionally use the same signals he employs with conspecifics, signals that can indicate conflict, stress, or overload.

▷ **Panting** is the dog's way of regulating his body temperature. If he feels hot or has a fever, he pants. The temperature is not always the cause, however. Panting can also be a sign of excitement, in both the positive and the negative sense. If the dog catches sight of his beloved ball, for example, he may pant in happy expectation of being allowed to chase it in the near future.

Panting can also be a sign of stress. If an insecure dog sees himself exposed to a situation that he finds highly unpleasant, he may pant because he feels stressed. To identify the cause of the panting, take a look at the animal's body language (→ page 47).

▷ **Yawning** due to tiredness happens to dogs as well as people. More commonly, however, a dog's yawning is the sign of an inner conflict, a so-called ◗ DISPLACEMENT ACTIVITY (page 261). An example: The dog wants to play with other dogs, but you ask him to sit at your side. The consequence may be that he yawns to express his inner conflict.

▷ **Scratching** is comparable with yawning. Certainly, the dog may have an itch now and then. But not infrequently he uses scratching as a displacement activity when he has an inner conflict. For example, you may say "Down" to your pet when he would prefer to do something else—and he starts scratching himself.

▷ **Licking his nose:** Here the dog licks the end of his muzzle. This behavior can also arise when an inner conflict exists, but it may also indicate uncertainty. Alternatively, the dog may be trying to appease or placate. Licking in combination with hunching and wagging his lowered tail is often interpreted as an indication of a "bad conscience." It is only an ◗ APPEASEMENT GESTURE (page 259), however, to mollify a complaining human.

▷ **Separating** is something the dog may try if he feels two humans are embracing too tightly. Then he will attempt to squeeze between them. If a dog sees his owner as "threatened" because another person or dog is approaching, he may place himself directly in front of his two-legged companion.

Reacting Correctly

Your specific reaction to such signals depends on the situation:

▷ If a dog displays uncertainty by licking or looking away when you approach, you should keep your distance.

▷ If the dog exhibits stress in everyday situations (for example, by panting), I suggest that

Research & Practice

Communication Ranges

2

Though it often seems that a dog is thinking the same way as a human—this is not the case. Many humans, however, think in their own terms when dealing with their four-legged friends, which is quite understandable. This not infrequently results in misunderstandings and our behavior ultimately achieves the very opposite of what we intended. This is explained in part by the fact that the dog can be guided only by your tone of voice and behavior—he or she does not understand what you say.

▷ Let's assume that your dog is barking too much when your doorbell rings. Annoyed, you call out, "Stop that right now!" and hasten to the door to stop the barking. From the canine point of view, what message has your reaction given your pet? Your excited tone of voice and the mad rush to the door have given the dog this signal: "Alert—there's something really exciting at the door." And he keeps on barking and also tries to get to the front door as fast as possible.

To get the dog to calm down, walk to the door in a calm, relaxed way. Alternatively, you can ask a friend to ring the bell a few times at five- or ten-minute intervals for several days in a row, while you show no reaction at all.

▷ Here's a similar situation: You come home from a shopping trip, your dog is beside himself with delight and jumps up on you like a rubber ball on a string, while the rugs slip sideways and the large floor vase goes flying. You try to set your shopping bags down as quickly as possible and then devote all your attention to greeting your pet, to put an end to the chaos. That teaches the dog that you'll respond the way he wants all the more quickly, the more he "goes nuts." You can remedy the situation, however, by entering the house

quietly, walking past the dog without comment, and calmly setting your shopping bags down. Finally, pick up the newspaper, sit down at your table, and read. Once your pet has moved down into a lower gear, you can show him some quiet attention.

◁

This dog is licking his nose. This may indicate an inner conflict or uncertainty. Look at the rest of its body language to determine the cause. Don't unconsciously reward your pet by "soothing" him when he displays undesirable behavior, such as signs of fear.

▷ When you give the "Come" command, similar misunderstandings can occur. Let's suppose you're out walking with your pet, and he runs ahead and sees something very interesting—such as a field to which liquid manure has been freshly applied. You call him as you walk along, but he looks up briefly and continues on his way. You run after him, calling out excitedly, "Hey, where are you off to now, come here right now!" But the dog gets this message: "Great, my owner's coming along and even urging me on. Now I can really check out that liquid manure!"

There's only one course of action here: turn around and head in the opposite direction! If your bond is a good one, the dog will soon follow.

you accustom him slowly, step by step, to the pertinent situations or stimuli, so that stress is avoided. For ways of doing this, see page 261.

▷ Displacement activities (→ page 261) during training are indications that the level of distraction is still too high or that the exercise itself is still too difficult. Reduce your demands for the time being, or redo the exercise and train at a slower pace.

▷ If your dog is "protecting" you, you need to think about the extent to which you want that to happen. Depending on the animal's temperament and on whether he is consciously or unconsciously being rewarded for his behavior, difficult situations can result: for example, when the dog regards another person as an enemy. A dog with a strong protective instinct should always obey implicitly. Besides obedience training, a muzzle can offer additional security. For more on this topic, see page 227.

Use "Dog Talk"

You can use some of the signals listed on page 62 to communicate with your pet or with another dog. For example, you can separate two dogs promptly if dissent arises, that is, before things get serious. This is not advisable in every such situation, however, and you should try it only if you feel confident enough.

Here's another example of a way to use these signals in daily life: If you are approaching a dog that seems insecure, you can move aside and look away to give him a signal that you have no bad intentions toward him.

Spotting Problems in Time

Most dogs lead a problem-free life with their two-legged friends. They adapt to their living conditions, fit into their "pack," and enjoy the comfortable life of a house pet. If incidents with other dogs occur, in most cases there will have been signs of problems long in advance. Often, however, these signs are not detected or not taken seriously by the dog's owner. Of course, not every precarious situation results in a momentous incident, but even less serious things can become a burden in living with the dog.

If you detect the signs early on, many minor problems can still be solved before they become a real nuisance or even a danger.

 INFO

A Guilty Conscience

If the dog reacts to criticism—for example, when he or she comes to you only after being called repeatedly—in a very submissive, conciliatory way, it is often interpreted by humans as a sign of a guilty conscience—as if the dog knew what he or she did wrong. No way is this true. Rather, the dog is expressing uncertainty—he obeyed the command (albeit rather slowly) and was then punished. In the future, he will be even less likely to come.

What Are the Alarm Signals?

▷ **Ignoring** the human partner, for example, is an indication that the owner-pet relationship is not harmonious. The dog totally disregards his owner unless he or she happens to have something of burning interest. He ignores commands and more or less does his own thing. If you look closer, it often turns out that the dog is the focal point of the family and is thoroughly encouraged and spoiled, with every family member intent on making the dog's life as comfortable as possible.

△

This dog is probably threatening another member of its species. On the one hand, he is expressing an offensive threat—the front teeth are visible, and he is looking straight at his opponent—but he is also making a slightly defensive threat, since his ears are laid back.

leader. After all, only someone who can dominate others can be dominant.

Such a dog may have no scruples about walking right on the tables and chairs, helping himself to everything edible, or protesting when you're on the phone instead of giving him your undivided attention. In an advanced stage, this assumption of privilege can mean that the dog's freedoms encroach on the human's. He may claim certain privileges exclusively for himself, and try, for example, to force you off your own sofa or bed by nudging you, staring fixedly at you, or threatening you. Then your warning bells should sound, if they haven't done so already.

▷ **Defending and protesting,** too, are threatening gestures and as such should serve as alarm signals. If the dog, for example, defends his food or a chew bone by growling, you need to seek help. By no means should you "respect" your pet's behavior and keep your distance. I also think there is reason for concern if the dog defends his toys or gets too wound up when playing tug-of-war with you, and bites the toy with a deep growl or even tries to bite you.

If he protests or even snaps at you when being brushed or having his paws cleaned, that, too, is unacceptable. This is also the case if the dog snaps at you because he is unwilling to obey a command.

▷ **If the dog attempts** to take control of strategically important areas, this too is problematic. If, for example, he has made your front hallway his main napping place and wants to decide who can or can't come in the door, then every visit degenerates into a stressful event, with the result that soon nobody will be willing to visit you.

Dogs often try to monitor staircases as well, and then they warn unwelcome users by barking loudly. This behavior may also be extended to areas where there may be food, such as the kitchen or the place where the dog's food is stored. Here it often helps to move the dog's

If a dog cannot be managed and controlled, problems in everyday life will crop up sooner or later.

▷ **Demanding behavior** by the dog in every conceivable set of circumstances can also result in a precarious situation, especially if it is reciprocated by the human, who thus assumes the role of the reacting partner—possibly even adopting the routines of encouraging and spoiling described above. That only makes the dog more independent and, depending on his type, continues to expand the latitude he enjoys. As a consequence, the dog becomes the dominant pack napting place to a strategically "insignificant" area.

▷ **If your pet tends** to threaten people, whether out of fear or an overdeveloped instinct to guard and protect (→ page 267), this is a very serious problem. It is especially serious if the dog behaves this way toward children, whether they are your own or someone else's. If this is the case, your cardinal rule has to be prevention of danger. This means that the dog absolutely must wear a muzzle. In addition, I urge you to seek professional help quickly, to avoid accidents. It may even be better to part company with such a dog.

Is the Hierarchy Clear?

If you've identified one of the above-mentioned warning signals in your life with the dog, I recommend that you take a close look at the hierarchy in your home. Does everything or almost everything revolve around the four-legged family member? If so, then ask yourself whether you're unconsciously letting yourself be manipulated by the dog. For the next few days, make a conscious effort to look at every possible situation of daily life. If you conclude that your dog enjoys too many privileges, you need to change the way you behave toward him. Please avoid any kind of physical confrontation with your pet, however. Not infrequently, some problems resolve themselves once you adopt a more dominant approach. Suggestions for solving specific problems are found in the section beginning on page 228.

▶ TEST

Do You Understand Dogs?

To understand a dog and communicate with him so that he understands you as well, you must be able to interpret his behavior correctly. This test will tell you how well you understand dog language at this point.

2

Yes No

1. You come out of your bedroom in the morning and see that your dog has gnawed on your rug during the night. Annoyed, you go over to him and give him a piece of your mind. He hunches over, tucks his tail, licks his nose, and lays his ears back. Does he know why you're fussing at him? ○ ○

2. A dog that threatens humans or other members of his species or exhibits other aggressive behaviors is always dominant. Is this a true statement? ○ ○

3. Your four-legged friend is lying on the sofa. You come close, and he stares at you, his body tensed. Should you declare the sofa off limits, since the dog exhibits a tendency to defend it? ○ ○

4. Your dog is chasing a cat at full gallop, and the cat takes refuge behind a fence. The dog stops in his tracks and stands in front of the cat, wagging his tail. Does this indicate that he wants to greet the cat in a friendly way? ○ ○

Answers:
1) NO → page 62
2) NO → page 46
3) Yes → page 66
4) NO → pages 45

10 Questions About Dog Language

When giving us a friendly welcome, our dog often briefly bares his upper teeth. Is that a reason for concern?
Some dogs "laugh" when greeting someone. The rest of the animal's body language remains friendly, while he briefly curls his upper lip so that his teeth are visible. We suspect that this is due to a genetic pre-disposition—Dalmatians, for example, are especially prone to display this trait. This behavior has developed over the course of the domestication process and is exhibited only with humans.

During a walk, an older dog threatened our three-month-old puppy. But he should have "puppy license" until the age of six months, shouldn't he?
◗ PUPPY LICENSE (page 271) is enjoyed in the wild only by puppies from the same pack. Dogs that you encounter while out for a walk, however, are not members of your pack. Though most dogs are more or less tolerant toward puppies, there are great differences within this range of tolerance. And some canines simply can't deal with puppies and want nothing to do with them. The way a dog treats puppies depends on the individual animal, but also on its specific experiences.

Our Rocky is a self-confident dog. Sometimes he lifts his leg against mine and marks me. Is this normal?
You definitely need to look closely at the established hierarchy and make a change. If he marks you, this is a sign of a gross lack of respect and an indication that something is wrong between you and your pet. The dog considers you his property, to a certain extent.

Our dog Sam often has reacted uncertainly to other dogs since his coat grew so long that it hangs in his eyes. Does that play a role?
If he did not exhibit this behavior when he was younger and his coat was shorter, and if he has had no really negative experiences with other dogs, his insecurity may very well be due to his restricted vision. Help Sam by using a barrette, or clip his coat so that he has an unimpeded view.

If we're out with our dog, he sniffs at every scent mark and lifts his leg everywhere, even when he's on leash. Does it have to be this way?
When your dog runs free, he can "read" messages to his heart's content and leave behind some of his own. But when he hears a command from you, such as "Heel," then he has to quit marking and stop checking out scent messages—whether he is on leash or not. You can also make it a rule that when on leash he absolutely does not mark or sniff—provided he has sufficient opportunity to roam free every day. If not, occasionally let him "read" and mark, without interrupting him with commands. But you should never allow yourself to be dragged around by your dog, and

▷

An invitation to play, a warning, or a greeting? Look at a dog's overall body language when you want to interpret its barking, as well as its tail wagging, correctly.

Grabbing a dog by the nape and shaking it is not a species-appropriate training method. The muzzle grasp, on the other hand, is something a canine understands— it is practiced by dogs themselves.

How can I tell whether our dog feels comfortable?

You can determine that by his so-called comfort behavior, including whether he rolls around lazily on his back, sleeps on his back, or stretches luxuriantly. Many dogs also moan and groan while thus occupied. A dog also signals that he feels comfortable by shaking himself. Many dogs do this when they wake up or when a walk is imminent.

Do I have to give my dog commands as loudly as possible, if I want him to obey?

Dogs have far better hearing than humans, so a low to normal volume, combined with the right energy, tone of voice, and facial expression, is perfectly adequate—except when you're calling your pet from a distance. Try deliberately varying the loudness of your voice—you'll be surprised to see how low the required volume is. Save your loudest voice for real emergencies.

you should usually be the one who decides when it's time to move on.

How do I behave if I'm approached by a free-running dog with no owner in sight?

Here your decision should be based on the situation. If the dog is threatening you, possibly because you're in its territory, then stop in your tracks and look away. If it calms down a little, walk away slowly. If the dog maintains a low profile, keep on going without paying it any notice. If the animal makes you uneasy, change direction promptly to avoid direct contact.

My puppy is afraid of other dogs even if they're friendly. What can I do?

Puppies react almost like children—some blithely go up to other children or adults, while others need a little more time to unbend. Since dogs tend to look to their owner for guidance, it will help if you yourself act happy and relaxed and pay some attention to the other puppies or to an older dog that crosses your path. That way you'll show your little pet that it has nothing to fear. A certain reserve when encountering strange dogs is quite appropriate, however.

Do your very best to get out of the way of a dog that is threatening you. Look away, and move slowly and calmly.

Can I discipline my puppy by grasping his nape and shaking him?

A dog will not understand that. Extensive research by behavioral scientists has determined that this "educational measure" is not used by wolf parents with their young and is obsolete. Puppies exhibit this behavior when playing with their peers; it is a playful way of practicing the technique of shaking their prey to death, for use on later hunting expeditions.

Basic Training— Learning for Life

▶ You want your puppy to grow up to be a dog that is capable of handling everyday situations, trusts you, and can be relied on to obey you. With the right training, that goal can easily be achieved— provided you remain involved and committed. The process of systematically, consciously working on socialization and training takes time, patience, and perseverance, however. But your efforts will be rewarded in the end: you'll see that your endeavors to develop a good, healthy relationship with your pet pay off in a great many ways. And besides, training your puppy is a lot of fun!

3

Preparing the Puppy for Life

When a little pup joins the household, the daily routine is turned upside down at first. And for the puppy, it's the beginning of a new, exciting life.

AS MENTIONED in the first chapter, when a little puppy comes to live with you, she or he is in the midst of a sensitive, highly significant phase of development, during which her or his way of learning is comparable to imprinting. I strongly urge you to invest the necessary time and effort to take full advantage of this phase, with careful consideration of its potential. Later on, this will pay off in a number of ways for you and your pet. Don't be misled by the puppy's appearance. This cuddy little creature is already a real dog, full of curiosity and interested in its surroundings, and equipped with a great willingness to learn.

Socialization—The Crucial Phase

Socialization means familiarizing the puppy with her environment. The stimuli and situations related to this environment should become and remain something entirely normal for the animal. In the wild, a wolf pup becomes acquainted with its habitat, among other things, during this phase. It explores the nearby area with all its terrain features, plays with its siblings, and learns what it can get away with where the "grownups" are concerned and what it had better avoid.

What a little puppy now must become familiar with as her habitat depends on her individual setting. If you want a family pet (→ page 22) that accompanies you everywhere, the socialization process has to be different from that appropriate, for example, for a "yard dog," which presumably will only stay near the house. If you want to train your puppy as a gun dog, her socialization phase will include familiarization with feathers and pelts, while a future companion for a rider should be given an opportunity for early contact with horses that are used to dogs.

Most canines, however, spend their lives as so-called companion dogs. They go almost everywhere with their owners—shopping in town, jogging, on vacation, to outdoor cafes, and along for the car ride when the children are being driven somewhere. This means that a wide range of situations must be "normal" for the dog, so that her behavior toward humans and her surroundings will be faithful and reliable. Moreover, this will expand her horizons, so to speak, and later on she will also be able to cope with unfamiliar situations easily and with a minimum of stress.

Familiarizing the Puppy with Humans

Here, I hope the breeder has already laid the essential foundations and given his or her puppies plenty of positive contact with a wide variety of people. You should continue that process now. After a few days, once your puppy has settled in and gotten to know her new caregivers, I recommend that you afford her contact with all sorts of human beings—including people with normal mobility, others who use crutches or a cane, men with full beards, children of various ages, and so forth. You need to allow for your dog's individual temperament, however. An outgoing, extroverted puppy that generally enjoys everyone's company is less likely to find this overly stressful than an insecure puppy.

Familiarizing the Puppy with Different Surfaces

Socialization also includes letting the puppy become acquainted with different ○ FLOOR AND GROUND SURFACES (page 264), so that she won't be afraid of slippery floors, stairs, or the like in later life. If your pet is fearful and is too heavy to be quickly picked up and carried when necessary, you may have a problem later on. Now is the time to show the puppy smooth stone and wood floors, narrow footbridges, woodland terrain, flower filled meadows, and various types of stairs.

Depending on the length of the staircase, carry the puppy two-thirds or more of the way

3

◁

Socialization also includes learning good canine manners. While playing, puppies practice social behavior. Sometimes one is on top, sometimes the other. If one of them gets too rough, the other won't play anymore.

▶ WHAT DO I DO IF . . .

. . . the puppy lacks confidence?

Reward even the tiniest steps. Let's say the puppy lacks the courage to walk across a compost sifter screen that is lying on the ground, or to get close to an object that seems scary, such as a lawn mower.

While holding a tasty treat in front of your puppy's nose, encourage her to step on the screen or to come close to the lawn mower—while the engine is switched off—to get the reward. Do all this without a leash or commands, using only an encouraging tone of voice. As soon as the puppy puts a single paw on the screen or moves in the direction of the lawn mower, hand over the treat.

Now use another treat to coax her to take another step closer. She may go ahead and walk across the screen or help herself to the dog biscuit on top of the lawn mower. If the puppy won't budge, don't force her; instead, try this exercise again later.

up, and then let her climb a few steps (more is not good for a puppy) on her own. Use treats to motivate her to walk on the unfamiliar surfaces.

Important: Reward your puppy with the treat while she is on the unfamiliar surface; don't wait until she returns to a "normal" one.

Field Trips for Socialization

Keep taking the puppy into town or to other fairly busy, crowded places. Ideally, keep the focus on the puppy, and don't try to get any errands done. And at first, don't choose the rush hour; that would only overtax the puppy. Your plans should also include an occasional trip on public transportation. Alternatively, find a seat at a sidewalk café and let the little puppy experience the sounds and people. Take the puppy along when you're visiting friends, shopping downtown, or visiting a flea market or street fair.

Plan outings of these kinds, and don't try to get too much done at one time. For example, it's not advisable to combine a lengthy meal in a restaurant with a trip to town on the same day. It's better to spread out more ambitious plans over the course of several days.

Getting Ready for an Outing

Whenever you're going downtown, be sure to take some bags along so that you can easily dispose of your little puppy's "urgent business" if necessary. Don't forget to take treats too, as a reward (→ left). When you're going to a restaurant or to the home of friends, I also suggest that you take your puppy's bed with you. Try to schedule such outings for a time when the puppy will be a little tired, and give her a chance to relieve herself beforehand. Then it will be easier for the little dog to stay quiet for a while.

The First Lessons

Among the first things you need to consider when a puppy joins your household are housebreaking and teaching your new pet her or his name. These two items are really quite important if dog and human are to coexist in harmony.

Housebreaking a Puppy

At the start, housebreaking is uppermost in the minds of a puppy's new parents. But here I can reassure you: Every puppy becomes housebroken. Whether the process takes one or four weeks, however, depends primarily on how attentive you are. It can also take a little longer if the breeder has given the puppy no opportunity to go some distance away from her bed to do her business, or if the surface there resembled the texture of the floor covering in your home.

How to proceed: This works best if the puppy is always in the same room with you. That way you can tell when she gets restless or walks around in circles with an unmistakable intention. Pick her up immediately and take her outside. While the puppy relieves herself, say a certain phrase each time, such as "Hurry up" or "Potty." Then she will link your signal with the corresponding activity, and after some time the signal will serve as an encouraging stimulus. Make it part of your routine to take the puppy outside first thing every morning, as well as every time she wakes up from a nap, after every meal, and while she is playing. Let her outside for the last time relatively late, close to midnight. Praise your pet every time she is "successful" outdoors.

If a little accident happens indoors now and then, remove all traces without saying a word. If you catch the puppy in the act, pick her up and hustle her outside without making a fuss. Criticism is not helpful, especially if the mess was left some time ago. Indeed, it can even be harmful, if the puppy links the fussing with carrying out these body functions in general. Then the poor little youngster may crawl away somewhere to eliminate.

Use the Crate for Training

Some puppies sleep through the night from the very start, some have to go outside only now and then, and others need to go out every night for quite some time, maybe even more than once. But that too will get better! Here are some ways you can improve the situation.

At night, let the puppy sleep quite close to you, with only a small radius of action. Then she will let you know when she has to go, because she normally will not want to soil her bed. If she can leave her bed or if she sleeps in another part of the house, then at night the puppy will simply go a little distance from her bed and eliminate there. Then the housebreaking process will be prolonged. I have had good luck with having the puppy sleep in a ○ CRATE (page 261) at night. If she feels pressure, she will move around or whimper, and then you can carry her outside.

A crate can be useful during daytime hours as well—for example, if you're alone with the puppy and want to shower or make a phone call without being disturbed by your pet. During the day, put the crate, with the puppy's little bed inside, in the living area. At night, place it next to your bed. Dog crates are available in different models, made of plastic or metal wire. The plastic crates are more enclosed, making they seem "den-like," a feeling some dogs like. In a wire cage, the dog can see everything going on around it (some dogs like that too)— if necessary you also can lay a blanket over the top to create a den-like effect. Choose a crate of adequate size. The dog should be able to lie down in it and stretch out, as well as stand up. If you want the crate to be used later on, you should base your choice on the dog's size when fully grown.

Getting used to the crate: First, make the crate nice and cozy with soft bedding and a dog toy. If the puppy gets tired during the day, coax her into the crate to nap, using treats or a chew stick. Leave the door open at first. Once your pet goes into the crate voluntarily, you can close the door for a few minutes. At night, always close it when you go to bed.

If the puppy is really tired, she won't put up a fuss at night—unless she needs to potty. If she complains at first in the crate in the day-

 TIP

Slow Adjustment Process

When the puppy joins your household, all your friends and neighbors are sure to be curious about her. This is understandable. But the little dog first has to get over the separation from her mother and littermates. Give her time during the first few days to get used to things and concentrate only on becoming acquainted with her new caretakers.

time when the door is closed, make sure to stay nearby, but ignore the little puppy. Open the door only if the puppy has been quiet for a few moments. Otherwise she will learn that she can accomplish something if she just protests loudly enough. To avoid problems with the correct interpretation of whimpering, I suggest that you let the puppy eliminate before you put her in the crate.

Important: The stay in the crate must always be cast in a positive light. Never shut the puppy in her crate as a punishment!

The Puppy Learns to Answer to Her Name

The name belongs to the puppy from the very start, so to speak. It goes without saying that everyone has to call her by the same name.

Choose a name that is as short and terse as possible: ideally, no longer than two syllables. This kind of sound is easiest for the dog to commit to memory. If your puppy has a ◯ PEDIGREE (page 270), then there will already be a name on it. If you like it, you can call the puppy by this name. Often, however, these names are quite long and elaborate. If so, simply pick another name (→ Useful Literature, page 285).

If the little dog is to learn her name, she first has to connect the name with herself. If you choose a name and want to use it to summon the puppy right away, your pet won't react to it at first. After all, how should she know that you're talking to her?

To get the puppy used to her name, make a point of using it when you're spending time together—that is, when you snuggle with the puppy, pet her, give her a treat, or play with her. Use her name only when you're engaging with the dog in a positive way, and always say it in a friendly tone of voice. That is, don't use it to reprimand your pet, for example, if you catch her tugging at the carpet fringe.

After a few days, you can test from time to time to see whether the puppy is reacting when you call her by name. If she does react, you should always have something positive ready for the puppy (such as petting her or playing with her). If you frequently simply say the puppy's name for no reason, over time she will stop paying much attention to it.

Establishing a Positive Bond

A ◐ BOND (page 260) of trust between you and your four-legged friend, in which you are the partner in charge, is the basis for training and for every kind of subsequent schooling. Having a bond means that the dog looks to you for guidance and enjoys working with you; that is, you are the center of her life. However, the dog should not be so dependent on you that she immediately has a nervous breakdown if you're not there at some point. That would be too close a bond.

How can you foster an optimal bond? Well, a puppy has all the makings for it—a dog is inherently a pack animal, and a puppy left entirely on her own could not survive. She is dependent on care, and at this age she innately has a very pronounced inclination to bond. Usually, however, that is true only if she has been adequately socialized with humans before she left the breeding facility.

The first few days: When the puppy comes to your home—ideally, at the age of eight or nine weeks—she should spend the first few days becoming acquainted only with her direct caretakers. That way she will know where she belongs and can start forming a relationship with you. Go with your new pet as she explores its new home and yard, and get her used to her name (→ page 76). In addition, she should learn where she is supposed to eat and sleep.

From the very outset, please follow the rules you and your family have established for the puppy. If, for example, the puppy is not supposed to go into certain rooms or to get up on the sofa, then don't make any exceptions at the beginning. Don't let your household get too noisy at this time. A puppy needs lots of sleep, and when she is tired, she often will simply collapse. These breaks are important for her development, so make sure she is not disturbed when resting.

Very Important: Body Contact

As you read on page 47, body contact plays an extremely important role in the development of a feeling of belonging together. Pet and scratch the puppy often and in a relaxed way—for example, when you're lying on the rug or outdoors on the lawn with your pet. Many puppies cuddle up close to their humans to take a nap. Snuggling (→ page 47), like petting, is highly conducive to bonding. Brushing with a soft brush or a special massage glove for dogs also serves the purpose of social communication. But please make sure you don't pull the hair of a longhaired puppy, because then she would associate being brushed with something negative!

Playing also promotes bonding. Go ahead and romp around with the puppy, with or without a toy, but don't let her get too wound up. If she tries to bite your hands or clothing, stop the game immediately.

Taking Walks as a Way of Bonding

A puppy has a strong instinct to follow, because she "knows" that she can't survive on her own. Thus she will be very intent on

▷

A puppy has a great innate willingness to learn, usually is quite ready to bond, and is very curious. You can use these qualities deliberately, to give your pet the best possible preparation for life in your home and in our natural environment.

maintaining a connection with you when you're out for a walk. By systematically following through with this routine, you create a good basis for ensuring that later on, the dog will check on your whereabouts of her own accord when you're out together—and not the other way around, with you constantly having to look for your pet.

Start the "bonding walks" as soon as the puppy has had a few days to become acclimated and knows that you're now her new mama or papa. Keep the following points in mind:

▷ Only the primary caretaker should take bonding walks with the puppy until the dog is at least 18 weeks old. Ideally they should be taken on a daily basis, or at least every other day.

▷ The length of the walk depends on the dog's age. For a nine-week-old puppy, I suggest a length of five to seven minutes. Then gradually increase the time to about 10 to 20 minutes.

▷ Keep varying the terrain, because the more unfamiliar the surroundings, the closer the dog will stay to you. This is especially important for more independent puppies.

Here's how it works: Carry the puppy into the countryside, far enough away from your house, or drive out in the country. At first, choose an area that you can see clearly, such as a field with only a few bushes, far away from traffic and as free of distractions as possible. Set the puppy on the ground. She should be wearing only her collar, with no leash. Now walk away from her in an authoritative way. The puppy will follow you. Change direction every few steps without warning, especially if the puppy is about to pass you (don't wait until she has passed you), or if she otherwise is not paying attention to you. Don't wait for her. To put it bluntly, the puppy needs to learn that you're gone if she fails to pay attention to you. Hide somewhere

△

Take advantage of the puppy's natural instinct to follow. Make it a habit to take regular bonding walks. They will get the puppy used to always paying attention to your whereabouts.

if she's not concentrating on you, perhaps behind a small bush. If she has "lost" you, don't call her immediately, just observe. Go ahead and let the puppy search a little, then call her in a quiet voice. Only if the puppy reacts by panicking should you let her see you right away. Over the course of time, the puppy will learn to pay closer attention to staying in contact.

Now you can start taking your bonding walks also in areas with more terrain features, that is, with a lot of bushes or a stand of trees. Normally a puppy won't run away, but if you're unsure or if the puppy is especially afraid of environmental stimuli, you can tie a thin, roughly 9-foot-long rope (with no loop at the end) to her collar and let the puppy drag the rope behind her. This will make her easier to "catch" if necessary.

Exploratory Walks Are Educational

These systematic walks serve to familiarize the puppy with the realities of her environment and encourage her to check out unfamiliar things. If she learns that she can cope with unfamiliar situations, this will strengthen her self-confidence. Especially for slightly insecure dogs, that has a favorable impact. I suggest you take such exploratory walks several times during the socialization phase.

If you keep the following points in mind, your puppy will not only learn faster, but will also enjoy the learning process even more.

▷ Always start the walk with a hungry dog and a suitable supply of interesting treats. This way, if the puppy feels uneasy about something, you can use some tidbits to persuade her to show a little courage.

▷ If the puppy has a certain toy that she likes especially well, take it along too. You may be able to use it to distract your pet's attention from something.

◉ WALK IN THE CITY

Carry the little puppy, on leash, to the center of town—ideally, at a time when the sidewalks aren't crowded. Along the way, she will meet other people. If someone wants to pet the puppy and she is willing, then let her make contact. If you decide to take a rest on a bench, for example, the dog should stay on the floor at your side. If she is really tiny, you also can hold her on your lap.

When you reach the center of town at first simply stand there for a few minutes and let all the commotion sink in. Nearby, a street musician may be playing a tune. If the puppy is eager to explore, let her walk around on leash and sniff at objects or make contact with other people.

If the puppy is fearful, first walk several feet away to a somewhat quieter corner and let her observe everything from there. You may be able to get the puppy in a happier mood by playing with her. Once she has relaxed a little, give her a treat and gradually move in a casual, good-natured way somewhat closer to the busier area again. Don't leave the location until the puppy is in a relaxed frame of mind and has overcome her fear.

Next, head for a sidewalk café and treat yourself to a cappuccino and your little dog to a rawhide chew. Then, for example, you can explore a pedestrian zone with shops and street vendors. If allowed, carry the puppy inside a store with a smooth floor. If she is cheerful and not intimidated, walk around with her and let her explore the new surroundings. But if the little dog is unsure of herself on the smooth floor, roll a few treats across the floor for her to pick up. In this way, hunger and the stimulus of motion will put the dog in a positive frame of mind. Once she has relaxed to a large extent, you can leave the store.

If the music seems a little suspicious to the puppy, try to put her in a more relaxed mood by playing an energetic game together.
▽

This puppy is not exactly enthusiastic. But because of her bond with you and trust in you, she will voluntarily follow you into shallow water.

Well, that's enough for today. At home the little creature will take a nap right away—use this as an opportunity for a snuggling session!

▶ WALK OUTDOORS

Take your leashed puppy into the countryside. For the walk, choose an area where you can explore a few interesting things such as tree stumps, brushwood, and a little stream. If the "experience stations" are far apart, you should carry the puppy from site to site.

Look for a little wooded area. Take off the puppy's leash, and let her run behind you. Coax her over to a fairly low stump and encourage her to climb on top of it. If necessary, use treats as an incentive for the puppy. Once she's on top of the stump, show your pleasure and praise your pet. If she's not interested at all or if she's really afraid, don't force her to get on the stump. It's important for the puppy to do everything voluntarily.

Now take a little break on a "normal" surface or on a park bench. Leave the puppy on leash at your side. The break is over and you've rested long enough? Continue with your walk. Hey, what's that? Your puppy stops in her tracks, her tail lowered and the hair on her back slightly raised, and wonders whether it's time to shift to reverse gear. Perhaps there's a hard-to-miss bale of hay in front of her? She's never seen anything like that before. Now you should walk up to the bale, touch it, and thus, show the puppy that it's not something dangerous. If the dog comes close and seems interested in the "monster," reward her. If she's uncertain, stay near the bale of hay with your pet and start a game to put her in a relaxed mood and divert her attention. Once she has relaxed, continue the game while trying to get closer and closer to the bale. Don't go on with your walk until the puppy has relaxed in full view of the scary object. She doesn't have to go right up to the bale, however, if that's asking too much of her. And now it's time to go back home. On the way you see another walker approaching. If the passer-by wants to make contact, let the puppy go up to him or her if she's so inclined. The other person should squat down, so that the puppy doesn't jump up.

Now your little puppy has had quite a lot of experiences and needs to rest and recover. Back home, let her sleep as long as she wants.

3

▷

Voluntarily exploring different kinds of terrain improves motor function and self-confidence and also strengthens muscles. Even though this puppy still looks a bit skeptical—in the end, her curiosity and pleasure in trying things out will triumph.

Basic Obedience Training for Your Do

Socialization in the context of daily life is not the only important thing. Now is the time when the puppy can easily master the first few obedience exercises as well. You can best accomplish this by using positive motivation.

THROUGH POSITIVE MOTIVATION (→ page 33), the puppy learns in a stress-free and positive way that listening to you is always worthwhile. In addition, he or she learns in a manner that resembles imprinting (→ page 25), as you now know, so that systematic practice at an age-appropriate pace also has a beneficial effect on subsequent schooling.

The structure of the following exercises is suitable not only for puppies but also for older dogs that are still "beginners." The belief that obedience training should be postponed to a later stage and that nothing should be undertaken with a puppy is now outmoded. So go ahead and get started!

Meaningful Training—With A System

Do you want your four-legged friend to serve as your companion? Above all, he will have to demonstrate good ○ BASIC OBEDIENCE (page 259) in that context. What good does it do if your pet wins trophies in dog sports competitions, but at other times drags you through the neighborhood while you cling to his leash? Or if he can't lie quietly under the table while you eat in a kitchen or dining room or visit the home of friends? All training exercises are related in some way to everyday situations.

Here's something you need to keep in mind: Drill during your daily walks or, if the weather's "not fit for a dog," practice at home. Have the puppy wear a leash, and always hold it loosely in one hand. It's not meant to force the puppy into a certain position, but to keep him from running off somewhere so that you have to catch him again.

Three-Step Lesson Planning

1. Plan the lesson correctly: Think about the drill you plan to execute. What goal do you want to accomplish, and what steps lead to it? Take all the time you need for this step, and don't try to teach your pet anything unless you're in a good mood and feeling well. That goes for the dog too, of course. Schedule the lessons at times when the dog is hungry, that is, probably before a meal. Where necessary, use "upscale" dog treats.

2. Follow the lesson plan to the letter: Always have the dog perform the drills exactly the same way. Only then will he be certain what you want of him and master the exercise to the extent you wish. If you are lax about execution, the dog will not obey reliably. Your own attitude is also significant, because the dog will respond only if you are energetic and committed. Your body language will express only what you really feel inside. But if you really don't care, for example, whether your

dog actually lies down when you practice the "Down" command, then your behavior will reflect that and your body language will seem correspondingly "wishy-washy" to the dog.

3. Decide when to start and stop: As a matter of principle, you must be the one to decide when and how long to practice. Here, however, you also need to keep in mind your dog's age and ○ ABILITY TO CONCENTRATE (page 258). For puppies, a few minutes are enough. If your dog's interest flags, just have him do one more simple exercise that he already has mastered, and then conclude the session.

How to Make Training Positive

Teaching your dog is easier when you have a positive attitude, and this applies to your dog as well. Always start the training session with an exercise that your pet already can do well. Then you can start a new drill or keep working on a more difficult one. At the end of the session, do an exercise that the dog can perform successfully, so that he will remember the lesson in a positive way. If a drill simply isn't working, abandon it without showing any irritation. Then end the session with an easier version that the dog has mastered.

From hitting the books yourself, you already know that repetition is essential if you want to retain the material. That is also true for your pet. For you, this means, for example, that you can practice the "Sit" or "Down" commands ten times over the course of the day—but no more than two or three times in succession. Mindless repetition at a single stretch will bore not only you but also your pet.

Increase Demands Slowly

Experience shows that a lesson is more successful if you structure it in small steps, moving from easy to difficult. Don't go to the next level until the dog has reliably mastered the previous one. If something just isn't working, I suggest that you do the exercise again in small steps, instead of repeatedly correcting your pet. Quite likely he has failed to grasp what you want of him, and the constant correction will only cause him stress.

This can be illustrated with the example of the "Stay" command. For this, the dog is supposed to sit or lie in a certain place while you walk away from him. If you go too far away or for too long a time too soon, he will get up, because he is unable to cope. If you correct him at this time, the dog will not understand why he should stay where he is, because he lacked an opportunity to learn step by step.

Cutting Back on Treats

At the start of every lesson, you have food in your hand to motivate the dog to follow directions. However, you don't want the dog to spend his life doing something only if enticed by a reward. To gradually eliminate the treats, you should retain the motivating hand gesture once the dog has correctly understood what it's all about and reacts promptly and reliably every time—but without holding a tasty reward in your hand. If he obeys the visual and audible signals, use your other hand to give him a treat after a short while. Gradually switch to giving your pet only ▶ VARIABLE REWARDS (page 276): that is, sometimes he gets a treat, sometimes he doesn't. For a simple exercise he is rewarded less often, for a harder one, more often at first. A normal "Down" command, for example, no longer entails a big reward. But if the dog lies quietly at your side despite a real distraction, he should receive a treat when it's over.

As soon as you call or whistle, a helper releases the puppy. It comes happily to you. Once it is close to you, put the bowl on the floor.
▽

The Dog Comes When You Call or Whistle

In daily life, there are a great many situations in which it is crucial for your four-legged companion to come at once, if possible, when you call or whistle—and to come without first thinking it over: for example, when someone on a bike is approaching.

Prerequisites: The puppy must already know where his food bowl is located, and he has to be hungry and/or be fond of certain tidbits. He also must have formed a certain bond with you.

This is important: As you know, during the puppy phase a dog learns in a manner that resembles the imprinting process. Therefore, during this important stage he has to learn that there is no other response to this audible signal than to come to you immediately and cheerfully. If he sees, however, that he is equally acceptable to first make a quick stop at a mouse hole, then he will be slow to respond properly—with the result that later on, he will come only when he feels like it. In my classes, I repeatedly see that many dog owners also fail to use an unambiguous signal. Sometimes they say "Come," but at other times they say "Now come here," and so forth. Often the dog has no idea what he really is supposed to do. Thus, you need to use the same audible signal every time.

Making It Work

First, choose an audible signal. The best one is "Here," because it is otherwise seldom used, and the dog can relate to it without getting confused. Also useful is a dog whistle (→ page 40). I recommend that you raise your puppy in a "bilingual" environment, by first saying "Here" and immediately thereafter giving two short blows of the whistle.

▷ If feeding time is approaching—your puppy probably is already aware of it—then you, as the primary caretaker, should go to the kitchen and prepare the meal. You can also comment on this in an enticing tone of voice. Meanwhile, another family member should hold the puppy by the collar several feet from the spot where his bowl will be, without giving any command at all. The puppy will feel a strong urge to come to you, and at this moment he is in a state of positive anticipation—ideal prerequisites for coming to you happily.

▷ Once his food is ready, call the puppy by saying "Here" and blowing the whistle, while holding the bowl or the tidbits in your hand. The family member releases his or her hold

▶ INFO

Audible Signals to Finish the Session

You need this signal ("Go on," "Over," or something of the kind) to tell your four-legged friend that he's free now, and he doesn't have to obey any more commands at the moment. It can be used whether the dog is on or off leash. For example, if you've called your pet to come, he has to stay with you until you release him again with the finish signal. If you complete an exercise and don't follow it with another, use this audible signal to end the session.

on the puppy, and he will race up to you. Now you should shower him with praise and serve him food without delay.

Don't ask him to sit first; otherwise, the reward for coming will be too far in the past, and you'll actually be rewarding the puppy for sitting. Keep doing this at every meal for approximately one week.

▷ Phase 2 follows: During the day, arm yourself with a supply of tasty treats and the

1 *Don't say "Here" or blow the whistle to call the puppy when you're outdoors until you've done enough training indoors and are absolutely certain that he will come to you at once, without making any detours.*
2 *Once he has come, give the puppy his treat right at your side, within one or two seconds, and lavish him with praise. Then ask him to sit.*

Here too, the puppy must not be so far away from you that he loses track of things. If you don't have a yard, call the puppy to come from the balcony into your apartment.
▷ If things are going like clockwork thus far, you can gradually move the lessons outdoors. If you're out somewhere with the dog and want him to come, always use a voice full of excitement to get his attention, but omit the "Here" or the whistle blow. If the dog looks your way, walk in the opposite direction. Keep encouraging him to follow you, keeping your tone of voice interesting. Once you notice that your four-legged companion is heading toward you, is only three or four feet away, and is displaying no tendency to change course, you should give the audible signal.
▷ In time you can give the command when the puppy is even farther away from you—but only if you're sure that he will come to you directly and without veering off course. And you mustn't forget the praise and treats! Don't take hold of his collar until the dog is eating his reward and being petted by you. If you immediately reach for the collar while he is still in his "approach pattern," he may stray off course. In conclusion, you can ask him to sit, if required. If you want to send your pet away again, don't forget to use whatever finish signal (→ page 85) you've chosen! The puppy should stay with you until he receives the signal.

If It Just Isn't Working

Ask yourself whether the puppy is familiar enough with your household by now, or whether a real bond has been established yet. This may well be the case with a puppy that has had inadequate contact while at the breeder's. Is he being overfed, or was the treat not enough of an incentive? Experiment with different kinds of sausages and cheeses (small pieces only), or cut back a little on the dog's food servings. If the drill isn't working outdoors yet, systematically go over everything again at home for a few days. You may have rushed things.

whistle, if you use one. In addition to feeding times, now you should occasionally call the puppy at other times as well, but only indoors, when he is not very far away from you—without any distraction, of course. The distance between you and the puppy should not be too great; the puppy must be able to come to you without having to really search for you.
▷ If that works, then Phase 3 should follow: If you have a yard, call the puppy to come from there to the patio or into the house.

If the puppy is not concentrating on his owner, or vice versa, communication between the two parties is impossible. An audible signal at this point would be meaningless. The little pup has to learn to concentrate on you when required.

Use a voice full of excitement (say, for example, "Look here!") to capture the puppy's attention. He will look up at the treat and thus automatically see your face. After a few seconds, give him the reward. In this way he learns that it's worthwhile to look at you.

Getting the Puppy's Attention

To be able to communicate with your four-legged friend, he has to pay attention to you. If he has learned to focus on you when he hears a certain audible signal, then he is ready to learn the command "Down," for example. If you give the "Down" command just as the dog is watching a butterfly with great interest, however, he is unlikely to lie down.

Prerequisites: The puppy must have established a good bond with you and must be hungry, but not too ravenous.

This is important: Practice without any distractions, and train in a room, if possible.

How to Proceed

▷ Take a treat, and arouse the dog's curiosity by saying "Look here" or some such words in an encouraging tone of voice. The dog will turn toward you. The first few times, you can combine the audible signal with your pet's name. Then it is preferable to omit the name, because you usually say it too often anyway.
▷ Next, hold out a treat so that it's directly between the dog and your face. Then the puppy

will automatically look at you as well. At first, give him the treat as soon as you get his attention. This always has to seem worthwhile to the dog.
▷ After the first few times, delay the reward for a few seconds while repeating the audible signal, but give your pet the treat while he is still looking at you. Over the course of the next few weeks, gradually extend the length of the eye contact. Perhaps you can also introduce a slight distraction, such as a person nearby, at this stage. That depends on your pet, however.

If It's Just Not Working

Test to see whether the treat is attractive enough. Or is your voice not inviting enough? Experience shows that many dog owners still need to do some work on their voice. Possibly the puppy is simply tired. Try the exercise again when he's really in good shape. Is there really no distraction nearby? This is very important.

The Puppy Learns "Sit"

In daily life, it is frequently necessary for a dog to sit quickly in response to an audible or visual signal, for example, when the doorbell rings and you want to keep your pet from being the first to race to the door, or when the veterinarian wants to examine the dog's ears.

Prerequisites: The puppy must be hungry and must have established a certain bond with you.

1 *Hold a treat above the puppy's head. Don't say anything, because at this point he can't link the right behavior with an audible signal.*

2 *As soon as he sits down of his own accord and has all four paws on the ground, say, "Sit" and give him the reward. Then end the training session in your usual way.*

Making It Work

Dogs learn this lesson very quickly.

▷ Show the puppy a tasty treat, and then hold a small piece right above his head. Don't use an audible signal yet; the dog isn't familiar with it and won't get the message you want to send.

First, the puppy may try to jump up or use similar methods to get at the tidbit. Leave your hand right where it is, but close your fingers around the treat to conceal it. If you wave your hand around, you'll only introduce an element of agitation.

▷ Be patient! Within a short or relatively short time, your dog will sit. As soon as that happens, say "Sit" and give the puppy his reward. Now, while he sits for a few moments, repeat the audible signal once or twice. Then give your finish signal—"Go on," for example—and let the little creature race off again.

▷ After just a few days, your puppy will sit when he hears "Sit." Now you can move on and gradually increase the waiting time for the reward, first, by a few seconds, and then for longer periods, depending on the dog. This way the puppy will learn to sit quietly for longer and longer lengths of time.

Don't forget—never give the puppy his rewards until the exercise is coming to a close, that is, just before the finish signal!

If Problems Crop Up

Does the puppy fail to show enough interest in the reward? Then you can try the drill again when he's hungry, or try using a more "upscale" treat. Perhaps the puppy is too restless or anxious. Then you yourself are probably too restless or anxious. Make a deliberate effort to teach the lesson calmly. Or is something distracting the puppy?

Have the puppy sit at your side and hold a favorite treat right in front of his nose. Let him sniff at the treat, but don't hand it over yet.

Next, bring the treat slowly down to the ground, right in front of the dog or next to him. The puppy will follow your hand with his muzzle and lie down.

3

Teaching the "Down" Command

"Down" is a command you need whenever you are staying somewhere for an extended time and want the dog to lie quietly at your side, for example, in an outdoor cafe or at a friend's home.

Prerequisites: The dog must already have mastered the "Sit" command and must be hungry.

Making It Work

▷ Tell the dog to sit. Hold a treat right in front of his nose. If he shows interest, bring the treat straight down to the ground, but not too quickly. The puppy will follow your hand and thus, end up lying on the ground. Instead of moving your hand straight down, you can also move it at an angle or slightly to one side of the dog. That will force him to crouch slightly to get at the treat, and he will almost automatically fall into the *down* position. But if you move your hand away from the dog's head at an angle, he will stand up!

▷ As soon as he is lying down correctly, repeat the audible signal "Down" a few times and give the dog his reward. Leave your hand on the ground. While your pet is eating, gently stroke his back with your other hand.

▷ Shortly before he finishes the treat, instruct him to sit up again and then go away, using the signal "Sit" and an upward hand motion. Make sure you end the lesson promptly—don't let the puppy get up without "permission."

▷ After a few days, if your four-legged companion lies down in response to "Down," don't present his reward immediately; wait until he has stayed in the down position calmly for a few moments. Then conclude the lesson as usual, with "Sit."

If It's Not Going So Well

Does the puppy lack the necessary staying power because the treat is not enticing enough? Pick something better. Does your pet have too much energy? Practice when he is tired. Make a conscious effort to stay calm and patient, and move your hand calmly. Leave it in the spot you want the puppy to go to.

Important: Stop rewarding your pet for obeying the "Sit" command.

Doing the First "Stay" Exercise

The puppy needs to learn to stay in the *sit* or *down* position in a certain place, even if you are some distance away. This is useful, for example, when the dog is dirty and you need to leave him outside the door briefly, sitting or lying down, so that you can go inside and get a cloth to wipe him off.

Prerequisites: The puppy must already be able to sit or lie next to you for about one minute without any further influence from you. Only then does he have the necessary composure to stay in one place while you move some distance away. In addition, he must be able to retain eye contact with you for a few moments. For this exercise, the puppy must not be too young, since the younger he is, the harder it will be to keep him from running after you.

This is important: Teaching a dog the "Stay" command requires a great deal of composure on the animal's part, because he must stay at the appointed spot alone, while remaining relaxed and tranquil. For these reasons, make a conscious effort to keep your body language

calm, move in an easy, relaxed way, and don't rush. The audible signal, too, must sound calm and soothing. Don't unleash the puppy; if he really does get up, you'll have him immediately under control again. The leash should always hang loosely, however, to avoid straining. The dog would yield to the tug and stand up.

"Stay" in the *Sit* Position

▷ Have the dog sit on the side where you want him to *heel* later on (→ page 94). Next, get his attention briefly, say "Stay," and stand up straight, right in front of your pet, so that you are directly opposite. Thus you are "blocking" the dog—although you've changed your position, your pet can't run after you. In this way, you design the lesson from the very outset so as to build in an almost automatic success for the little dog.

▷ After a few seconds, go back to your pet's side. Praise him in a quiet voice; your return is reward enough—your four-legged friend likes to be near you, after all. If you move away from the dog with the treat in your hand, or

To start the lesson, stand right in front of your dog so that he or she has almost no chance of making a mistake. It will automatically learn to stay in a spot if you are not next to it.

Once he or she has mastered the first step and stays sitting calmly in its spot, you can move a little farther away, still facing your pet. Very slowly, extend the time and distance.

3

rummage around in your pocket for the treat right in front of your pet, he will have trouble staying where he is. If you're absolutely set on rewarding the dog, don't take the treat out of your pocket until you're back at the dog's side.

▷ If the exercise is successful at this elementary level, then you can slowly extend the time you spend standing in front of the dog. Let your dog guide you here. If your pet is one of the more easy-going, calmer types, then you can prolong the time more quickly than with a more high-spirited or fidgety animal. Always end the lesson while the dog is still relaxed and seated.

▷ Once you've extended the time, you can take the next step and increase your distance from the dog. Move one or two steps away. Then extend the time a little more, and once that works, increase the distance again. With a puppy, however, be sure not to move farther away than the length of the leash.

"Stay" in the *Down* Position

▷ Follow the procedures described above for the "Stay" in the *sit* position, but give the *down* command before you move away. Stand up straight in front of your pet, and don't bend over. When you go back to the dog, he should remain in the *down* position. If necessary, use the audible signal "Down" right before you stand next to the dog. Once you are there, wait a few moments and then use a gesture to encourage him to sit (now you want the dog to move again), as well as an appropriate tone of voice.

If It's Not Working

If the dog leaves the *stay* prematurely, this usually is due to the fact that he hasn't learned the normal *sit* or *down* well enough yet. If that is the case, go over the basics again. Or you may have increased the time and the distance from your dog too quickly. Then, the best thing is to go back one or more steps and

1 *For the "Stay" in the* down *position, first stand right in front of the dog. Make sure the leash is not taut. Slowly increase the level of the exercise.*

2 *At the end of the lesson, go back to the dog's side while he or she remains in position. Saying "Down" shortly before you reach its side will remind it once more to stay where it is.*

carefully run through the drill again. Think about whether you may have talked to the dog during the *stay*, possibly even calling him by name. That can easily cause a dog to stand up and come to his owner. Don't go so far away or for such a long time that the dog becomes restless or needs additional support from you.

No matter whether it's a puppy, an older dog, a scent mark, another canine, or a human—if you give in to the tug at the leash (even one or two steps are enough), your dog will learn that this method works. And he or she will use it again and again.

Every time the leash gets taut, stop in your tracks without comment. And ignore the dog: that is, don't say or do anything. Baffled, your four-legged friend will turn slightly—and the tension on the leash will be relieved.

As soon as the leash is hanging loosely again, continue walking with your dog. In this way you give your pet a signal: if the leash is loose, I can keep going, but if I pull on it, I won't make any headway.

The Puppy Learns to Walk on a Leash

Although a puppy is not yet able to *heel* for an extended period of time, he still should learn that he's not allowed to tug at the leash. When you walk, the leash should always hang loosely between you. Older dogs, too, have to learn to walk on a loose leash even when they aren't being required to *heel*.

Prerequisites: The dog must be accustomed to the leash and collar.

This is important: Like "Coming When Called," this exercise is also very important for dog owners. Usually, however, serious consequences unknowingly creep in quickly.

Make it a rule to walk only relative short distances with the puppy on leash. The fewer opportunities he has to pull and drag, the better. As you now know, dogs learn predominantly through a sense of achievement. If your pet strains at the leash and attains his goal in this way, he learns that this behavior is

profitable. Consequently, he will start to tug again, and increasingly hard.

Making It Work

To illustrate the procedures you can use, I want to describe two examples from my own experience:

▷ When your dog is on leash, whether he's a puppy or an older dog, don't let him have any contact with other members of his species. When owners come to my puppy class, the little dogs, which for the moment are on leash, naturally want to get close to each other. But that's not allowed. "Oh, just for a second to say hello," the owners sometimes say. Right away they give in to the tugging—and the puppy has a great experience. But the puppy is supposed to learn that tugging at the leash doesn't accomplish anything. To get that across, in this situation you should simply do nothing. The puppy owners, therefore, stay about three or four yards apart, keep the leash at its normal length, and say nothing to the puppy—he wouldn't react to it now anyway. There's also no need for him to execute a command, since he's still too little to be able, for example, to sit calmly at his owner's side for a few minutes. So the puppies are still straining at their leashes, hopping around, or whimpering. But none of this helps; they can't get any closer to each other. Usually, after not too long a time, they stop and calm down.

▷ If a puppy tugs at the leash while you're out walking, the best thing is to stop immediately, without comment. Wait until he acts differently and the leash is loose again. He may sit down in bewilderment or take a step or two toward you. Only now should you resume walking and praise your pet briefly. You may have to stop again two steps later and simply can't be in a rush about this.

▷ Another possibility for older dogs, not for puppies, is for you to quickly spin on your heel shortly before the leash becomes taut. If the dog is walking on a loose leash again, praise him, and turn around again to walk in your original direction. Match the crispness of your about-face to your particular dog. You want him to feel the jerk created by your turn, but not to go flying through the air.

▷ Sometimes an admonitory cough can also help to stop the dog just before the leash becomes taut. Praise your pet if he reacts to it. Whenever the dog is walking on a loose leash, you can reinforce this behavior with friendly, quiet words of praise and a soothing audible signal such as "Slow" or "Steady."

If Problems Arise

Does your dog have too many undesirable experiences of success? You need to cut them out, as far as possible. Have you tried only one method and not used it long enough or consistently enough? Then try the others as well, because not all dogs react the same way. Does your dog basically have a surplus of energy? Keep him or her busier, and let them have plenty of time to run free. If no method is working at all, a Halti training head collar (→ page 223) will help.

▶ WHAT DO I DO IF . . .

3

. . . the dog pulls at the leash?

Think about this: Are there some situations in which you're allowing the dog to pull—for example, if it's suddenly attracted by an odor in the shrubbery? Or is he pulling from the start of your walk until the moment you reach the area where he can run free off leash, and then he is still rewarded by being allowed to run free?

Solution 1: Try to have the dog walk at heel in such areas while concentrating on a treat. If the distance is still too great for your pet, you can drive to another area in your car. Make the walking lessons more interesting, so that the dog is motivated to pay attention. With an older puppy and, later on, an adult dog, include a good many left-right turns, and always walk in a decisive way and at a brisk pace. Also good are little circles to the side, with the dog heeling; this helps you practically cut off his path. As soon as your pet looks at you in confusion, lavish him with praise.

Solution 2: In "hard cases," the Halti (→ page 223) will help.

The Dog Learns to *Heel* Correctly

If you're walking in a fairly busy area—in town or along a road, for example—the dog should stay close by your side.

Prerequisites: The dog must be hungry or must be especially fond of a toy. In addition, he must have been trained to sit, and he has to be able to give you eye contact.

This is important: Decide which side you want your four-legged companion to walk on when heeling—either always on your right or always on your left.

Making it Work

▷ Let's assume you've chosen the left side. Take a treat in your left hand, and put the dog on your left. Now, let him see the treat. Hold the leash in your right hand, letting it hang fairly loosely. Your left arm, with the reward, should hang straight down next to your leg. Then the dog will walk along next to you, on the correct side.

▷ If your puppy is interested in the treat, start off at a fairly brisk pace. If he runs along and pays attention, give the audible signal "Heel" and encourage the little pup with a few words of praise.

As you walk, let the dog lick and nibble at the treat. It is important to hold your hand still: if you keep raising it in the air, the dog will start jumping up to reach it.

▷ The length of the exercise should be appropriate for your pet's ability to concentrate and his current level of training. The younger he is, the shorter the lesson should be. For a puppy, a few yards are sufficient at first, or even just a few steps. End the lesson before he stops paying attention. Then tell him to sit, and give him the whole treat. If you give him the snack while you're walking, he may stop to eat, and thus would feel rewarded for stopping.

▷ Practice heeling straight ahead at first, but quickly introduce little circles, weaving movements, and turns.

▷ If your four-legged friend is keeping up nicely after a certain amount of training, gradually stop offering a reward. When you get your dog's attention and start walking, keep your hand in your pocket. If your pet heels properly and stays attentive, praise him after several feet or even a few steps, using a friendly tone of voice. Then, before his attention strays elsewhere, take a treat out of your pocket and give it to the dog. Ideally, tell him to sit first. Then gradually extend the reward-free distances.

If the Lesson Doesn't Go Well

Check to see whether something may be distracting your pet. Is the reward not enticing enough, or is the dog not hungry enough? Then schedule the lesson before a meal. If your dog is more motivated by a toy than a treat, you can hold a toy in your hand. If he moves along without losing his concentration—at first, for just a few minutes—throw the toy and use the finish signal "Go on" to send him running after the reward.

▷
First, call the puppy's attention to its treat. If he seems interested, let the hand holding the reward hang down next to your leg. Then the dog will be walking in the correct position. The leash should hang loosely.

Leashing and Unleashing the Dog Correctly

If you want to leash or unleash your dog, this should always be done in the same way and without any rush. You may want to leash your pet, for example, because a bike rider is coming toward you and the dog is wildly jumping around in front of you, which could be dangerous.

Prerequisites: The dog must have been trained to sit and must make eye contact with you in response to an audible signal.

This is important: Never be in a rush when putting on or taking off your pet's leash.

Making It Work

Leashing: If you want to leash your pet and have called him to come, first tell him to sit. Once he is sitting calmly, put the leash on equally calmly, and then praise him. This will turn putting on the leash into a highlight. Many dog owners reach for the collar more or less hastily while the dog is still moving. Dogs don't like that, and they will try to resist the leash. That will make leashing a negative experience, which it never should be.

Unleashing: Use the same procedure described above for leashing. First, ask the dog to sit, and then remove the leash (at first, keep a light hold on the collar). Now leave him in the *sit* position until you give permission to go, using the finish signal "Go on." Don't let your pet take the clicking of the leash as a signal to race away—later on, you will want him to do his exercises even after being unleashed.

It would be ideal for your canine friend to give you eye contact briefly before you wind up the session. Then getting his "freedom" will be a reward for waiting patiently and concentrating on you. There's surely no need to tell you what your dog will learn if you go

△

It's best to have the dog sit before you attach or remove his leash. He should stay in the sit *position until you release him by giving another signal.*

ahead and unleash him even though he's tugging and pulling at the leash!

If Problems Arise

If your dog tries to avoid being leashed, let him wear a rope or leash several yards long, which he drags along behind him. Before you try to put on the leash, step on the end and then call the dog to come. Use the procedure described elsewhere on this page, and make a conscious effort to stay calm. Then your four-legged friend will learn that he can't "escape" from you and that wearing a leash is not a bad thing.

If unleashing isn't working, there may be too much distraction. For now, practice without any distractions at all. Perhaps your dog hasn't really mastered the *sit* command and the attentiveness exercise yet. Then you can repeat these lessons.

What Else the Puppy Must Learn

You may have worked on bonding and practiced basic obedience exercises, but your little rascal still has a lot to learn.

Letting The Body Be Examined

The puppy has to allow you to explore any part of his body at any time. After all, he may get a thorn in his paw or pick up a tick. Or he may have to be examined by the veterinarian because of an ear infection. If he's unaccustomed to being examined and on top of that is in pain, then the visit to the veterinarian will be stressful for all concerned.

Making it work: Perform a preventive check of your puppy's ears, eyes, and mouth several times a week. Examine his paws, making sure to feel between the toes, and run your hands through his coat. That will help your pet get used to being touched in this way. To announce this activity, come up with some kind of audible signal to use every time, so that the puppy knows what awaits him. The best time for such check-ups is when the puppy is tired.

Important: Shower your pet with praise for being a good dog and "putting up" with everything.

If it's not going well: If the puppy is reluctant, keep on with whatever you're doing—checking his paws, for example—until he has calmed down completely or at least to a certain extent. Then call a stop for now. If the dog learns that he can get out of check-ups by wiggling and fussing, he will redouble his use of such tactics. Next time, make sure that your pet is really tired.

Eating Garbage: Prohibited!

Many puppies are living "garbage disposals." This can be dangerous. Besides, it's usually quite unappetizing, though corrective action often is difficult.

Making it work: Try using a stop command. This will also help in other situations when you want to call a halt to undesirable behavior.
▷ Fill one hand with treats. Give the puppy a few, one at a time, from your hand. Once he has eaten four or five, lay the next one on your palm. Just before the dog takes it, abruptly close your hand and then say, for example, "Stop." Frustrated, your pet now will sit there and wait. If he tries burrowing his nose into your hand, wait until he stops. Then praise him and use your other hand to give him a treat.
▷ Do this several times a day for several days in a row. This will teach the dog not to take anything from your hand, even from your palm, when you say "Stop."
▷ Once your pet has mastered this lesson, drop a treat on the ground right next to you, and then say "Stop." If the dog still tries to snatch it, quickly step on the treat—don't let the dog get it, whatever you do. Then give him another treat from your hand.

▷

Your dog should let you touch him or her anywhere at any time. Practice checking your pet's ears, paws, teeth, coat, and more on a regular basis, ideally starting while it is still a puppy. This will also keep your trips to the veterinarian from being stressful.

▷ When your dog has learned to ignore the treat once he hears "Stop," and at various places in your home, it's time to move the lesson outdoors. While your pet isn't looking, set out some "bait" on a path or in a field. Then you know exactly where it is and can react in a systematic way. Finally, with your puppy on leash, go to the area you chose and observe your pet closely. As soon as he gets a whiff of the enticing bait, say "Stop." If he reacts and looks at you or even comes to you, praise him loudly and give him a reward. Then you can also tell him to sit and reward him for this desirable behavior.

Alternative: If this procedure is too time-consuming, you can also try to impress your pet with a gentle pull at the leash plus a "No" spoken in a growl. But always before he has the bait in his mouth!

If it's not going well: In extreme cases, for example, if the dog keeps trying to eat rocks, you may—for your pet's own safety—have to make him wear a muzzle (→ page 227) until he gets used to not eating anything, even if he can smell it and see it.

Learning to Give Up Objects

No matter how careful you are, your puppy may get something in his little mouth that is not right for him—such as one of your children's toys or a dead mouse that the cat brought home.

If you come up close and fuss at the dog, all you'll do is ensure that he beats a hasty retreat, along with his "prey." You won't be able to catch him unless he's still really young. In addition, I advise against such attempted captures, especially if you want the dog to fetch later on. You would only be teaching the dog ahead of time not to bring any objects to you.

Making it work: If the dog is carrying something that he's not supposed to have, you should do no more than try to coax him to come, using your most enticing voice. Move slightly away from your pet as you do so. If it

△

This dog willingly relinquished his toy when he saw the delicious treat. This method works equally well with puppies and with full-grown dogs.

comes near, offer something in exchange, depending on your pet's preference, a yummy dog treat or his favorite toy. As an audible signal, say something such as "Out" or "Thank you."

If it's not working: If the puppy really won't let loose of something and can't flee, use the muzzle grip to get him to open his mouth. Put your hand around his muzzle from above, and press your fingers into the area behind his canine teeth, toward his flews—not too gently, but not too hard either, and while remaining calm. Give the audible signal "Out," and gently remove the object from the dog's mouth, making sure to praise him afterwards.

Defending Something Is Prohibited

As pack leader, you have to be able to take something away from your pet at any time without having him growl at you. Take preventive action.

Making it work: As soon as your puppy has learned to come to meals when called (→ page 85), have him sit before you and set his bowl on the floor. He should sit until you give the finish signal (→ page 85) that grants him permission to eat. From time to time, stir the food in the bowl while the dog is eating, and stay nearby.

Occasionally, you should also take your pet's toy or chew bone away from him. Use the method outlined on page 97, "Learning to Give Up Objects."

If you're having trouble: If the puppy growls, don't let this deter you. If you don't keep on, the score is now 1:0 in the dog's favor. Don't let him have the chew bone or toy again until he behaves in a friendly way.

What I have just described applies only to puppies. If an older dog defends his food or similar things, read the section beginning on page 251.

Learning to Stay Alone

Since your four-legged friend can't go everywhere with you, he has to learn to spend a few hours alone now and then.

Making it work: While your pet is still a puppy, make sure he can stay a certain distance from you while indoors. When you go into the bathroom, for example, he doesn't need to come along. If he whines, stay in the bathroom until he is quiet again. Then he will learn that making a racket accomplishes nothing. If you go to him when he yowls, he may just intensify the noise, to your neighbors' "delight." Most puppies, however, accept this distance from the outset.

You can also practice with a pet crate (→ page 75). First, stay near the puppy, and then you can also leave the room briefly. You can say something such as "Wait," using this same signal later as well.

Once the puppy can stay alone indoors with no problems, go outside without him for

▶ **TIP**

At the Veterinarian's Office

Plan a "socialization trip" to the veterinarian. The puppy should become familiar with the veterinarian and the office without getting a shot, being in pain, or having any other negative experience. If you've already practiced examining your pet's body, a "practice exam" by the veterinarian won't bother it either.

a few minutes. Ideally, choose a time when the little pup is tired but not yet asleep; otherwise, he won't even notice the lesson. Say "Wait," take the trash out, and stay outside for a few minutes. If the dog is quiet, come back. If he howls, don't come back until he has been quiet for a few moments.

Gradually extend the time spent alone, and don't make a big deal out of leaving or returning. Staying alone should be something quite normal for the dog. Make this your rule of thumb: at the age of six months, the dog can stay alone for roughly three to four hours.

If you're having trouble: Have you reacted to his howls? Or was the puppy still too wide-awake? Wait until he's tired. Here's another trick: Try it in the car first. Get out to do some quick shopping and say, "Wait." For many dogs, staying alone in a car is not problematic. After a few "shopping trips," you can try again at home.

Little Exercises for Several Puppies

While still a puppy, your pet should learn that seeing other dogs doesn't always mean that it's time to party. Even if another member of its species is nearby, the puppy needs to concentrate on his or her owner. It's ideal if you know one or two other dog owners with puppies; then you can go through a few lessons together. I know that it's more fun to chat with each other and watch the adorable puppies play. But believe me, later on you may regret your failure to train a little with your puppy amidst the distraction of other animals. Overcome your wish to talk, and include a few little exercises with all the puppies both before and while you let them play. These should be exercises that the puppy already can do alone.

Practicing paying attention: Stand a several feet apart. If the puppies tug at their leashes, just ignore them. Once they've stopped, each owner should get the attention of his or her puppy and practice eye contact.

Sit **and** *down:* Practicing the *sit* and the *down* together. Make sure the distances are great enough that the puppies aren't distracting each other.

Heel: Practice heeling together. Using treats will help. Don't make the exercise too long, however. Here too, make sure you keep enough distance from each other. Don't walk directly toward, or too close to, each other.

Owner-dog game: Each owner should play with his or her own dog—on a loose leash, ideally, to keep the puppies from trying to get close to one another. Encourage your pet to play by using a toy and a friendly tone of voice. It's important to keep enough distance between your team and the others. Stop while your puppy is still enthusiastic. That may be

1 *The puppies are tugging at their leashes, trying to get closer to their playmate. Right now it's important for the owners to stand there without comment, not moving a step and not lengthening the leash.*

2 *After a short time, the puppies have understood that tugging doesn't accomplish anything, and they stop. Now each dog is readily concentrating on its owner.*

only one or two minutes of play. If he or she is not in the mood, try to get them to play at home (→ page 187).

Unleashing it correctly: Please don't forget to unleash the puppy in a controlled way after the little exercises (→ page 95). If need be, keep a loose hold on his or her collar. Encourage it to give you eye contact, and then let it race off to play with the other puppies.

Becoming a Family Dog

If you've put the puppy's early months to good use, you've laid the foundation for a good life with your pet from here on. Now you can take his or her basic training to another level.

NOW IT'S IMPORTANT to stay on the ball, to reinforce and expand on what your pet has learned. Everything the dog has mastered thus far must be taken to another level in the next few months as you train while your dog is increasingly facing distractions. Never train in such a way as to overtax your pet, however. If at all possible, your four-legged friend should obey your signals at once. Positive reinforcement has taught the dog what exercise it should do in which way. Now you can gradually discontinue the practice of offering treats as a reward. For "everyday" exercises such as the *sit*, use only your voice as praise. A simple *down* can be rewarded with a treat on an infrequent basis, not every time.

Deepening the Bond

The bonding walks with your puppy and the systematic engagement with your pet through play, cuddling, and other activities have paid off. Your little dog has become thoroughly attached to you. Now she's getting older, however, and thus also more independent. Therefore, this is not the time to rest on your laurels. Playing with the dog and participating in social communication through snuggling, brushing, or petting continue to be important throughout your dog's life, in fact. Do as much as possible with your pet alone, and interact with her while you're out in public. Play with her and explore certain types of terrain, just as you did when she was a puppy. Let her walk on fallen tree trunks like an acrobat, and call her to come, making her way across fairly undemanding obstacles (such as a fallen limb, snowdrifts, and the like). Now and then, include a few lessons. Everything the dog enjoys and needs you for will strengthen the bond.

Changes of Direction

As in puppyhood, you still can incorporate changes of direction in your bonding walks. A young dog will no longer stick to your heels like glue, as she did only a few weeks earlier, and now it is fine for her to run a few yards ahead, though she should keep looking back at you of her own accord. I know that it's difficult to always find unfamiliar places for your walks, so my advice is to work in a few "surprises" on your customary route. For example, you can suddenly do an about-face without saying a word and continue in the opposite direction. That is a practice I recommend if the dog has seen something interesting at a distance. Alternatively, at a fork in the path, don't take the direction your four-legged companion appears to prefer. If she follows you, after several feet you can reverse direction, heading down the path you originally wanted.

Tip: Don't always present your "surprises" at the same spots!

Contact with Other Dogs

Certainly, it's important for your pet to have contact and a chance to play with other members of her species (→ also page 17). But why must that be so at every encounter? Part of her learning program is playing with other dogs only when you give permission and walking

▶ INFO

Playing Is Learning

Fun is not the only thing that counts when a dog plays. Playing with "its" human strengthens the bond, but for a young dog this also means learning how to interact socially. Thus, it is part of the training process. The bite inhibition, for example, is also something that must be acquired (→ page 260). For these reasons, playing should be a fixed part of your daily routine.

past other leashed dogs without making contact with them. If you let your pet go up to every dog, she will soon insist on doing so even if the other animal is on the opposite side of the street.

If your young dog is playing with another canine, I suggest that you not stand and wait every time until the game is over. Just keep walking. If your dog is used to making sure that she maintains the connection to her "pack leader," she will continue to do so even when playing with other dogs. And quite probably your dog will follow you on her own after playing for a bit.

How to Introduce Visual Signals

As I explained on page 45, body language plays a great role in communication between dogs, as well as between dog and human. This form of communication is something you can use to great advantage by incorporating ○ VISUAL SIGNALS (page 276) with your hand into your dog's training program, in addition to unambiguous body movements in general.

Visual signals have the advantage of adding variety to the training process and promoting the dog's alertness. Visual signals can also emphasize a verbal signal. For example, when practicing the *stay* in the *sit* or *down* position from a distance, you can use the appropriate visual signal for added support. You can also substitute it for the audible signal. Visual signals can be used, for example, to indicate that you want the dog to *heel* without having to interrupt your conversation.

This is important: The individual visual signals must be so unmistakable that your four-legged friend can understand them with no problems. You lay the foundations for this almost automatically when teaching the basic commands, through systematic use of treats and the way you move your hand when offering them.

Making It Work

▷ To teach the dog a visual signal (→ right), always use it together with the verbal signal at first. After a certain time, the dog will react to either the visual signal or the verbal signal alone. You will be training her "bilingually."

▷ If you want to teach visual signals to an older dog that knows only verbal signals thus far, you should first give the audible signal and then the visual one. The prerequisite is that she must have good mastery of the verbal signals.

Try to complete a visual signal in timely fashion by changing your hand position as soon as the dog has assumed the desired position, but no later than the time the lesson ends or another command follows. And don't forget, once an exercise is working every time, gradually cut back on the treats or use them only occasionally, as described for the exercises on pages 83 to 95.

Important Visual Signals

▷ *Sit:* Your hand is clearly raised, whether you're holding a treat or not. Whether you now use the "raised index finger" or lift your whole hand is up to you. The whole hand is a clearer signal, however. You can also decide how high you raise your hand. If you want the dog to sit at a distance (→ page 137) or want to support her in the stay, the higher, the better—the dog will look up, and her hindquarters will go down.

▷ *Down:* Your dog has mastered the *sit* in response to a visual signal. Now, as you did with the puppy, make a downward movement with your arm and open palm and say "Down." At first, the movement is very distinct and your hand goes all the way to the ground, but over time a less sweeping gesture is enough. It also is a way of optically "pushing" the dog down.

▷ *Heel:* When starting and carrying out the *heel,* keep striking your thigh with a treat held in your hand, and simultaneously say "Heel." However, do this only if your canine companion is concentrating on moving along with you. Even without the treat, over time she will come to understand this signal as a request to *heel.* This signal will give additional motivation, especially if you make a turn that keeps the dog moving on the outside.

▷ *Stay:* At the moment you say "Stay," briefly hold your open palm horizontally in front of the dog's face. You don't need a treat for this. The dog should follow neither your hand nor you; the visual signal serves as a kind of stop sign.

▷ *Here:* When you call the dog to come to you, you'll do it primarily with words, because if she isn't looking at you, you can't give her a visual signal. But by using visual signals in addition, you can support the dog while she's in the process of coming to you. Here's how: Pat your abdomen (→ photo, page 112, top) or stretch out your arms at your sides, pointing slightly downward. If your pet has learned the signal after a time, you can occasionally use the visual signal alone to call it to come from the *sit* position, just as a training exercise.

▷ **Other visual signals:** Basically, you can teach your canine companion a visual signal to go with every audible signal. Beforehand, however, plan the signal carefully, to ensure that the dog will understand it.

If It's Not Going Well

Maybe you've taken on too many visual signals at one time. Or your dog may not be familiar with them yet, and that means the exercise is probably too much for her. Teach your pet one signal after another. Check to see if the dog has reliably mastered the verbal signals and can easily tell them apart.

If problems arise, you can also check to see whether you're employing "sign language" clearly enough. I repeatedly see the raised index finger in particular being used for everything you can think of. Many dog owners tend to use this signal unconsciously, whenever they want to tell the dog something very emphatically—no matter what lesson they're trying to teach. Then, of course, it's difficult for the dog to find out what she is supposed to react to and how.

1 *Here's how the visual signal for "Sit" looks. Seeing your upward hand motion, the dog also looks up—and her rear end almost automatically goes down.*
2 *The visual signal for "Down"—a downward hand motion—causes the dog to look down and thus, to lie down.*
3 *For the "Stay," hold your open palm briefly in front of the dog's face as you move away; it will act as a kind of stop sign.*

Training When Other Animals Are Near

Your dog can get into a dangerous situation or even cause harm, for example, by chasing a chicken or another animal. Usually this happens when you're not prepared for it, and the shock slows your reaction time. Through deliberate training, you can reinforce your dog's obedience skills so that you have better control over your pet in such situations.

Prerequisites: Your four-legged companion should be able to reliably obey all the basic commands, at least without a great deal of distraction. Is there a farm with fowl, a pond with ducks, or perhaps a wildlife park near your home? Or do cats that are accustomed to dogs live in your neighborhood? These conditions would be highly favorable for training.

How It Works

First, get your dog in the mood for "work" by doing a few drills without any distraction from other animals. Once your pet is focused, go with her in the direction of your "training objectives," but don't go too close yet. You want your pet to notice the animals but still to be able to concentrate on you. Make sure to keep the dog on leash, so she can't take off like a flash.

▷ **Paying attention:** Now place your dog at your side, and encourage her to give you eye contact for a few moments. Reward her for doing so.

▷ **Heeling:** Next, practice heeling with your pet. Walk away from the animals at first. If that works, try to walk parallel to the "prey." The dog will get a better view of the animals. If that is working as well, take a few steps toward the animals. If need be, use treats to help for the time being.

▷ **Practicing the *sit* and *down*:** Now practice having your dog quietly *sit* or also lie in the *down* for an extended time, right next to you. This will be more difficult, because the dog is no longer moving, as she was while heeling, and is not being distracted by your request for eye contact. Thus, she has time now to concentrate on the prey. Make sure the dog always sits or lies parallel to the animals and right next to you (→ page 106). Now practice as described

Despite the sheep in the background, this dog is keeping her eyes on her owner. You should use "animal encounters" as training sessions, especially if your dog is interested in chasing.

Practice heeling, for example, so that you are walking between the dog and the sheep. Keep enough distance from the distraction for the dog to move along at your side in a relaxed way.

above under "Heeling," first with your back to the animals, and then parallel to them. If your dog can sit or lie quietly in the *down* position without craning her neck to see the prey, you now can practice with the animals in her field of vision. But always at an appropriate distance, please!

▷ **Stay:** Sit and *down* in the *stay* are a bit more difficult, because your dog needs to quietly sit or lie while you are some distance away. Use the sequence of steps outlined in the previous training variations—that is, first practice with your back to the animals, then parallel to them. Only when these versions are working well should you tell your pet to sit or lie down with the "prey" directly in view. First, practice with a shorter distance between you and your pet and for a shorter length of time than is possible without the distraction of the animals. With increasing progress, you can gradually lengthen both elements.

Is the Exercise Not Going Well?

Test to see whether your pet really has reliably mastered the drills without the distraction of animals. Unless that's the case, it's understandable that things aren't working with such

an attractive distraction. Then, if need be, it's time to go back to the roots. Maybe you were too willing to take a risk and thus, ventured too near the distracting animals. For the time being, keep more distance.

Does your pet have a tendency to race off and head for the prey? A dog owner once asked me what she could do when her dog started scaring ducks. On her daily walk, she passed a stream where there were always ducks, and every time her dog would take off at a run and not come back when called. Actually, this problem is easy to solve by leashing the dog in time, if necessary 600 feet or more before reaching the spot in question. That will prevent any undesired success on the dog's part and also make good use of the situation for purposeful training.

You must also keep your four-legged friend from flushing and chasing crows and other birds, an activity many dogs enjoy. If, despite her training, your pet occasionally has such exciting hunting experiences, this will substantially lessen the success of the training. Instead, make such situations into training opportunities (if the birds stay on the ground for any length of time), or divert your pet's attention in time with a toy or a treat. If both of these solutions are not possible at this point, avoid such locations or leash your dog in good time, as recommended above.

If things just aren't working at all, then your pet is probably one of those dogs with a very strong hunting instinct (→ page 266), or other factors may be contributing as well. Read more about hunting on page 243.

For the "Stay," first down *your dog so that she has no direct view of the sheep. If your pet obeys very reliably, you can practice without the leash.*

Staying in the *Sit* and *Down* for Extended Periods

This lesson always comes in handy when the dog has to sit and wait quietly at your side for any length of time: for example, when you want to cross a street and the light is red or the traffic is too heavy. Otherwise, both you and she could be in danger. If you're in a café or visiting a friend, the dog can't run around there; she must be able to lie next to you. Otherwise, things could end as they did for a friend of mine: Her visitor's dog ran around in the unfamiliar apartment and happened to come across the apple cake for the afternoon coffee in another room. Unnoticed, she wolfed down more than half of the cake.

Prerequisites: Your pet must be able to perform the *sit* and *down* reliably and without treats. In addition, it's a good idea to let her get enough exercise and activity beforehand, if you're planning to go to a café or to visit friends. Then it's easier for the dog to stay calm and quiet for any length of time. For both versions of this exercise, it is crucial that you yourself exude an air of calm.

Making It Work

▷ **Sitting:** At first, you can resort to using treats as a positive reinforcement. Have the dog sit at your side, with no distraction and no treats. Make sure she sits parallel to you, so that later on, when you practice with more distraction, she doesn't sit where she has a good view of the distraction and concentrate on that. Once the dog is in the *sit*, wait a few moments—just how long depends on the dog. A quieter type will sit longer at first than a high-spirited one. End the lesson with a treat before your pet gets restless. Remember, don't hand over the treat as soon as she sits; wait until the end of the exercise. The dog will learn that sitting for a longer time is worth its while.

Slowly extend the time to a few minutes, and gradually incorporate distractions. For example, if you're out in public and run into someone you'd like to chat with, tell your four-legged friend to sit next to you. For a while, reward the dog for this every time, and then use treats only from time to time.

▷ **Down:** Here, apply the principle described above for an extended *sit*. If you want to reward the dog, wait until the end of the exercise—that is, shortly before you release her from the *down*. Put the treat on the ground to keep the dog from looking up. Here, too, use the treats only on occasion (→ above). If the drill is working without a distraction, start incorporating small distractions, for example, by training with people nearby.

If the Exercise Is Causing Problems

Ask yourself whether you are exuding a great enough sense of calm, or whether the dog may still be too full of energy. Did you possibly introduce a distraction too soon or extend the time too quickly? If you have the impression that your pet doesn't want to sit or lie down although she has learned to do so and is not being overtaxed, you have several options. With sensitive, insecure, or fearful dogs, I recommend that for the time being you keep on offering treats as a reward for correct execution. Praise and positive reinforcement encourage obedience and a willingness to cooperate.

Stubborn dogs and other hard-boiled canine types also need "firmer" kinds of correction. Still, a person can reestablish trust and cooperation even with a supposedly hopeless case.

▷ **Sitting:** Push down on the dog's rear end, for example, in combination with a stern, but quiet "No" to force her into the *sit* position.

▷ **Down:** If the dog leaves the *down* position, redesign the exercise so that your pet has to

3

The dog has to learn to lie quietly next to her human for a few minutes without repeatedly getting up or having to be reminded again and again.

If your four-legged friend has stayed in the down *long enough, at the end of the exercise— that is, just before you tell her to* sit *again—she should get a reward.*

In daily life, it's helpful if your pet can sit calmly beside you for an extended period—for example, when you're out walking and would like to have a brief chat with someone.

A well trained dog stays calmly at your side in the down *position while you treat yourself to a pleasant reading break on a park bench.*

assume the *down* under your bent leg. Then she can't get up again. But it's a little tiring.

Instead, while the dog is still in the *down*, you can put your foot on the leash in such a way that it remains loose when the dog is lying down, but becomes taut if she tries to sit up. The dog itself can decide whether she wants to put up with that or would prefer to lie down again comfortably after all.

Important: For this correction, use only a relatively wide collar that does not pull, because physical force is not desirable here.

Longer "Stay" at Greater Distance from You

This exercise is useful, for example, if you want your dog to lie down at some distance from the table while you eat, or if you're mopping and want to keep your pet from running across the wet floor.

Prerequisites: Your pet must have learned to stay in the *sit* or the *down* at a distance of three to four yards and for approximately two minutes.

Your dog is now probably used to seeing you stand in front of her. Next, get her accustomed to seeing you move around while in front of her.

Making "Sit and Stay" Work

▷ The dog is leashed. Have her sit at your side. Give the signal for stay (verbal and visual signals), and take a few steps forward. Stretch out the leash at full length on the ground in front. Then, if necessary, you'll have an "emergency brake" if the dog stands up, and you can quickly bring her back to the original spot.

Now, just stand there quietly for a moment. If the dog is relaxed, walk parallel to her, slowly moving back and forth a little. The length of time depends on your dog. Go back to the dog before she shows any sign of impatience. At first, extend the length of the exercise, and then increase the distance as well.

▷ Once you can walk back and forth at a distance of several yards for two or three minutes, start walking in a semicircle around the dog. Once that also works without the dog getting restless, you can keep extending the exercise until you can make a complete circle around your pet. In the process, she will lose sight of you for a moment. If she stays where she is without turning her entire body around to follow your movement, then she is performing at a very high level of difficulty. Congratulations.

▷ Now you can begin to teach this exercise while incorporating a distraction as well. For example, train in a field next to a path where several walkers are passing, or at home, when

If you want to extend the "Stay," first get the dog used to seeing you walk calmly back and forth in front of her— at first only a few yards away, and then at a greater distance.

Once that works, start walking in a circle around the dog—at first, fairly close to your pet, then farther away. The dog is allowed to turn her head, but she must not leave her place.

Start "Stay" with distractions at a lower level again. Stop several feet in front of your dog, off the path, while walkers go past.

Once your pet has reliably learned to stay where she is, tell her to lie down on one side of the path while you stand on the other; now the walkers are moving between you and your four-legged friend.

other family members are walking through the house or yard.

Training "Down and Stay"

▷ In the *down*, the drill works just the way it did for the *sit*. And please keep this in mind—when you return to the dog's side, she must remain in the *down*. To be on the safe side, you can use the hand signal for *down* as you walk back or say "Down" again. The dog should not sit until you are back at her side and have given the appropriate signal. I recommend that you vary the procedure—let her sit up right away at some times, at others have her stay longer in the *down*. The stronger your pet's tendency to sit up too soon, the longer you should wait to give the *sit* signal.

▷ In the *down*, too, gradually incorporate distractions once you can circle around your pet without seeing signs of restlessness on her part.

If the Exercise Isn't Working

If your canine friend won't retain the *sit* or *down* positions, she probably hasn't yet learned the *stay* well enough. If your pet is one of those dogs that can hold the *sit* longer than

the *down*, for the time being you should practice only the normal *down* for awhile before beginning the *stay* in the *down* position.

If the dog is not staying in position while you move, it may be that you're moving too quickly and jerkily. It's important to walk up and down very calmly and quietly in front of the dog. If your pet gets restless during the lesson, help her by using the hand signal for *sit* or *stay* (→ page 102), and return to her side.

If the dog is restless or stands up, ask yourself whether you may have unconsciously caused her to do so. Don't talk to your pet while you're away from her and while she stays in the desired position. If she looks in a different direction, that's okay, provided she doesn't get up. If you talk to the dog, possibly even using her name, or make an enticing sound in an attempt to make her concentrate, she may misinterpret that as a command and get up in order to come to you.

1 When you practice heeling in the face of distractions, first keep some distance between you and the walkers or other distractions, and stay a little off the path.

2 As your pet becomes more proficient, reduce the distance to the objects of attraction. Walk on the path, and practice even when there's more activity there, as in this photo.

"Heel" Near a Distraction

This exercise is definitely something the dog should have mastered if you take her out in public—for example, into town, or if someone on horseback or a jogger comes along.

Prerequisites: Your dog should be able to *heel* reliably, with no distraction and no treats. Only then can she learn to *heel* when the distraction level is greater.

Making It Work

▷ For review, briefly practice with your dog on leash and with no distractions. Then look for a path, for example, where you will find walkers or an occasional cyclist. Stop next to the path, and first practice heeling at some distance from the events on the path. Since this is a more difficult situation, at first you can reward the dog for correct, concentrated heeling with a treat or a toy—depending on her type, for a shorter or longer distance. Again, keep in mind that you should reward your pet only if she gives you her uninterrupted attention.

▷ If the exercise is working, gradually increase the distraction level. Now go closer to the path. You can practice parallel to the path or at a right angle to it, alternating between facing the people and turning your back to them.

▷ If your canine companion is not reacting to the distractions, practice right on a path where several people are approaching you or passing you. It gets even more difficult if you go past people with a leashed dog. If it lunges toward your dog or barks, the training session becomes a real challenge. Increase the distance if need be. If your pet still resists being distracted, she has earned an extra helping of treats while she is still concentrating on heeling.

If You're Having Trouble

Ask yourself whether the dog has really understood heeling when there are no distractions and has practiced it long enough. If not, do more training before you go to the next level. Possibly you also are too passive and thus, too "uninteresting" to your pet. Show your commitment and use your voice to motivate the dog so that she pays attention to you. Did you increase the distraction level too quickly? Correct heeling requires a great deal of practice.

The Command to *Come* and *Sit Front*

3

Let's suppose that you've seen a cat and were able to call your dog to *come* in time. Once she's near you, for her own safety it is crucial that she not immediately turn around again in the cat's direction and thus perhaps race off again.

Prerequisites: Your four-legged companion basically must respond reliably to "Here" or "Come" by coming to you cheerfully, and she must be able to perform the "stay and sit" for a considerable time and at some distance from you.

This is important: In daily life, you mainly will call the dog to *come* when she is running free. To practice the ● SIT FRONT (page 272) systematically, start the exercise from the *sit* and *stay*. Practice in a distraction-free setting so that your dog can concentrate on you.

Here's How

▷ Tell the dog to sit at your side, and then walk several feet away. As you move away, put a few treats in one hand. Turn around toward the dog and wait a few moments. Call her now, by running away and slapping your abdomen with both hands. Running away, as you know, has a catalyzing effect on your dog. Since dogs tend to focus on motion, your pet will concentrate on your hand movements while she runs toward you. Use an enticing tone of voice to call her, or use a dog whistle. Don't stop moving, and stand up straight until your dog has almost reached you.

Don't lean toward your pet; otherwise she will apply the brakes while she's still too far from you. Keep holding your hands at stomach height, and the dog will smell the treat. Many

● WHAT DO I DO IF . . .

. . . the dog doesn't come?

If the dog fails to come reliably when you recall her, it is not always an isolated problem; it can, for example, be related to excessive independence on your pet's part. Often changing the way you deal with the dog can be helpful here. There may be other causes, however.

Solution 1: Does your voice sound clear and convincing enough? Women especially often have a voice that sounds rather "thin" and faint even at a distance of 10 to 15 yards, and it may not sound really motivating and interesting when the dog is distracted. If this is the case, it's best to use a dog whistle.

Solution 2: Does the dog "know" that you'll wait for her anyway and gladly repeat your command seven times more? Change your behavior, and walk away quickly after the first call. Fall back on the "hunger" principle and reward your pet with special treats, which she gets only after she comes, however.

Solution 3: In stubborn cases, split up her entire food ration into small servings throughout the day—available only if she obeys your signal to come.

1 *Call your dog to* come *from the* sit *position, and quickly run backwards, encouraging your pet with "Here" or a whistle blow. As you do so, slap your abdomen with both hands.*

2 *When the dog gets very close to you, stop and stand erect to keep her from putting on the brakes too soon. Then the dog sits and gets her reward right in front of you.*

dogs now will sit of their own accord because they're looking up toward the treat. If this doesn't happen, simply say "Sit." Now, give your pet the treat and praise her, but she has to stay in the *sit* position! Don't let her take her reward and race off again.

▷ Since the dog is now right in front of you and concentrating on you, you've interrupted her show of interest in the cat, for example. At this moment she can't easily get past you, even to one side.

▷ While she's enjoying her reward, put on the leash again. Finally, call her to your side once more with the "Heel" signal, and tell her to sit there. Another treat will help you accomplish that. Say "Heel" and shift your pet around by moving the treat in a curve pattern, first outward, then to the back, so that the dog ends up parked next to you again.

▷ Only now is the exercise over. Either you continue heeling or you let your pet run free again, depending on the situation.

Always use this sequence, so that the exercise really succeeds every time. In practice, unfortunately, I repeatedly see that most dog owners get negligent over time and eventually settle for having the dog come more or less close in response to the command. But then you don't really have the animal under control, and should the occasion arise, she will quickly be off again.

Important: Don't always call your dog out of the *sit* and *stay* position. You don't want her performance of the *stay* to be impaired. About half the time, call her the usual way.

If You're Having Trouble

Is the dog running past you? Then you probably have your hands at your sides rather than at stomach level. If your hand position is correct and the dog still runs past you, I recommend practicing in front of a wall or a hedge to keep her from running any farther. Does she sit at an angle to you? Here, too, the cause often is an incorrect hand position. Keep your hands in front, near your abdomen, and run backwards again, calling or blowing the whistle. Then you can correct your pet's position.

Biking with the Dog

If there's not enough time for a lengthy walk, you can still give your pet some exercise by letting her run along next to your bike. Besides, most dogs pay especially good attention, because you move faster on the bike.

Prerequisites: Medium-sized to large dogs are best suited for running next to a bike. They mustn't be too huge, however. In addition, they must have healthy joints. The dog should know how to *heel* and should demonstrate good basic obedience (⟩ page 83). In addition, she should be about one year old when you start this exercise.

This is important: If you want your dog to run next to your bike on busy streets, she must learn the command "Bike" or "Right." She should always run on the right side of the bike, because then she will be away from the traffic. If you already have your pet *heel* to your right, you need no additional command.

Teaching Your Dog

▷ First, push your bike on your right and use the audible signal "Bike" to tell your leashed dog to run on the bike's right. At first, practice as described above for heeling (→ page 94)—that is, initially with treats, discontinuing them gradually.

▷ If that is working, look for a quiet path, and ride slowly for a bit while the dog runs along beside the bike. Let your pet romp a little beforehand, so that she isn't bursting with energy on your first outing and doesn't get some nonsense in her head. It could be dangerous for you if she drags you off your bike. Hold the leash loosely in your hand so that you can release it quickly if necessary. As soon as you stop, the dog should sit. Don't overtax your pet. Extend the distances slowly, and don't ride too fast or in really hot weather. The dog should be able to trot alongside you at an easy pace. On dirt roads with no traffic,

you can let the dog run free next to the bike. This will give your pet a chance for a little sniffing or a game with other dogs, but she will still be careful not to lose sight of you.

If you're quite often out with your dog and bike, I recommend that you buy an attachment specially developed for bikes, the so-called Springer bicycle jogger. The device is available in pet stores and in certain bike shops as well.

▶ INFO

Make Biking Fun

Once your dog is used to the bicycle, start out by riding slowly for about ten minutes. Match the duration and distance of the ride to your pet's condition and age. Your canine friend should not always run on asphalt, which is quite hard. Try to ride on dirt roads in the country or on paths in wooded areas. If it's a warm day, bike with your dog only in the morning or evening. If your pet is overweight, she needs to lose some before she starts bike training.

If Biking Isn't Working

Is your dog too high-spirited? Keep her active before you start training with your bike. Is she not yet able to *heel* reliably enough? Until she has mastered heeling, it makes no sense to get her accustomed to biking.

Important Exercises for Several Dogs

Does this sound familiar? Your dog obeys as long as no other dogs are in sight, but tunes out once another canine appears on the horizon, insisting on heading in that direction? That behavior can get tiresome, even dangerous—for example, if you're walking along a street and your dog won't obey "Heel" or "Sit," but pulls on her leash in the direction of the roadway because she has glimpsed another dog on the other side. And if you're sitting in an outdoor cafe or on a park bench and other dogs are nearby, it's nice if your own canine companion lies quietly instead of constantly trying to get the attention of her fellows.

Prerequisites: The dogs must have reliably learned all the basic commands, combined with a low level of distraction or none at all. If their levels of training are different, each dog should do only those exercises that she already knows thoroughly.

This is important: Make it a rule that when your dog is on leash, she can have no contact with other dogs. I have repeatedly pointed out that dogs learn from success. They also learn what happens when they're on leash and lunge toward another dog and you go right

 TIP

The Right Motivation

When doing exercises with other dogs, remember to give your pet plenty of positive motivation so that she gives you her attention. You might take along really interesting treats. If your pet keeps straining at her leash, or if you constantly have to repeat the commands, then the dog is not learning effectively.

along, so that your pet can "say hello" briefly. The result is that your dog learns that with the right amount of effort she can accomplish her objective, and concludes that she will try this again every time an opportunity presents itself. If your dog is also used to being unleashed right away so that she doesn't miss a chance to play, you're only making your situation worse. If necessary, read page 95 once more. Apart from that, not all other owners are exactly happy when you let your dog greet every dog she encounters. For more on this, see page 166.

When you're out for a walk, take advantage of "oncoming dog traffic" to practice in a purposeful way. It's even better if you get together with one or more other dog owners whose pets are at roughly the same level of training as yours. Then a few highly useful training segments can be worked into your daily walk without taking additional time. Your conversation time may be slightly reduced, but perhaps you can make up for it by having coffee together afterwards.

Making the Exercises Work

▷ Always keep the dogs on leash during these training sessions so that none of them has an opportunity for an undesirable success, that is, for a quick visit with another dog.

▷ For each meeting, don't take on more than one or two exercises. In between it's fine to take a break. You can use the break to play with your own dog, for example. If it's a warm day, you can use the break to lie down in the grass with your dog and snuggle.

▷ Start the first training segment right away—without letting the dogs play together first. After all, your pet is supposed to learn that she must concentrate on you, without being allowed to greet other dogs sufficiently or play with them. In your daily routine, that frequently is just not possible. Dogs accept this very quickly and are in no way annoyed with their handlers.

▷ The only thing to overcome when you practice in a group is your own weaker self. Naturally, it's more appealing to take a walk together and chat while the dogs race across a field. Joint practice sessions are also fun, however, and useful as well.

If you've ever attended a good dog training school, you've surely noticed that your pet relatively quickly gets used to following your guidance even when other dogs are present. This holds true even when she's allowed to play with her "fellow students" for a few minutes now and then.

Staying Concentrated Despite Other Dogs

To guarantee that you're on the same wavelength as your dog even when other dogs are present, she must be able to concentrate on you even in the face of canine distraction. To accomplish that, first arrange all your teams some distance apart. The distance should be large enough that the dogs don't distract each other. Now each handler should get his or her pet's attention and make eye contact. If necessary, at first you can hold a treat or a toy in your hand. In the beginning, make the sessions a little shorter than the amount of time your dog can already do the exercises in with no distractions. Reward your pet in any case, provided she maintains eye contact with you. Over time you can increase the duration of the eye contact and reduce the distances between the teams.

When this is no longer difficult for the dogs, you can increase the level of distraction. Now one team can practice maintaining eye contact while another practices heeling. Keep the distances between teams large enough, and reduce them very gradually! Plan the exercises to ensure that the dogs make as few mistakes as possible.

1 *First, practice around only a slight distraction: Only one owner-dog team is in motion; the other two dogs are concentrating on their owners.*

2 *If that is successful, increase the level of distraction. Only one dog should concentrate on its owner, while the other two teams practice heeling nearby.*

Practicing in three teams: Two teams practice attentiveness while the third walks around. If that works, then two teams can walk around while the third works on concentration.

Here, too, make sure to keep the distances great enough for the dogs to do the exercise successfully.

Heeling in Random Directions

Take positions with sufficient distance between them. The distance between the human-dog

1 *Before these three teams practice* heel *work in random directions, it is important for each owner first to get his or her dog's attention in peace and quiet, ideally in the* sit *position.*

2 *These teams have already been practicing for some time, and the distances are now rather short. Be sure to start the training with greater distances.*

at first and gradually reduce it. Here, it is advisable for the dogs to walk on the outside at the start. With increasing skill, the dogs can walk right past each other, with the humans on the outside.

When practicing heeling in a group, always keep it in the back of your mind that you now have tempting competition to some extent. Always walk in a resolute, energetic way and praise the dog whenever she heels correctly. You need to put some "oomph" in the exercise, so that your enthusiasm carries the dog along.

"Down" and "Sit" with "Heel"

In the previous exercise, all the teams did the same thing. Now it gets a bit harder: One team stays quietly in place, with the dog sitting correctly at her owner's side. The other team does *heel* work. This raises the distraction level for the dog that is not in motion. To keep the dogs from distracting each other, the team in motion must stay at a sufficient distance from the waiting team in this exercise. Gradually reduce the distance, but only by amounts small enough for the dogs to have no problems. Since each team naturally wants to practice sitting and heeling, you should alternate regularly.

Incidentally, the distances may depend on the individual dogs. It may well be that one dog, for example, can maintain a shorter distance from another dog when heeling than when sitting while the other walks past. As soon as one team is doing a good job with the exercise in the *sit* position, it can go on to "Down" while the other team does *heel* work.

My tip: Even if this is working well in the *sit*, start the "Down" segment at a greater distance from the walking team. Too short a distance may cause the dog to leave the *down* position.

Practicing in three teams: Here it's advisable to structure the exercises so that at first only one team is heeling and two teams have their dogs *sit* or assume the *down* position beside them. If this is going well, you can increase the level of difficulty. Then two teams

teams is adequate if the dogs can concentrate on their owners with little trouble. If necessary, rely on treats at first.

First each owner gets his or her pet's attention. Once the dogs are concentrating, each team should start off. Move in random directions. As you walk, keep the distances between you fairly large at first. If no dog is straining toward another, you can gradually start passing each other at less distance. When directly approaching each other, keep more distance are in motion and only one is doing the *sit* or *down* exercise, which again means more distraction for the "motionless" dog.

"Stay" in the *Sit* or *Down*

As a starting position, all the teams should be at least six feet apart, more if necessary. The dogs sit correctly parallel to their owners. Now each owner gives his or her pet the signal to *stay* and walks away as far as the leash will reach. Place the leash on the ground in front, as an "emergency brake." Now stand calmly in front of the dogs for a few moments, longer if their training level warrants it. Then go back to the dogs. If that was successful, do the same exercise in the *down* position.

Whether you finish this exercise now or after a few more training units in the *sit* position depends on the dogs' level of training. For an exercise to go well, it is important for the dog, even under this distraction, to stay in the *down* position until you are beside her again and give the "Sit" command.

If the dogs have understood the exercise, increase the action. The dogs should sit or stand next to each other in the *stay*, while the humans again walk away as described above. Now, however, stand close together in front of the dogs and talk a little. The dogs will hear your voices, which represent a greater level of distraction for them. After roughly half a minute, go back to your dog. Gradually lengthen the duration.

Variation: This adds more movement to the exercise. The dogs sit or lie next to each other in the *stay*, while each human walks back and forth a little in front of his or her dog. Over time you can certainly decrease the distance between the dogs, but always start again by standing quietly in front of the dog

Perfectly trained. Even though another dog is going past at a relatively short distance on a loose leash, this dog maintains the down position nicely.

1 "Stay" with several dogs: At first, each owner stands quietly several feet in front of his or her dog. Don't talk to each other.

2 If all the dogs stay in a relaxed sit position, their owners get together in front of them for a short chat. Each one unobtrusively keeps an eye on his or her pet.

3 If that succeeds, each owner should walk back and forth in front of his or her dog. Then extend the exercise: Each owner walks back and forth in front of all the dogs.

as she maintains the *sit* or *down* position. If the exercise is successful—that is, if the dogs stay relaxed and don't get up—walk back and forth in front of your dog. If that, too, is working, then the owners should walk up and down in front of all the dogs, not just their own. Overall, a lot of movement is going on before the dogs' eyes.

One Dog Is Down, the Others Move

With this exercise, the stay can be made even more challenging. Give your dog the "Sit" signal. Then walk two or three yards away and lay the leash on the ground in front. Stand calmly in front of your pet. Meanwhile, the other team practices heeling at least nine feet away from you at first. You can try the same thing with the dog in the *down* position. In addition, the teams should switch roles.

If the dog maintains the *sit* or *down* despite distraction, the team that is just practicing heelwork can also pass between the dog in the *stay* and its owner.

Practicing in three teams: First, two teams practice "Stay" while the third does a heeling drill. If that works, one team does "Stay" and two walk around. Here too, keep switching roles.

If each dog does a good job, turn up the distraction level another notch: Your dog sits or lies, the other team heels, and you walk back and forth in front of your dog at a relatively close distance. Now everything around the dog in the *stay* is in motion.

As the dogs become more skilled, increase the distance between the human and the dog in the *stay*. The distance between the waiting dog and the passing teams, however, can gradually be decreased.

Come Under Slight Distraction

In the previous exercises for several dogs, each owner still had his or her dog nicely under control—either because the dog was next to you or because you "glued" her to a certain spot with "Sit" or "Down" and "Stay." Now, train your pet to come to you when called, in the process having to pass by one or more other dogs.

If you can't assess the other dogs successfully because you don't know exactly what they've already mastered, I recommend beginning with an easier version. All the teams take positions at appropriate distances. Then, one after another, each asks his or her dog to do the *sit/stay* and calls him or her as usual. As I explained on pages 111 and 112, it is important to pay attention to a good *sit front* and to end the exercise correctly.

If every dog comes happily to his or her owner with no intermediate stops, you can increase the level of difficulty somewhat. One team stands still, the dog sits, and one or more teams position themselves as a distraction about halfway along the route the dog will have to take when called. Thus, it has to pass another dog. Depending on the level of training, the distraction team can stand right in this area or a little away from it at first.

Now, when you call your pet to come, try to sound especially involved, and run backwards in the opposite direction as you call. The more interesting you seem now to your dog, the better she can resist the temptation to make a detour to the other dog on the way to you. Observe your pet closely on her way. If there's even the hint of a glance in the direction of the other dog, repeat the *come* signal immediately.

Practicing in three teams: With three teams, you can make the exercise even more interesting by having one team standing on either side of the route as a distraction. For the distraction teams, of course, it is important that the dogs sit or lie quietly, even if the dog being called races past them. Take turns, so that each team has the chance to play the role of a distraction and then practice the "Come."

1 *First the dog learns, in the face of a slight distraction by other members of its species, to stay in the* down *position: Two dogs are down, and only one human-dog team is heeling nearby.*

2 *If the dogs retain their position and stay relaxed, increase the level of distraction by the other dogs. Only one dog practices "Stay," and two teams practice "Heel" not far away.*

If the Exercises Aren't Going Well

If the dogs are accustomed to being allowed to play together when they meet, it may be that to begin with they will persistently try to get close to each other. If so, you need to choose large enough distances and start out, if necessary, as described on page 99 in reference to puppies. That means that you can't give into pulling and tugging; you simply have

△

Not altogether easy—a dog responds to her owner's request to come, walking past other dogs that remain in the down *position. Start with more distance between the waiting teams and the dog that is coming when called.*

to ignore all that until the puppies have quieted down. If the group includes some real "mule heads," then you can keep meeting with the other teams and practice "ignoring tugging"— and without letting the dogs play together before or after the event. Train this way until the little group has been distinctly calmer for a few meetings in a row. Don't start the real training until you notice that your dogs are concentrating on you.

If an exercise isn't working, the cause may be that the lesson hasn't been sufficiently learned without any distractions involved. Then, it's advisable to review this exercise thoroughly without distraction for the time being. You may also have increased the level of diffi-

culty too quickly, or reduced the distances between the dogs too soon, or increased the distance between dog and owner during the *stay* by too much. If so, take your time and cut back on your demands again. It is also very important to match the level of difficulty to the individual dog. What one can already do well, may take another quite a while to learn.

Are you making the exercise exciting enough for your dog? If you're too passive, there's not enough incentive for your pet to give you her attention. As soon as your dog shows signs of being distracted by another dog, use the method described on page 87 to get her attention. Don't forget to use your tone of voice and treats to praise her when she complies.

Getting the Most Out of Walks

Learning for life—that applies to your canine companion as well. Everything you've taught her in the past months should become a regular part of your daily routine and your walks together. In addition, make the walks so full of variety that your pet doesn't lose her interest in you or her sense of your importance when you're out together. Then the dog will have no need to look for pointless activities to keep busy.

▶ NATURE WALK

At home, you ask your dog to sit, put on her leash, and go out the door with her on a loose leash, carrying treats and toys. On your way, you pass a yard where a dog is running up and down next to a fence, barking loudly. You tell your dog to *heel*, distract her with a treat, and walk past the property quickly and in an unflustered way.

Now you pass a public green space. Let your pet *heel* for a several more feet. Now she has a chance to run free. Tell her to *sit* and remove the leash. She stays in the *sit* position. To keep her from always knowing what to expect next, occasionally you can let her wait a few more moments and then leash her again. After a few more moments, unleash her again. When your four-legged friend briefly makes eye contact with you, give her the finish signal (→ page 85). Now she can run around. After a few minutes, while the dog is not distracted, you call or whistle for her to come to you. If she doesn't come right away, you walk away. She comes, sits, and you praise her. End the exercise and let her run free again.

You walk past a small wooded area and, without warning, quickly turn and stand behind a large tree. After a short search, your pet finds you and is relieved. You greet and praise her. Oh, there's a wonderful fallen tree

trunk! You tell the dog to sit not far away and step over the trunk. After waiting briefly, you call (or whistle) the dog to *come*. She steps on the gas and enthusiastically clears the obstacle. That's fun! End the exercise correctly again, with *sit front* and the leash.

Finally, with your dog at *heel*, you wind around through the trees for a bit. You leave the woods, and then you see a friend with her four-legged playmate. You say hello and talk for a few minutes. Both dogs *sit* at *heel*. Now you unleash the dogs and let them romp for a while. Then you continue on your way. Your pet follows of her own accord, since she is accustomed to keeping an eye on your whereabouts.

After some time, a couple of people out for a walk come toward you. You take advantage of this situation and practice the *down/stay* next to the path for a little while. Finally, you

Use the natural surroundings to spice up your walk with a few exercises. "Here across an obstacle"—and the dog comes running, her ears flying.
▽

△

Calm and relaxed, this dog stays in the down *position despite the distractions she faces in the busy pedestrian zone, while her owner waits for someone.*

3

let your dog run off leash again. A bit farther away you see some crows on the grass. They've already caught your pet's eye. You distract her with an enticing tone of voice and run away. As soon as the dog faces in your direction, you signal it to *come* by calling or blowing the whistle. Once she reaches you, you give her a generous helping of treats. After ending the exercise in the usual way, you take your pet's favorite toy out of your pocket and play together.

Now it's time to go home. On the way, you fool your pet again by suddenly branching off in the wrong direction. Your dog notices this quickly, however, and follows you. Before you get to the street, you leash her again and walk home with her at *heel.*

◉ WALK IN TOWN

Your four-legged companion has had a chance to romp to her heart's content and to do her "business." Then it's time to leave: You go to the car and tell your pet to sit. Then you open the door and in response to a signal, such as "Hop in," the dog jumps in. Everybody else gets in too. You all drive into town. Once there, you're lucky enough to find a

parking place on the main shopping street. Everyone gets out, the dog waits until the door is opened, and you put on her leash. Now you wait a moment and then say "Hop out" to give her permission to leave the car. You tell the dog to *heel,* and walk along the street. In front of a display window, you slow your pace, since you want to look at the latest fashions as you pass. You say "Heel" in a soothing way to get your pet to slow down too. She stays at your side on a loose leash. You've seen the window display, and you say "Heel" more enthusiastically and resume your normal pace. Oh, there's a delicatessen coming up! The other family members want sandwiches with cold cuts and go inside. You stay in front and wait while the dog lies down next to you.

Once they've all returned, you resume your walk. You come to a red light. The dog sits at *heel,* and someone else with a dog is across the street. Your pet has noticed the other animal, so to play it safe you say "Sit" once more. The light turns green and you cross the street. Just before you meet the other dog, you briefly ask for your pet's attention, if necessary. Now you stroll through the pedestrian zone. The children are whining because they want to try out the newest computer games in a store. While they do so, you'd rather sit in the sidewalk café across the street and treat yourself to a latte macchiato. You *down* your dog at your side. Suddenly, two tables away, you see a good friend. You give your pet the *stay* command and go over to the other table to exchange a few words. Your dog stays nicely in position, even when you come back. Now the children have come back too. The dog still retains her position. Now tell her to *sit* so that she can greet the rest of the family. If you've finished all your errands, you walk back to the car with the dog at *heel.*

Attending a Puppy Class and a Dog School

Probably you're groaning by now, as you gradually realize what has to be considered in the training of a dog—more than in the case of other house pets. Well, theory is fine and decidedly important as well. It's even better, however, if theory and practice complement each other. For this reason, I suggest that you start attending a good ○ DOG SCHOOL (page 262) while your pet is still a puppy. To find a suitable one, however, you need to look for certain things. After all, anybody can offer training courses and puppy classes. A colorful obstacle course or a fabulous homepage alone will tell you nothing about the quality of the instruction, however.

Puppy Classes

Let me start by saying that it's better not to attend a puppy class at all than to go to a bad one. Ideally, a puppy class consists of four to six puppies of different breeds, no more than 16 weeks old. Fearful puppies or small breeds may stay in the group until they're older than that, while especially rambunctious or self-confident ones may possibly leave the group sooner. Young dogs, however, do not belong in a puppy class under any circumstances, since they have a different, more boisterous play style. When playing together (with intervention by the trainer, if necessary), puppies practice social behavior with their own species and become familiar with the various outward appearances and behavioral modes of dogs. Playing together, however, occupies only part of the time in the group.

In a puppy class, the little animals systematically learn that their human is very interesting and important even when four-legged playmates are present.

▽

Also important are bonding exercises, such as play involving puppies and their owners, as well as recall exercises. Then the puppy, while still young, learns that her owner plays an important role and is thoroughly interesting even when other dogs are present. That's crucial. Another lesson involves learning about different kinds of unfamiliar situations, such as walking on a strange surface or across little obstacles, and becoming acquainted with unfamiliar noises. It entails no compulsion, no pressure to perform. If it helps, the puppy is motivated with treats or toys, and even the tiniest steps are rewarded. The initial obedience exercises also involve no tugging on the leash or similar measures. All the training is done through positive motivation and in such a way that the little animals don't distract each other.

The trainer also provides an adequate amount of theory, answers questions, and can always explain why something is being done in a certain way. Pay attention to the trainer's tone as well. Sometimes dog owners are treated with relatively little respect, or the puppies' behaviors are too hastily "diagnosed."

Professional Training Courses

The statement about the tone of conversation applies also to ○ TRAINING COURSES (page 276). And the dog is not the only one positively affected by praise! Here too, as with the puppies, there should be no more than four to six teams in a group. That's the only way the trainer can spend enough time with each one. He or she must be able to adapt to each dog (and to its owner too, of course) and must be informed about breed-specific characteristics. In addition, the trainer imparts theory, structures the exercises systematically, and can explain something is being done in a certain way. "That's how it's always done" would be anything but professionally exhaustive. At the start of the training session, the dogs should not be allowed to play; if they play at all, then only during the break or at the end.

○ CHECKLIST

3

Puppy Classes and Training Courses

How can you tell whether a facility is good? Here are the most important criteria:

Puppy Class

- ○ No puppies older than 16 weeks are accepted.
- ○ There are no more than four to six puppies in a group.
- ○ The puppies' playtime is only part of what goes on.
- ○ Bonding exercises between puppy and owner are essential.
- ○ The trainer intervenes if, for example, one of the puppies is being dominated, or if one always dominates the others.
- ○ Positive motivation is the only method used; no overt physical force and little distraction are involved.

Training Courses

- ○ There are no more than four to six dogs in a class.
- ○ At the start of the training session, the puppies are not allowed to play together.
- ○ The exercises are systematically structured; no strong-arm methods are involved.
- ○ Breed-specific characteristics are taken into consideration.
- ○ The trainer must have a feel for the individual human-dog teams.

10 Questions About Basic Training

Our Dino, at the age of ten weeks, is still not house-trained. Should we stick his nose in the mess he's made?

On no account should you do that. It's awful for the dog, and he won't be able to understand it at all. At most, he'll learn that it's very bad when he has to "go," and he'll go off and hide somewhere to do his business. The trust between you and the puppy will be seriously impaired.

Paul does come when we call him, but he always hops around us at arm's length. What can we do?

Do you always reach for him right away or hold out a treat for him? Don't give him the treat until he comes really close. If he still tries to evade you, tie a rope—a good six feet long, but not too heavy—to his collar and let him drag it along behind him. If he won't come close enough, you need not keep clowning around—just put your foot on the "emergency brake" by stepping on the rope without showing any emotion. When he looks at you in bewilderment, call him and praise him.

How long can you leave a dog in her pet crate, if she has gotten used to it?

An hour now and then, perhaps if she needs a timeout because she's really rambunctious, is no problem. When she's tired, she can stay in the crate even longer, overnight if need be. After all, the dog frequently lies in her bed even longer than that to sleep. But "storing" a dog in a crate for hours on a regular basis is inappropriate.

What training method should I look for when choosing a dog school?

The training should be based on recent findings in the field of behavioral research. Military-style drills, impassive running in a circle, and any training involving yanking on the leash, wearing a prong collar, or other such methods of coercion are absolutely out and are not species-appropriate. Otherwise, much depends on your own requirements and on what is suitable for you and your dog. Therefore it's good if the trainer doesn't act like a guru and adhere to one method alone.

Our Ben is a little fussy and doesn't like taking treats as a reward when around any distractions. Can we change that?

Is he really hungry enough? Is his bowl of food possibly available all day? Feed him at fixed times, and train before mealtime. If you're going to the dog school, don't feed him beforehand (even if the interval is a long one). If Ben accepts normal treats at home but not at school, check out the assortment available from your butcher—often, cooked chicken or little pieces of cheese will be big hits. There almost always is some type of treat that a dog can't say no to!

▷

If you ever find yourself with little time to pay attention to the puppy—possibly because you have to make an important phone call—she will be safe and secure in a pet crate.

△
Make yourself as interesting as possible to your dog when you call her. Experiment to see what gets the best reaction from your four-legged companion.

When we would like to go for a walk with our puppy, she doesn't want to get far from the house. Why is this so?
Puppies develop a strong attachment to a place at the beginning—your home is their "den," where they can seek refuge if threatened. For this reason it's best to carry your puppy part or all of the way to the spot where you have your bonding walks and little exploratory outings, or to go there by car.

My husband would like our dog to *heel* at his right, but I prefer my left side. What's the best way to solve this problem?
You can teach your pet to *heel* on both sides. You'll need a separate signal for each side so that the dog can tell the difference between the sides. It would be a good idea to teach her to *heel* on only one side at first. Once she has mastered this, start working on the other side.

Our Ina is six months old, and until now she has stayed nicely in the *down* position at my side. However, recently she started getting up again. What can I do?
She may be testing your consistency at the moment. You can put her back into the *down* with a firm tone of voice. Possibly she will stay there. If not, put her into the *down* while on leash, and then put one foot on the leash. The leash should be only loose enough that

Ina doesn't feel any pressure when lying down, but can sit just halfway. If she gets up, do nothing and keep your foot on the leash. At some point that will be uncomfortable for Ina, and she will lie down again.

3

When we call Nico, he comes, snatches the treat, and is off again. How can we change this?
Owners usually concentrate while the dog is coming to them, but tune out once it is there. Stay focused even after Nico has reached you. Don't let go of the treat; hold it so that he can nibble at it but can't take the whole thing. Meanwhile, pet him while keeping a hand firmly on his collar. Now leash him. You can also tie a 1- to 2-yard-long, thin rope to his collar and pick it up as soon as Nico has come and is nibbling at the snack.

◁
"My home is my castle"—a puppy feels safest at home. That's why many don't want to leave the house at the beginning.

Can you teach puppies and young dogs the basic commands without using a leash?
Yes, provided you train at home and without any kind of distraction. If you're in the yard or out walking, I suggest leaving the dog on leash. Then, if she gets up and runs away, the leash will allow you to get her under control right away, and you can immediately repeat the exercise. This is more effective than calling your youngster back, praising her, and putting her in the starting position.

Training with "Advanced" Dogs

▶ In the past few weeks, you've learned that although training your four-legged friend sometimes takes a lot of work, it's also a lot of fun nonetheless. And besides, you've reinforced the close relationship between you and your pet. The daily routine with your dog, too, is becoming largely stress-free at this point. To build on these good results, here's my advice: Don't rest on your laurels; keep your eye on the ball and keep on training.

4

Important Exercises for Everyday Life

Your efforts have paid off: Your dog's training now has reached a good, serviceable level that enables you to successfully handle a great many situations in everyday life.

THIS LEVEL CAN BE even further increased, however. In the following chapter, I present additional exercises that build on what has already been learned. For one thing, they add variety to the training sessions, and for another, they make daily life with your pet even more comfortable in many situations. This is true for the dog as well, since he or she enjoys more freedom in the end. My tip: To avoid overtaxing your four-legged companion, before starting the following exercises you should make sure that the basics have been thoroughly mastered. This will also contribute to smooth, trouble-free training.

The Dog Comes to You Despite Distraction

This exercise is useful, for example, when your dog has seen children who are playing with a ball, or when fast "objects" like riders on horseback or joggers are approaching.

Prerequisites: Your pet must come to you cheerfully and immediately when not faced with distractions. He has a good bond with you.

This is important: As soon as the dog reaches you, he should always *sit front* (→ page 111) and then come to your side again.

Making It Work in Daily Life

If you're practicing in "real life," make sure always to call the dog in sufficient time. Normally you know exactly how far away the distraction can be without risking loss of your influence over your pet. Don't push that distance! Always recall the dog while he is still at a distance where you have him safely under control—and it's better to call too soon rather than too late.

If you're not certain whether your pet hears you, you have several possibilities:

▷ Don't call the dog right away; instead, without saying a word, go up to him immediately and in a neutral way, and then leash him. This is advisable, for example, if the dog is totally disconnected from reality while busy investigating a mouse hole.

▷ Use an inviting tone of voice or clap your hands to get your pet's attention, but don't use the "Come" or "Here" signal. As soon as he looks briefly at you, run away quickly—go behind the nearest patch of shrubs, for instance. Once he is unmistakably headed in your direction, add the verbal signal or whistle blow as well.

▷ You can also get your canine companion's attention by using an enticing tone of voice to comment with great interest on some place on the ground ("Well, what's this?"). Here

too, use the verbal signal or the dog whistle only when the dog is moving toward you.

The method you select depends on the dog and on the situation. If you have a speedy dog and if the distraction is also moving slowly, then I recommend that you run in the opposite direction—that is, take some action, instead of recalling your pet.

Making It Work with a System

▷ Take a food bowl or several favorite toys along— depending on your pet's preference.

 TIP

Training with Helpers

If you're not sure whether your four-legged friend will veer off course toward the distraction instead of coming to you, you can practice with another person. Your helper should quickly pick up the toy to keep the dog from succeeding. You yourself should run away quickly, to give the dog additional motivation to come to you.

Tell the dog to sit, and set the food bowl, containing a few bites, a little distance behind him. Alternatively, place a toy behind him. The closer the bowl or the toy is to the dog, the more challenging this exercise. Therefore, you need to select a distance that will guarantee success. Then walk several feet away from your dog, wait a bit, and call him in the usual way.

▷ If this works, you can increase the level by placing the bowl or toy closer to the dog.

Variation for Adept Pupils:

Put the dog in the *sit* position and walk a several feet away from him, as usual. Place the

1 *The food bowl is behind the dog, and a toy is lying in the path he must take to reach you. If you call your dog now, you'll be competing against some very attractive distractions.*

2 *Now the food bowl and toy are to the left and right of the dog's route to you. Call him in a really enticing way, so that he comes straight to you.*

toy or the food bowl a little to one side of the "recall route" (the farther to the side, the easier the exercise). At first, the distraction should be closer to you than to your pet. Now call him with the customary audible signal and the necessary action.

▷ If your dog comes cheerfully and without any intermediate stops, gradually reduce the distance between the bowl or toy and the dog.

▷ If that is presenting no problems, you can put toys or food on both sides of the route and call your dog.

Another tip: Instead of using a toy or bowl, you can also place the dog in a field where a mouse hole can serve as a distraction.

If nothing is more interesting to the dog than you, it's all right to feel a little pride at this point!

Variation for Advanced Pupils: As the crowning touch, so to speak, you can try your hand at a very exciting variant—you call your dog after he has seen his toy fly through the air.

▷ You put your pet in the *sit* position and move away as usual. Next, throw his toy behind you and then call the dog. At this easier level, you are still standing between the toy and the dog.

▷ If your pet shows no inclination to run to the toy, but comes to you instead, throw the toy next to you.

▷ If he still comes reliably, throw the toy to one side, but in the dog's direction. The closer the toy lands to the dog, the harder the exercise becomes.

If you still haven't had enough, you can throw two toys, one to each side. Don't forget, special achievements deserve special rewards!

If the Exercise Isn't Working

Quite likely you've increased the distraction level too quickly. Take your time, even if takes several weeks to reach the highest level. Possibly your pet has not yet learned the *come* well enough, and under distraction it is hardly likely to work. Go back a few steps. If playing is a bigger reward for your dog than food, keep a toy with you and play with your pet after calling him to come.

Heeling Off Leash

Even if your four-legged friend will stay near you while off leash, it's a good idea to tell him to *heel* briefly when small children or a leashed dog are approaching.

Prerequisites: When on leash, the dog must *heel* reliably without treats and for an extended period of time.

This is important: Practice without the leash only part of the time, keeping the dog leashed for most of this exercise. If you train too much off leash, your pet may get a bit sloppy about heeling.

At the beginning, go only fairly short distances without the leash, and always end the exercise while the dog is still attentive and in the right position. His head or, at most, his shoulders should be at the height of your knee. Give rewards only occasionally, more frequently at the start.

Making It Work

▷ Choose a setting with few distractions, and at first practice a few exercises, including heeling, with your leashed dog and without treats. This way you'll get your pet in the mood for a training session.

▷ Next, lay the leash over the dog's back and walk away, giving the audible signal "Heel." Move off just as decisively as when your pet is on leash, and then he will come along with you. Walk straight ahead at first, and then include some curves in your path.

▷ If that is working well, you can dispense with the leash altogether. To put a prompt stop to any undesirable attempts on your pet's part to run off, however, you can build in a kind of safeguard: In addition to the normal leash, put a roughly 9-foot-long, thin leash or rope on the dog. To keep him from noticing anything, put both leashes on him before you leave home. If you want to train outdoors, remove the normal leash, and start out as usual with the dog at *heel*. He will drag the other leash or rope behind him, and if he doesn't stay at your side, you can activate the "emergency brake" by stepping on the end if need be.

▷ Once your pet is heeling correctly for some length of time without your intervention, both straight ahead and when there is a change of direction, you can dispense with the second leash or rope.

First, however, train without any major stimuli and possibly with treats for the time being. Gradually you can also train under distraction as well.

Solving Problems

Does the dog really *heel* well enough when he's on leash? Work on improving heeling first. Ask yourself if you're setting out more hesitantly without the leash because you're waiting to see whether the dog is really coming with you. If that's the case your pet will sense it. Was the distance you asked him to *heel* off leash perhaps too long? End the exercise in good time, and practice with the dog on leash more frequently.

◁

If your pet heels reliably even when off leash, you can cope with many kinds of encounters with no stress at all. Here, even a jogger doesn't ruffle the dog's composure. Begin this exercise without any distractions, however, and increase the level of distraction very gradually.

4

Heeling Across Obstacles

When you go up or down a staircase with your leashed dog, he should stay nicely at *heel* instead of tugging you upward or downward, because that could be dangerous. In addition, this exercise will add variety to your training sessions.

Prerequisites: Whether you walk at a normal pace or very slowly or run, the dog must at least stay at *heel* when on leash, though doing so off leash is better.

This is important: Avoid anything that entails a risk of injury for you and your dog.

Here's How

Choose suitable terrain, such as thinly wooded areas with some fallen tree trunks or heaps of brushwood, short, fairly steep slopes, a low railing next to a park path, and similar minor obstructions.

▷ At first, on easy ground, get the dog in the right mood for heeling. Then change to terrain that is more challenging.

▷ First, for example, you can weave in a kind of zigzag course around trees with trunks that are not overly thick, staying close to the trees. In this way, the dog learns to stay right at your side. Keep varying your pace. Match the duration of the exercise to your dog's level of concentration.

▷ Next, look for a fallen tree trunk that is not too large in diameter. Walk over it with your pet at *heel*. Make sure he doesn't jump ahead, but coordinates his movements so as to stay right next to you. If necessary, use treats at first. Then it will be easier to keep the dog in the desired position.

▷ Practice at a normal pace first, and then slow down. Go across piles of brushwood, for example, with the dog, or go up and down a slope. Especially when going down again, make sure the dog keeps up with your pace and leaves the leash loose.

▷ If everything is working well thus far, do some practice on stairs that will help in your daily routine: short flights of steps at first, then longer ones. As your dog's skills increase, you can practice on longer staircases and on different kinds of steps as well.

▷ If the dog is right at your side and the leash stays loose, start practicing without the leash.

If you've been using treats for the exercise as long as necessary, gradually start omitting them from your sessions.

If It's Not Going Well

Has your pet thoroughly mastered normal walking at *heel*? Work on improving that first. Perhaps your dog just has surplus energy and is a little boisterous for that reason? With the necessary calm and quiet, he can concentrate better. Or have you picked an overly demanding obstacle? Try choosing an easier one.

▷

Walking at heel across obstacles is fun for a dog and helpful in everyday situations. Make sure your pet stays right at your side, on a loose leash, and doesn't try to pull ahead or even clear the obstacle before you do.

The *Down* with You Out of Sight

Let's suppose you're in an outdoor café with your dog and want to order some cake at the counter, or you want to run into the corner store for the paper. At such times it's helpful if you can put your pet in the *down* position at a certain place and be sure that he will reliably stay there, even though he can't see you at the moment.

Prerequisites: Your dog must have no problem staying in a *down* or *sit* position while you're in view, even if you go some distance away for an extended time.

This is important: If you want the dog to wait for some time without seeing you, I suggest that you *down* him. For one thing, that position is more comfortable for the dog, and for another, he can stand up from the *sit* faster than from the *down*. If he should have to wait for a longer time, he must be able to lie on his side as well and even take a little nap. However, he must not leave the place where you downed him, for his own safety as well. For this reason, it's important never to call him out of the *down/stay*. The dog needs to completely internalize the fact that he must stay in the *down*, no matter what he hears or what is going on nearby, and that you will always come back for him.

With this exercise, increase your demands very slowly. At first, train with no distractions, and then gradually increase the distraction level. Over time, practice in different places too, so that the dog will reliably stay in the *down* later on in any environment.

Both with this exercise and in daily life, you should never leave the dog in the *down* position for any length of time in the blazing sun or on a damp, cold surface.

How It Works

For this exercise, choose terrain with a single bush or something similar behind which you can hide.

▷ Put your pet into the *down* position a few yards in front of the bush—the more advanced the dog is, the farther from the bush he can be. If your dog has an easier time with the "*down* while out of sight" exercise when a personal object of yours is lying nearby, then you can put your sweater, for example, next to him. Then walk calmly back and forth in front of it.

▷ Now walk in a circle around the dog, moving between him and the bush. Next, expand the circle to include the bush, so that you

▶ TIP

Out of Sight, Silence Is Preferable

Don't go out of sight unless the dog can do the *stay* while in sight without getting tense. Don't repeat a command when you're out of sight, because hearing your voice could easily cause the dog, at least at the outset, to come to you.

briefly vanish behind the bush, and thus, from the dog's field of vision.

▷ If this is successful, go on to the next step. When you make the circle, stop behind the bush so that you can still see your pet, but he can see you only with difficulty or not at all. Next, count silently to ten and then come back out. If your dog becomes restless, come out of your hiding place sooner, before the dog stands up, if at all possible. Extend the duration and the distance from the dog only very gradually.

4

1	**2**	**3**
Put the dog in the down position near a bush. Walk around your pet in a circle, so that he still can see you. Then expand the circle to include the bush. Then you will briefly disappear from the dog's view.	*Next, circle around your pet once more, but stand behind the bush, first only briefly, then gradually for a longer time. For a few moments, the dog will lose sight of you completely. Don't talk to your pet during the exercise; he might leave his position.*	*Now go back to the dog as usual. he seems a little impatient, say "Down" while walking toward him, and give the appropriate visual signal. Praise him quietly while he is lying beside you.*

Incorporating Little Distractions

Once the *down* without distractions is working well, you can practice at a short distance from a path with some foot traffic, or at home when other family members are present. First, decrease the duration of the *down*, and then lengthen it again, depending on your dog's progress in training.

If that too is going well, your four-legged friend is ready for everyday situations. Next time you're invited to the home of friends, try the *down* while out of sight there, in a different room.

If the Exercise Is Problematic

Is the dog not yet able to lie or sit long enough or calmly enough while you're in sight? If that's the case, practice this drill again. Extend the duration of the *down* and the distance to the dog. Were you possibly out of sight for too long? No misplaced ambition, please. At the start, a few short moments are sufficient under some circumstances. Suit the "dosage" to your particular dog. Are you using hesitant body language as you walk away from your dog, because you're really not confident that he can do the exercise yet? Then your dog will become uncertain as well, and he may follow you. Have you gone too far away to perform your vanishing act? Put the dog in the *down* closer to your hiding place, and don't increase the distance until he can retain the position for some time. Is there too much distraction nearby? Make sure there's nothing distracting in the vicinity, and then increase the distraction level in tiny steps. Adapt the exercise to your dog's temperament.

"Sit" While Far Away from You

This exercise is very useful in daily life, since there are always situations in which it's better to stop and sit the dog immediately than to call him to come. If, for example, he were to cross the path of a bike rider or jogger while coming to you, that could be dangerous. The same would hold true if he were to chase a cat and in the process perhaps run into the street. In such high-stimulus situations, it's sometimes easier to bring the dog to a halt than to recall him.

Prerequisites: Since stopping at a distance is quite an advanced exercise, your four-legged friend must have a very good level of basic obedience, also in the face of distractions. In particular, he must immediately obey the audible and visual signals (→ page 102) directing him to *sit*.

This is important: Here, it's best to use a dog whistle. Your voice usually doesn't make enough of an impact, especially at a greater distance and when distractions are present. I recommend using a long whistle blow as your signal. When the dog stops, he should sit immediately, always turn to face you, and give you his attention. This also interrupts his eye contact with the potential "prey." To accomplish that, promptly sitting and turning around must always be worthwhile for your pet: You should immediately praise him, using your voice and treats. If your dog prefers a toy to a treat, you also can opt for that type of reward. As soon as he has held the *sit* for a few moments, toss him the reward and simultaneously give the finish signal. It would be best for your pet to bring the toy, because that will establish a connection with you, and furthermore he won't run off with the toy.

If your pet likes toys and treats equally well, I recommend using the treats at first. The advantage here is that the dog will already be sitting in the desired position and will receive the reward while maintaining it.

How the Dog Learns *Sit*

▷ First your dog must learn that a long blow of the whistle also means "Sit." You can practice this from the heeling position, for example. As soon as you stop, give a clear hand signal (raised hand or arm), followed by the long whistle blow. If your pet has learned to *sit* in front of his filled food bowl until he gets permission to eat, practice the *sit* in response to a long whistle blow in this situation too. Leave your arm in the air until you give the finish signal (→ page 85).

▷ Once the dog has understood that, you can proceed to the next step. You're out with the dog, and there are no distractions in sight. The unleashed dog, calm and relaxed, is running two or three yards ahead. Now get his attention by clicking your tongue or the like—only long enough for him to pause and look at you. Now the whistle blow follows, along with the clear visual signal. If you have the impression that the dog wants to move in your direction, take a definite step toward him in addition. By now you know that this body language will "put the brakes on" your pet (→ page 51).

▷ At the moment the dog sits, say some words of praise, go quickly to him, and give him a few treats. Depending on the situation, let him go again or put on his leash.

▷ Once this has been working well for some time, use the whistle to tell the dog to sit, without getting his attention beforehand. Now you should still be training without any distractions, with a short distance, and with a dog that moves along in a relaxed way. Gradually, increase the distance, and then incorporate distractions slowly. Under distraction, I

4

1 *Use an enticing tone of voice to get the dog's attention, but only enough for him to make eye contact, without starting to come to you.*

2 *Next, with one hand raised and a long whistle blow, take a clear step toward the dog. If necessary, also say "Sit."*

3 *To make the* sit *and the eye contact worthwhile for your four-legged friend, go up to him quickly, give him a treat, and praise him.*

suggest that you reduce the distance again at first. Then you can reliably control the dog and reward him again without delay.

Reward the dog for greater distances too. As soon as he sits, say a few kind words, followed up as soon as possible with one or more snacks, depending on its performance.

Stopping at a full run: This is the highest level of skill for real experts. You can tackle it once your pet can be reliably stopped, even in the face of distractions—for example, when it's heading toward another member of its species. At first, stop it while it's still closer to you than to its intended objective. If it obeys, a reward is due.

Once your four-legged friend is performing the exercise routinely, there's no need to bring or toss it a reward every time. Verbal praise is sufficient. Then you also don't need to come to it to release it from the *sit* every time. Instead, call or blow the whistle after a few moments or when the particular situation that required the *stop* is over.

If There Are Problems

If your four-legged friend runs to you in spite of your body language's message that it's time to stop, you can involve a helper and resort to using a leash several yards in length. Practice so that the dog is between you and your assistant, with the latter holding the leash in one hand. If the dog fails to stop in response to your signal, the helper can bring him to a halt with the long leash. In conclusion, reward the dog. If he ignores the whistle blow and keeps on going, you yourself can use the long leash as a brake. However, you should check to see whether the dog has understood the point of the exercise, and whether his level of basic obedience is adequate at this point. If not, work on that for the time being.

Paying Attention Despite Serious Distractions

4

The dog must learn to give you eye contact even in the face of serious distractions. Then you can have him execute drills even if there's a lot of activity nearby. In daily life, this frequently is the case and often it's especially important at such times for your four-legged friend to obey adequately. If the dog knows that concentrating on you pays off, you can use this drill to distract him from a strong stimulus such as a deer or a bike rider.

Prerequisites: Without distractions, the dog can maintain eye contact with you for a considerable time in response to your signal.

This is important: With this exercise, you can prevent your dog from chasing bike riders and the like, because he will connect "Something's moving over there!" with "I have to go to my owner, because there'll be a reward," and not with "I've got to chase that!" The prerequisite for making this connection is consistent training from the very outset. The dog also must be denied any experiences of success, to keep him from ever getting a taste for "pursuit" in the first place. In everyday situations, therefore, always call the dog in good time, that is, when the object is still far enough away for him to be recalled with no problems. If a jogger or the like approaches, divert your dog's attention to yourself until the jogger is well past you. Reward your pet with a toy thrown into the air in the opposite direction—but not until the jogger is far enough away.

Remember to reward your four-legged companion appropriately for an especially good performance, when he pays attention to you even in difficult circumstances. The payoff can be something edible or a chance to play with you.

Here's How

Whenever you practice around distractions, reduce the duration of the eye contact with you at first, and make sure that the distraction is not excessive or too near the dog. Make yourself as interesting as possible, and practice when your pet is hungry—you have to be much more interesting than the other stimuli. Train with your dog on leash.

▷ Choose a path where several people are walking. Stop next to the path and get your dog's attention. Have the treat ready in your hand at first; later, you can wait a while before getting it out of your pocket. Reward the dog once he has maintained eye contact with you for a few moments.

▷ If that's working, step onto the path when several people are nearby, and practice maintaining eye contact with your dog again. The duration of the eye contact around distractions should be suitable for the dog's level of training. At first, maintain eye contact only briefly, and then go back to your dog and reward him. Gradually extend the length of time.

▷ If that's successful as well, raise the level of distraction, for example, with faster-moving stimuli such as joggers or cyclists. However, just to be on the safe side, the distracting object must not speed past you too quickly.

Please note: Paying attention to you must be advantageous for the dog, so always give him a reward!

Is the Drill Not Working?

Maybe the dog isn't hungry enough. Or your voice may not sound appealing and interesting enough. Possibly the distractions are too close. Did you really insist on the eye contact? It doesn't help if the dog is near you but strains at the leash and remains fixed on the jogger, watching until he or she is out of sight.

Research & Practice

Targeted Training and Tests

4

If you've trained your dog to this point, you may have acquired a taste for the exercises and developed an interest in participating in one or more tests or trials, or in continuing to train your four-legged friend in a way appropriate for his breed. Here you can find information about doing just that.

If you have a purebred dog from one of the AKC recognized breeds, you can contact a specific breed organization. You can obtain addresses from your breeder or the AKC (→ Useful Addresses, page 284). There you'll learn what opportunities exist for training and what tests and trials are offered for your dog's specific breed. After all, not everything is suitable for every dog:

▷ The Canine Good Citizen Certificate is a good goal for any dog and dog owner. It can be taken by any dog, whether a purebred or not. An official test of this kind can be administered by an AKC organization; it is available through dog sports associations associated with the AKC to all dogs, regardless of breed and origin. Make certain that the specific training method is appropriate for your pet.

▷ Even for gun dog breeds, training as a hunting dog makes sense only if the dog subsequently will be used to assist a hunter. This usually is possible only if the owner has a hunting license.

▷ Training as a *Schutzhund*, or protection dog, requires special awareness of the responsibility involved. In general, the training includes subordination, protection work, and tracking. Obedience is absolutely essential here, of course, but the prey drive in particular is very strongly fostered. This type of training is unsuitable for dog breeds that were not bred for this purpose.

▷ For herding breeds, such as Border Collies, there are special herding dog-training courses and competitive events.

▷ *Most dogs want to stay busy. That means that they need not only adequate physical activity, but also mental activities. With special kinds of training programs, you can also ensure that your pet obeys you well.*

▷ For the various retriever breeds, hunting-related types of training with dummies instead of wild game are increasingly popular. Examples are dummy tests and working tests.

▷ For sled dog breeds—depending on the distance demanded, the breed, and the number of dogs hitched in a team—there are various classes of sled dog races.

▷ All dogs, whoever their breeder and whatever their ancestry, can participate in sports such as dog agility, obedience trials (→ page 202), and flyball (→ page 264). They are offered primarily by dog sports associations.

On the Move: Outdoors and in Town

An "advanced" dog behaves in many situations in a problem-free way and can be easily controlled. Such an animal contributes substantially to improvement of the sometimes justifiably tarnished image of dogs and their owners in public. A certain residual risk of disobedience or unpredictable behavior always remains, however, because a dog—despite the most conscientious socialization and training—is still an animal, not a computer.

In the material below, I present two examples of a possible outing in the country and a trip to town with an advanced dog.

▶ NATURE WALK

You leash your dog and, with him at *heel*, head for the woods and fields. On the way, you first walk along a street with traffic. Although your pet will *heel* even when off leash, you put the leash on now just to play it safe.

Now you've reached the free-run area and put the dog in the *sit* position to unleash him. Just as you're about to give him the audible signal "Go on," you see another dog owner approaching with a leashed pet, so you keep your unleashed dog at *heel*. Once you've passed the other animal, you let your four-legged companion run free, after first sitting. He sniffs and runs around in the field and is heading back to you. Here comes someone on a bike. To prevent a collision, you blow the whistle to put your dog in the *sit* position as a precaution. You stand and wait until the cyclist has passed. Now you go to your pet, praise him, and let him run again.

Then you see a couple of fairly slender tree trunks on the ground, and right away you decide to use them for an exercise. You call the dog and then ask him to *heel*. At first you walk several feet on flat ground, and next you tackle the tree trunks. First you walk at a normal pace, and then slowly cross over the trunks. Try to pause on the trunk for a few moments while the dog has his front paws on top and stays at your side. Alternatively, you stop just after clearing the trunk, with the dog having only his rear paws on it. From this position, you back up across the trunk, with the dog staying beside you. That was really well done! You praise your pet and let him run again.

Along the way he plays briefly with another member of his species. You keep walking, and your pet follows you voluntarily. Now a jogger is coming close. From experience, you know that your four-legged friend has a certain passion for chasing, so you blow the whistle to get him to *come*. The dog has seen the jogger, but comes to you nonetheless. He sits next to you, and you get his attention by using an enticing tone of voice and digging in your

Here, an advanced human-dog team is applying its knowledge in an everyday situation. The dog stops when he hears the sound of the whistle, and the cyclist can ride past safely.

▽

4

△

If your dog will stay in the down *position while you're out of sight, then he also will wait faithfully in a store when he can't see you.*

jacket pocket for his favorite toy. As soon as the jogger is far enough away, throw the toy in the opposite direction and give the dog the finish signal, "Go on" (→ page 85).

On the way home, you walk past a playground where children are playing badminton and soccer, and your pet has already pricked his ears. You recall him, praise him generously for coming, and walk past with the unleashed dog at *heel*. Now, you come back to the busy street and leash your pet for the last stretch before home.

◉ WALK IN TOWN

You've made a date with a friend for a stroll through town, and you take your dog along. You're still a little early, so you buy some ice cream and sit down on a bench in the city park to enjoy the sun. You *down* your leashed dog at your side. On the grass nearby, two other dogs are romping in spite of the leash requirement. Your pet stays obediently in the *down* position, and you enjoy the sun and the ice cream without feeling any stress.

Finally, you meet your friend and do some window-shopping. You and your friend sit at a table in a sidewalk cafe. Your dog remains in a *down* position while you drink coffee and talk. The waitress tells you that you have to pick out your cake at the counter. There's no problem, since your dog will stay in the *down*, and you can look in peace for something delicious.

After leaving the café, you and your pet continue your walk in a civilized fashion. On the way home, you pass a group of musicians in the pedestrian zone. A lot of people are standing around, with other dogs as well. You take advantage of this situation for an extra little exercise. You put your pet in the *sit* next to you and get his attention. He concentrates on you without feeling stressed, gives you plenty of eye contact, and in returns gets a special reward.

That's enough of a stroll, and now it's time to head home.

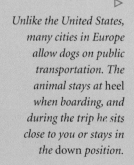

▷

Unlike the United States, many cities in Europe allow dogs on public transportation. The animal stays at heel when boarding, and during the trip he sits close to you or stays in the down position.

Exercises for Several Human and Dog Teams

Your dog needs to obey not only when he or she is alone when you, but also when other members of his or her species are present. Practicing in a group is fun!

TO REACH THIS GOAL, it's not enough to attend a group course at a dog school with your four-legged friend. Like all other exercises, obedience in the face of canine distractions has to be practiced constantly in everyday situations. If you've done that thus far with the basic commands, and if your pet has mastered the exercises for advanced dogs, you now can drill with other dog owners whose pets are at about the same level as yours. Seek out other dog owners in your neighborhood who have similar goals, get them organized, and start training together.

Heeling Independently Off Leash

4

The goal here is to keep your dog reliably at *heel* even when off leash. Then there's no need to leash him when you encounter other members of his species, should you want to prevent contact with other dogs.

Prerequisites: The unleashed dog stays perfectly at *heel* without other dogs as a distraction. When together with other dogs, he must stay equally reliably at your side while wearing his leash.

Making It Work

▷ In the beginning, each owner leashes his or her dog and puts him in the right mood for heeling jointly. If that is successful, put the dogs in the *sit* position and unleash them. Don't place them too close together. Next, get the attention of the sitting animals.

▷ Once every dog is paying close attention to his owner, each human-and-dog team starts out on its own. Start off just as decisively as usual—that is, without pausing to see whether the dog is really following. You already know that your pet has registered your intention and is behaving appropriately. Vary your distances from each other, but maintain fairly large spaces at first. Correct your dog if he even starts to look in the direction of the others—either by distracting or reprimanding him.

▷ Over time, you can also incorporate direct encounters with the other teams. The dogs walk on the outside at first. Once that is successful, they can pass each other directly. Here too, keep a greater distance between the teams at first, and reduce it gradually.

Incorporating variations: I recommend interchanging the following variations at first, so that each team takes turns standing still and moving.

▷ **Variation 1:** One dog owner stands still and puts his or her pet in the *sit* or *down* position, while the other teams practice heeling, alternating between a normal pace and a slow pace, or even jogging slightly. When you slow down, give the audible signal "Heel" in a muted drawl; when you speed up, make your voice encouraging and brisk.

▷ **Variation 2:** Two teams approach one another. Stop about 6 feet apart and chat a little. The dogs should stay either in the *sit* position or in the *down*, close at *heel*. Then the owners and their pets walk on again.

If Problems Arise

If all the teams are having problems, then it's still too soon for unleashed heeling. Practice a while longer with the dogs on leash. Alternatively, in your group, take turns walking with the dogs unleashed and go only short distances. If one dog or another is still having difficulties, their owners should keep them on leash for the time being. If one dog can keep running over to the others, they will be less obedient and have more trouble concentrating.

◁

When several dog owners are practicing heeling with their pets off leash, they should stay far apart at first, so that no dog is tempted to run over to another. Take firm, decisive steps to have a rousing, encouraging effect on your four-legged friend.

One Dog Is *Down* While the Others Train

Whether the dog can see you or not, he should stay in his place whenever other members of his species are nearby and in motion. This is useful, for example, when you *down* your pet briefly in front of a store and someone with a dog happens to pass by.

Prerequisites: *Stay* exercises in and out of sight, even with distractions, should pose no problem for the dogs.

This is important: Develop the exercise systematically. Only in this way can you gradually guide your dog toward the goal of the exercise: to truly stay reliably in the *down* position, for his own safety as well.

Making It Work

This drill is also suitable for two teams, but it is even more appealing with at least three human-and-dog teams. Even with three and more teams, only one dog is *down*, while all the others are in motion. Then the level of distraction for the dog in the *down* position is greater. At first, however, don't move too

△
Despite the distracting presence of other members of its species nearby, this dog stays in the down *position. At first, maintain greater distances when you practice this drill.*

energetically; stay as calm as possible. By degrees there is increasingly more movement near the dog in the down. At first the teams stay at a greater distance from the dog, but over time they pass closer and closer to him.

▷ One of the dogs is downed. Its owner doesn't stand in front of him, as described on page 117, but walks back and forth at a distance of several yards. The other teams practice heeling at least 6 feet away and then slightly closer to the dog in the *down*, walking around him and also between the dog and his owner. While you are still in sight, practice this drill in both the *sit* and the *down*. To provide additional distraction, two other dog handlers can also talk together in the vicinity of the dog in the *down* position.

▷ Now comes the more difficult variation: You *down* your pet and then walk around him, while the other human-and-dog teams also walk past your dog at a distance of about 3 feet. Your circles become larger. If the dog stays calm and relaxed in the *down* even then, go out of sight, only briefly at first, then for a longer time. The "distraction teams" should walk past the dog in the *down* at a greater distance at first. Keep in mind that when you're out of sight, your dog is always in the *down* position.

In this exercise, all the owners should alternate downing their pets. Practice the *stay* while out of sight only if the dog really stays calmly in position.

If It's Not Working

You may have increased the level of difficulty too quickly. It's best to develop the exercise again from the start. The distraction teams should stay at a greater distance from the dog in the *down*, while his owner maintains less distance.

Going Past Other Dogs

This exercise is helpful, for example, when your dog is running out ahead and a jogger with a dog at *heel* overtakes you. In such a situation, your pet should come when called.

Prerequisites: Your dog obeys the *come* signal when not being distracted by other dogs, even when you are some distance away. In addition, he has good basic obedience skills.

This is important: Make yourself interesting enough for the dog. Your four-legged friend must have the feeling that it's much better to come to you than to go to another dog. If necessary, use special treats to help you.

Making It Work

▷ Start with the lowest level of distraction. Put two teams in position some distance apart, with the dogs in the *down* or *sit* position. *Down* your pet crosswise to the other teams. Now walk several feet away, wait a bit, and call your dog. He runs past the two teams to reach you.

▷ It gets more difficult when everyone is in motion. Now you all weave past each other, not too far apart, with the dogs heeling. Next, in turn, each owner has his or her pet *sit*, walks several feet away, and calls the dog.

▷ Now all the dogs are called at the same time. Put all the dogs in the *sit* position about 6 feet apart, in a row. All the owners walk several feet away from the dogs, with those on the outside moving in a V and the owner in the middle moving straight ahead. Wait a little, and then call all the dogs at the same time. In this drill, the dogs may make detours toward each other, so don't try this variation prematurely.

▷ Now, try it with two-way traffic. Two teams stand side by side, while a third team positions itself several feet away, "between" the

△

Not an easy exercise. These dogs are sitting relatively close together. Next all three will be called simultaneously, and they should come to their owners happily and without making any detours. Use larger distances at first.

other two. The dogs stay in the *sit* position. Next, each owner stands opposite his or her dog. Owners 1 and 2 are on the right and left of Dog 3, and Owner 3 is between Dogs 1 and 2. Then all the dogs are called at once.

If It's Not Working

Has your pet learned to come to you reliably? Were the dogs too close together? Or did you increase the level of difficulty too quickly? If so, go back one or more steps. Don't let the dogs play together beforehand; that makes it harder for them to concentrate on you.

One dog owner is playing with his pet while two other teams practice heeling. The dogs should concentrate on their owners, not on the playing animal.

Two teams play while a dog is called to come to his owner, passing between the other teams to reach her. Use a friendly, encouraging voice to call your pet, so that he obeys cheerfully.

Training Near Playing Teams

Your pet must obey even when he has sighted some dogs at play. This can be useful, for example, if you're out walking with your dog but are in a hurry, so you can't let him play with the others.

Prerequisites: Basic obedience skills are reliably mastered, even in the face of serious distractions. The dogs must enjoy playing with a toy with their owners.

Making It Work

While one human-and-dog team plays together, the other two practice—and vice versa. Whether the dogs are on or off leash is something each owner must decide, depending on the level of the animal's training. Always stay far enough away from the other teams that neither the playing dog nor the practicing dogs are subjected to temptation and run toward the others.

▷ It's best to start with heeling. The practicing dogs should concentrate fully on their owners, who walk in the vicinity of the playing team.

▷ If that is successful, add on some *stay* exercises. Two teams do *stay* drills while the third plays again. The practicing dog owners walk back and forth in front of their pets and around them.

▷ Next, go out of sight. Two teams play (with the dogs on leash) while your pet is in the *down*. At first, don't go too far away when you're out of sight. The playing teams should not get too close to the dog in the *down* position. Come back for your dog in good time.

▷ Again, two teams are playing. One dog owner sits his or her pet, walks a few yards away, and waits a bit. Then he or she calls the dog, so that he has to pass by the playing teams when he comes.

If It's Not Working

Are the teams too close together? Or is your dog not interested enough in his toy? Have you started training off leash too soon? Does your pet have sufficient mastery of the exercises when not distracted by other dogs?

Calling the Dog Away from the Game

Even when playing with other members of his species, your dog should obey your recall command. This is quite practical when you're out for a walk and often necessary as well, when you don't want to wait around "helplessly" until your four-legged friend has played to his heart's content.

Prerequisites: He has good basic obedience skills. Under "normal" distraction, he obeys the *come* signal perfectly.

This is important: A dog whistle is especially effective here. It can be heard more clearly than your voice. The group must not be too large—two to four dogs are enough. The more there are, the more difficult the exercise will be. The canines must get along together and must not defend their toys or treats. If the exercise is working well, reward the dogs for their performance with a handful of treats.

Making It Work

▷ Put the dogs in the *sit* and unleash them. Once each dog has maintained eye contact with his owner for several seconds, release him with the customary finish signal: "Go on," for example. Then let them romp with each other for a few minutes.

▷ If you want to call the dogs now, you should all run in different directions. Blow the whistle and call your four-legged friend at the same time. Depending on his level of training, get his attention by clapping your hands before the authoritative audible signal or whistle blow. The owners need to seem as "irresistible" as possible. Don't give the special *come* signal, however, until you're certain that the dogs really will come directly to you.

▷ Now "step on the gas" and run away from the dogs until they're unmistakably heading

for their owners. As soon as they are so far apart that they aren't focusing on each other anymore, you should stop. Have the dogs *sit front* correctly; then no dog will have eye contact with any of his or her four-legged friends and he or she won't be so inclined to go off again. Now lavish the dogs with praise and give them generous rewards for their excellent performance.

▷ In conclusion, have the dogs *heel* correctly again. Always remember that the "Here" comes to an end only at this point. Depending on the situation, leash the dogs and practice something, play with them, or let them play with their canine friends again.

If It's Not Working

Ask yourself whether the group may be too large. Practice with only two dogs. Has your pet not mastered the *come* signal yet? Did you make the signal exciting and clear enough? Is your dog hungry? Plan the next session for a time when your pet is really hungry. If necessary, use special treats that he doesn't get for any other exercise.

4

◁

To call your dog away from a game with its canine friends, you need to take some real action. Get your pet's attention by using an exciting tone of voice. As soon as he looks up, run away from him. If he runs after you, he has earned a delicious reward.

10 Questions About Advanced Training

When I tell my Arco to *sit* in the *heel* position, he always sits at a slant and almost in front of me. Should I change this?

Yes, because if you're waiting at the curb, for instance, the dog will be sitting in the lane of traffic. Try practicing with a passive influence: walk along a boundary of some kind (fence, wall) with Arco, keeping him between the wall and you. Now, when you stop and tell him to sit, he can't scoot his hindquarters sideways. Which pocket do you carry your treats in? Always carry them on the side you've chosen for heeling your pet.

To ensure safety, I want to teach our four-legged friend to sit automatically at every curbside, if at all possible. Will that work?

In principle this is very useful, but it requires judicious, levelheaded training by the dog's owner. If you want your dog to master this truly reliably, then you really have to *sit* your pet at every curb and every roadside—even if it's only a narrow dirt road, or if there's no car anywhere in sight.

When I practice "Heel" across an obstacle, our Dino always jumps across before me, instead of staying at my side. How can I break him of the habit?

At first, take a treat in your hand and walk fairly slowly toward the obstacle. Before the dog puts his front paws on the fallen tree trunk, hold the treat a little higher. As you clear it on the other side, bring the hand holding the treat downward, right in front of the dog, so that Dino has to look down. Then the drill is sure to work.

Can I get my dog used to staying in the *down* while I'm out of sight, even when he can hear my voice?

Yes, but he absolutely must become used to having you come back to release him from the *down*, rather than being recalled. Plan the drill so that you first have a conversation with someone while your pet is in the *down* position within sight. At first, talk in a relatively "bored" tone of voice, and then more animatedly. If this works, try it when you're out of sight.

When we meet to practice with three teams, should we let the dogs play beforehand to burn surplus energy?

If you let the dogs play before the training session, you can forget about whatever goal you're trying to achieve through group training. The dogs must learn to concentrate on their owner when other dogs are present, even if they're not allowed to become acquainted or greet them. The owners should let them work off some energy in advance, without the others present.

▷

If your pet tends to walk too far from your side or to sit at an angle when you stop, then you can practice these drills while walking close to a wall or a fence.

Make sure your dog is leashed, and don't let him get away with tugging or pulling, especially when heeling.

Our Timmy heels just fine, but he quite often sniffs at the ground or pulls when he sees something really enticing. What can I do?

Use your voice to get his attention again right away, change direction, and praise him if he concentrates on you again. If that's not enough, then you need to "disrupt" Timmy by walking in a tight curve or several small circles on the side he heels on. That way you'll force him away and disrupt his sniffing. At some point he'll look at you in bewilderment, and then you should praise him and stop your "disruptive action." You can also combat inattentiveness by systematically changing directions with the leash (→ page 93)

How can I manage to keep Asta heeling close beside me even in the "curves," when she's running along on the outside?

The best thing is to deliberately get her attention with an encouraging tone of voice just before the turn. To do so, slap your thighs with your hand. Sometimes that is sufficient. It will be even clearer if you also turn your body in the direction you want to take. If you're working with treats, it should no longer be necessary to have them in your hand. Stick your hand "temptingly" in your pocket—if Asta focuses and stays right with you, she should get a reward when you finish the turn.

When Nicky is in the *down*, she usually looks "sloppy," lying there with both hind legs on one side or directly on her side. Is that okay?

In the *down* with and without "Stay," it's important for the dog to relax and not be always poised to rise. So it's fine for Nicky to make herself comfortable. That also indicates that she doesn't feel at all insecure when you go away, and knows that you'll come back.

When heeling off leash, my dog always stays a little too far from me. Can I also use the collar to correct him?

That's something you should do only in exceptional cases. If you reach for the collar to correct your dog frequently, you may well find that over time your pet tries to dodge your hand. It's better to resume training predominantly with your pet on leash, or at least more often on leash than off.

◁

If you want your dog to stay in one place for an extended time, it's all right for him to lie down in a comfortable position, or even to lie on one side.

If I *down* Xanthos for any length of time or go out of sight for a few minutes, he wiggles a little in my direction. Is this something that can be tolerated?

If Xanthos wiggles a little way now, there's always the possibility that he'll extend the distance and keep wiggling closer to you. That can have disadvantages in everyday situations, however. Correct him, and take one or two steps away again. He should stay exactly in the spot where you put him in the *down* or, depending on the drill, in the *sit*.

Out in Public with Your Dog

We dog owners have a tarnished image, often undeservedly. But sometimes, unfortunately, it's justifiably so. And all the rest of us get lumped together with the "bad" dog owners. As the saying goes, "Fly with the crows, get shot with the crows." With a little consideration and tolerance, and a well-trained dog, many disagreeable situations and conflicts in daily life can easily be avoided. Are you willing to do your part?

5

Two- and Four-Legged Animals—No Problem

Dogs are present almost everywhere—whether in natural surroundings or in an urban setting. But not everybody is a dog lover; many people are even afraid of dogs.

THAT'S SOMETHING YOU need to be aware of. A few years ago, some dog owners got together to plan a demonstration against an impending compulsory leash law. They chose to meet at a popular sidewalk cafe. Three dogs were running around off leash, and one of them was barking every time a new customer came in. One dog owner told us that her dog chased joggers but didn't do anything to them. The jogger only needed to stop and say a few friendly words to the dog. Someone else said that her two large dogs always ran free, whether in town or in the countryside. Is there any reason we should be surprised that compulsory leash laws are being contemplated?

A Few Words in Advance

5

In the ever-present debates, unfortunately, there's a tendency to polarize—dog owners against joggers, against hunters, against farmers, against mothers with small children, and so forth. It sounds as if "dog owners" were a separate species, and in fact we often feel excluded or sidelined when we're out in public with our pets. But some joggers, hunters, farmers, and mothers of small children are also dog owners. All the same—in our own interest, we must ensure that our four-legged companions don't bother or even endanger anyone.

"But he only wants to play!"

To put someone in danger, you don't need a "dangerous" dog. Even a dog that is dancing with delight can present a threat if she jumps up on or races around someone. Then it's no use to quickly call "He just wants to play" after your pet, which frequently happens when it's already too late for people to recall their dog. And what do you think happens when the "target object" notices that the dog owner doesn't have his or her pet under control at all? And on top of that, when the person in question has no experience with dogs or is afraid of dogs? Such a person will be negatively affected by this experience and in the future will have nothing positive to say about "these dog owners."

My plea is this: Take your four-legged friend out in public only if she can confidently deal with her surroundings and with strangers and displays a certain degree of poise. She should exhibit no uncertainty or fear where humans are concerned. After all, it's always possible that the dog will be accidentally jostled or petted without prior warning. Not everybody knows how to approach dogs properly. The dog, too, should not fall on everyone's neck out of sheer joy, but she also should not feel slightly threatened or cornered. If your pet's body language indicates that ordinary things like traffic noise or crowds of people cause her stress, then it's better to leave her at home. Try to get her used to the stressful situations bit by bit, by taking her into town at a quieter time of day and only for training for the time being.

Conversely, the dog must not constantly seek to protect her owner. This can be problematic, for example, if your pet is in the park or on a crowded street and wants to defend the surrounding area as her territory. If your dog exhibits such traits, you have to use due caution, keep an eye on her, and make sure that nobody gets too close to her. In addition, a reliable level of obedience is mandatory. A muzzle may make good sense as well. In some countries, dogs are required to wear a muzzle when using public transportation. If you're unsure whether you can control your pet in such circumstances, it's preferable to avoid these situations.

◁

Many dogs jump up on people, but are trying to be friendly or want to play. Jumping up, however, is quite understandably unlikely to go down very well, especially with strangers, and particularly if your pet belongs to a large or heavy breed.

Handbook of Etiquette for Dog Owners

Dealing with Dog Droppings

Dog droppings are a very common cause of annoyance and tempers that boil over. This topic appears with great regularity in the press in both summer and winter. In some cases it is presented in a slightly exaggerated way—after all, there are far more harmful things and worse types of waste in our environment. On the other hand, who likes to step in dog poop? Dog owners don't, and non-dog owners like it even less. Thus, it should be a matter of course to remove droppings in awkward places, such as on paths or in front yards. In fact, it's better to keep your pet out of front yards in the first place.

Every time I walk my dog, I have a few plastic bags in my pocket. Unfortunately, the dog license fee is not used for putting up bag dispensers all over the place. In some cases, however, you can get bags directly from the local authorities.

Taking Precautions

▷ **Trips to town** and the like are easy to plan for. Before setting out, walk your dog and give her a chance to relieve herself. Then you can prevent disagreeable incidents in the pedestrian zone. If your pet does happen to make a mess on the sidewalk, you should remove it. If you realize that she has to "go," quickly pull her to one side, if possible. From my kitchen window I once saw a dog owner whose leashed pet was defecating right next to our property. Naturally, the owner just kept walking. Believe me, I was outside in a flash. Urban green spaces also are not dog toilets, so please remove any canine waste in these areas too. If you fail to

Dog owners frequently are also involved in recreational sports. If a well-trained dog goes jogging with her owner, there are unlikely to be any conflicts along the way.
▽

do so, in many cities and communities there is the threat of a substantial fine.

If you live right in town and there's no park in the immediate vicinity, always carry plastic bags with you and pick up your pet's feces every time. That way you'll save yourself and others a lot of trouble. If your pet has learned a certain audible signal for permission to do her business (→ housebreaking, page 75) and her need is not urgent yet, then you can go to a suitable spot such as the base of a tree and give the signal there.

▷ **Playgrounds and sandboxes** aren't dog potties either. Not even in the evening or at night. Soiled sandboxes, however, are frequently the work of cats, not dogs. But in our society, cats meet with greater tolerance than dogs anyway.

▷ **The great outdoors,** too, should not unconditionally serve as a dog toilet. To err on the side of caution, make it a rule to dispose of your dog's droppings every time. Especially in winter, the unmistakable "objects" are visible in the snow from quite a distance, and in some places piles of them appear once the snow has melted. You've surely noticed as well that there are paths that every dog in the neighborhood appears to use. Many of their droppings collect there too, in proportionate quantities. In such a case, I would implore you to dispose of your pet's "business" without fail.

▷ **In agricultural areas,** dog droppings repeatedly are the subject of heated discussion. It is unlikely and debatable, however, that they present a real danger to cows' health. But it is a serious hygienic problem, since cows understandably refuse to eat soiled fodder. Possibly large amounts of grass become unusable, causing financial damage for farmers. That must be prevented, of course. In a freshly mown field, the droppings will decompose before the next mowing; in areas with higher grass, I advise you to dispose of the droppings in any event. Much unnecessary friction could be avoided in this way.

Did the feces land on the sidewalk or in a similarly inappropriate place? In any event, you need to remove the droppings. The best solution is to always carry a few plastic bags in your pocket so you'll be equipped for such incidents

Now you're surely going to ask where the dog actually is allowed to go. I think it's okay for your four-legged friend to defecate at the edge of bushes or in unplowed strips of land. Dog feces will decompose, after all, and after some time there will be nothing left.

Athletes, Watch Out!

Dogs and joggers, bike riders, and other athletes—it's an enduring love-hate relationship. Many dogs adore chasing everything that is moving fast. While most dogs "just" want to say hello or play, there are some with a strong ◉ PREY DRIVE (page 270) that will nip the legs of joggers or cyclists. But whatever motivation drives your four-legged friend—please keep her from chasing human beings. No jogger or biker can be expected to stop and spend time with your pet, or to wait until you've caught up with your dog again. If you are a jogger or biker yourself, you know from experience that on some routes you would have to stop almost every 300 feet.

So if you know or notice that your pet could get enthusiastic about chasing someone, I advise you to practice consistently with the dog until she learns to come in good time when called and to sit next to you or walk on at heel with you, instead of concentrating on the "prey." Otherwise, you'd do better to avoid routes that are especially popular with joggers and other recreational athletes. See page 243 for ways to keep your dog from chasing. Drills that teach the dog to *come, heel,* and pay attention are found in the exercise sections of Chapters 3 and 4.

But why not make a good impression on the athletes with your well-trained dog? You could, for example, stop your four-legged friend in her tracks when you see that all her sniffing has made it oblivious to "oncoming traffic" and she is now on a collision course. See page 137 for a description of ways to achieve that lofty goal.

Of course, there also are many dogs that don't care at all who or what is coming their way. If your pet is in this category and simply runs around without getting in the way when joggers or walkers approach, then there's no need to recall her. With all due consideration, the mere presence of a dog shouldn't disturb anybody.

What About Nervous Pedestrians?

You have to accept that some people are afraid of dogs—though there are many dog owners who can't imagine such a thing. Possibly such people have had bad experiences with dogs previously. Others are simply fearful, without having had concrete experiences. Perhaps the dog is unusually large and thus looks "more threatening." Among my friends, there are two of these "scaredy-cats."

If someone is afraid of horses, for example, it's easy to avoid them. Just don't go to a riding stable and don't take walks on riding paths. Running into a dog, however, is virtually impossible to prevent. Then, if a dog heads directly for a passerby who is afraid anyway, or perhaps barks loudly and runs toward or jumps up on this person, you can imagine that the level of anxiety is not likely to diminish—even if the dog has no bad intentions.

What you can do: When you realize that a passerby is afraid, or if he or she asks you to call your dog, then please recall your pet. Depending on the situation, a conversation may arise that allows you to remove some of the person's cause for concern. And he or she may even be confident enough to pet your dog if she sits quietly next to you and is friendly.

Here, too, a well-trained dog is the best way to advertise that there is no need to fear the majority of dogs.

Even if a passerby shows no direct fear but makes it evident that he or she wants no contact with the animal, you should keep your pet from engaging in direct contact. Not everybody will be wearing "dog clothes." Even during a brief greeting, in passing, as it were, your pet can leave saliva on the other person's clothing.

Speaking of clothing—if your four-legged friend has jumped up on someone and soiled or damaged his or her clothing in the process, then you should offer, of course, to pay for the cleaning costs or to make good the damage.

Many pedestrians feel uneasy around dogs, especially around larger breeds. Then it's better to recall your pet. Depending on your pet's level of training, leash her until the pedestrians have gone past. Alternatively, keep her unleashed but at your side.

Encounters with Children

Children's reactions to a dog are extremely diverse. Anything is possible, all the way from total enthusiasm to panicky fear. If you live near a playground or a school, you witness these reactions almost daily. But dogs also react in different ways to children. Some just can't get enough of children, while others are clearly afraid of them or seem mistrustful. Not infrequently, dogs—especially smaller breeds—are quick to feel threatened by boisterous children and can even snap at them at such times.

If younger children are coming toward you, it's best to keep your canine companion close to you, on leash if need be. Even if she has friendly inclinations, in her exuberance she can easily knock a child over. Children often have something to eat in their hand, such as ice cream or a pretzel. That too could tempt a dog to become somewhat more obtrusive and quickly snatch at the child's snack.

Recently I observed the following situation. A boy was playing in a meadow, and a dog owner came along with her thoroughly friendly Golden Retriever. The dog saw the child and ran toward him enthusiastically, while the frightened boy froze in his tracks. The owner called her dog, but she didn't hear her. The owner quickly called out, "She won't hurt you." You can imagine how such an experience affects a child who is not much bigger than the dog.

If you encounter children or families and your pet seems composed and well trained, frequently the mother, father, or children will ask if they can pet the dog. Here, the best thing is to leash your pet. Then you have more control over her, in case she gets in a playful mood or wants to lick the delicious traces of chocolate or ice cream off the child's face.

▷ **Your dog is afraid of children** or seems mistrustful: In this case, you should be very careful and keep your distance. The risk of something happening is too great. It is also

△

If your dog's behavior is basically friendly and she is receptive to attention from children, you can let her be petted. But stay close at hand!

difficult to use such a situation for practice, since it would be irresponsible to use children as "training objects." If it's impossible to avoid contact with children, I suggest that you have your dog wear a muzzle, but be sure to keep your distance anyway. Also quite important here is reliable obedience, so that you can control the dog even in critical situations. In addition to all your precautions, however, you also must try not to seem outwardly nervous or tense. That feeling would be communicated to the dog and ultimately would sensitize her even more to such situations. Here it is best to contact, as soon as possible, a veterinarian with a specialty in animal behavior or a professional trainer with similar qualifications.

In conclusion: You can never expect either children or adults to know the best way to act around a dog and how to approach it. You, as the dog's owner, must follow the situation and

1 *Most dogs live with their families without having any problems at all. They like to be a part of everything and enjoy being together with their "pack members."*

2 *There's no reason a well-trained dog can't be part of an outdoor picnic. This canine companion is well aware: The picnic cloth and all the tasty things on it are off limits.*

and then. Some dog owners only get together with other dog owners, but most people are likely also to have friends and relatives who have no dogs, and some of whom, moreover, are not exactly crazy about dogs. If you value such social occasions, your pet has to behave appropriately; otherwise, you probably won't be invited back, or people won't be accepting your invitations. This means that you have to train your pet properly.

What you can do: If you're expecting company or are invited out, I suggest that you give your pet plenty to do beforehand—provide her with plenty of physical and mental exercise. Then the dog won't have surplus energy, and she will have an easier time lying calmly in one place when necessary. If you're having visitors who aren't afraid and who like dogs, you don't need to worry about anything in particular. If that's not the case, it's helpful if you can *down* your pet next to you or in her special place for a time. For this purpose, the *stay* exercises described on pages 90, 108, and 135 are useful. Then your four-legged friend can't besiege visitors who may be fearful or who for other reasons don't necessarily want any contact with her.

This applies also if your dog is especially vigilant, for example. In this case, you should not leave her alone in a room with people who aren't "members of the pack." If your guests are staying overnight, it's best to put the dog in your room. If your children have friends over who are uneasy around dogs, it's also helpful if you can *down* your pet. My younger son has two or three such friends. Since we downed our bitch at first whenever they came to the house, they no longer are so fearful and even like her now.

In the end that is advantageous for the dog as well—she can still stay in the room. Often, in such situations, dogs that can't maintain the *down* position are locked in another room and thus excluded from whatever is going on. Over time, this can have a negative effect on the dog and lead to aggression.

explain this if need be or, depending on your pet's temperament, avoid making contact.

Guests and Parties

The term "family dog" says it all. The dog accompanies its family almost everywhere, and that's a good thing. Otherwise, she would often have to stay home alone or wait in the car—or you'd have to stay home with her.

In your circle of friends and relatives, there are certain to be parties or get-togethers now

5

If you're paying a visit along with your pet, she should likewise display good manners and stay quietly next to you. That's sure to meet with more approval—especially in households with no dog—than letting her make an exploratory round of the house or continually pester the other guests.

But even if your host and hostess are dog owners, good manners must not be taken for granted. Imagine the chaos that would result if both dogs get along well and race around the coffee-table or romp beneath it. To spare the furnishings, *down* both dogs, and now and then you can walk around with them and then let them run around and play outside to their hearts' content.

Going to a Dog Park

In many urban and suburban places in the United States, local organizations have formed dog parks that allow well-behaved and trained dogs to run free with other dogs in a fenced and safe environment. The accent here is on "well-behaved and trained."

To be safe and enjoyable for pets and pet owners, dog parks must have a number of rules. Before you go to such a park with your dog, thoroughly familiarize yourself with the environment and be certain that you and your pet can adequately abide by the park's rules.

Dog parks allow great opportunities for exercise and socialization. They also require that your dog be thoroughly trained and obedient to your commands. Imagine that a number of dogs are off leash and strangers to one another. There is no pack hierarchy here and aggressive pets can do real damage. Your dog must be completely under your control.

A dog off leash that will not come when she is called is a potential danger to herself and others. Therefore, the *come* command is extremely important if you and your dog want to partake of the fun and interaction at a dog park. You must stay constantly alert to keep your canine out of potentially hurtful situations.

Additionally, you are responsible for any injuries that your pet may cause.

It is wise to visit the dog park several times with your pet securely on leash. Walk around the outside of the park, then closer to the park, and then inside the park's fenced area. Allow your pet to sniff and introduce herself to other well-behaved dogs, but always keep a watchful eye for play that can become more serious. Try short sessions off leash, perhaps even trying out some of the lessons your pet has learned in your training time together. This will be a good test of your dog's capacity to be obedient with the added pressure of other free-running dogs around. After you have gone through heeling, *sitting*, and *down*, let your pet go to play with the other canines as a reward for good behavior.

Acclimatizing your pet to the new smells, sounds, and experiences of a dog park need not be strenuous. Remember that such a park, with all the new canine companionship, may be vastly different than anything your dog has experienced before. Introduce free-ranging and play with other dogs in a series of short visits in order that the whole experience remains fresh within your dog's mind. Gradually increase the time that you spend at the park

◁ *If you have to spend the night away from home, perhaps in a hotel, then a dog crate that your pet is already accustomed to can usually be quite useful. Your four-legged friend has a familiar place that gives her a sense of security, even if she has to stay alone in the room at any point.*

161

as your pet becomes successful at this new experience.

Dog parks allow special dog-to-dog (and human-to-human) friendships to develop. There may be one or more other dogs that become quite friendly with your canine and offer social outlets outside the park. Many dog owners find these playgrounds for pets to be excellent ways to make pets feel comfortable around other dogs and other people.

For hotels and other vacation facilities, the same thing applies. There are many vacation quarters where dogs are allowed, but even more places where you can't take your pet, in some cases because of bad experiences with dog owners. If you've made a reservation in a hotel that allows dogs, your pet should always be on leash there. An unleashed Rottweiler running around the patio and vigilantly eyeing every guest (a situation that I've experienced first-hand) doesn't exactly contribute to an improved level of acceptance for dog owners.

In your room, the dog should be as clean and quiet as possible. Don't leave her alone in the room unless she can stay alone for a while elsewhere, and unless you're sure that she won't start howling or barking, or even defend the room from the chambermaid or rearrange it to her own taste. For ways to train your pet to stay alone from an early age, see page 98.

Attitudes such as "It's all right for the dog to bark or get things dirty, after all, I'm paying for it" are inconsiderate and in the end only cause all dog owners to be increasingly less welcome.

If the hotel room or vacation rental has wall-to-wall carpeting, it's more hygienic to feed the dog in the bathroom and set up her water bowl there as well. That way, you can easily get rid of leftover food and take care of "overflows."

A word about sleeping arrangements: Take your dog's bed along on vacation, and put it in one corner of the room. A dog does not belong in a hotel bed—dog hair in the bed and possibly paw prints on the sheets are really not everybody's cup of tea.

Taking Your Dog Into Town

Most cities have an official leash law; for her own safety alone, your four-legged friend should always be on leash in town. Just imagine the following situation: your pet becomes aware of an interesting scent—and without warning jumps into the street. This can happen even to a really well-trained dog. Cars and other means of transportation are not anchored in the dog's ● INSTINCT (page 267) as sources of danger, because these things do not occur in nature. Therefore, in this instance you need to think for your pet.

An unleashed dog can present additional problems. She may, for example, run up to another dog that is more of an unfriendly type, and the result may be a scuffle or a hot pursuit. But even a rambunctious frolic that leads them through a busy pedestrian zone would not be really desirable. In addition, many people are simply afraid of dogs, especially if they are not on leash. And even dog lovers or dog owners are rarely wearing their "dog clothes" downtown, so contact that entails

▷

In busy areas like pedestrian zones, even a very well-trained dog should always be leashed for her own safety. Inner cities frequently have an official leash requirement anyway.

stormy, noisy though friendly behavior will not go down particularly well here either. But if someone wants to make contact with your pet, he or she can do that just as well with the dog on leash, if you are basically in agreement.

While for the most part dogs are not allowed on public transportation in the United States, or access is limited to only small dogs in carriers that fit on a lap, there are some exceptions. If you do take public transportation with your dog, I recommend that you start the adjustment process while your pet is still a puppy. The vehicles are often loud, relatively compact, and sometimes "wobbly." You don't want all that to be a problem for your dog. A stressed pet can be a danger to the other passengers. If trips to town or similar undertakings are stressful for your pet, then take her with you only if you can't avoid doing so. Otherwise, the dog is better off at home.

What you can do: Keep the dog close to you. It should stay calm. If you want to get an older dog used to public transportation, schedule your rides for times when there are relatively few passengers. Once your pet can manage that without getting nervous, you can slowly increase the demands.

Public beaches are another place where large numbers of people are found. At most such locations, dogs are not allowed. In some cases, however, they can still come along, but usually they can't go into the water. That is difficult to understand, but can't be changed. At the beach, obviously, your pet must be leashed and must stay close by your side. Here too, give your dog plenty of exercise beforehand and a chance to relieve herself—dog droppings on the beach would be a medium-sized catastrophe.

If the dog is allowed to get in the water, let her swim a little apart from the general tumult. But don't unleash her for swimming unless she really obeys reliably. She must not try to greet or "rescue" other swimmers. In some areas there are special beaches for dogs,

where they can race around on land and play in the water to their hearts' content. However, dog droppings are taboo there as well.

Out in the "Wild" World of Nature

In every dog there sleeps a hunter—and in some individuals the hunting instinct is fairly lively.

▷ **In nature preserves,** dogs are required to be leashed, in order to prevent stress and endangerment of wild and/or endangered animal species. Moreover, the density of the game population in these natural oases is often quite high.

▶ TIP

Keep Your Eyes Open!

If your four-legged companion starts sniffing at the ground with great interest or freezes in her tracks and gazes in a certain direction, recall her without delay—without first trying to identify the object of her desire. You might already be too late, if she has seen or scented wild game.

In one nature preserve, I once overheard a person in charge of this area and a concerned tourist talking about compliance with protective measures such as the ban on trespassing. The biggest problem, the official said, was uncooperative dog owners. There it is again, the often justifiably bad image!

The natural world does not come to a stop for the canine. Even if the areas in question usually are decidedly tempting free-run places for dogs—abide by the regulations. Especially in brooding or breeding season, a dog can cause a lot of harm, and not only by capturing "prey." Sufficient damage is done by the disturbance alone, since the dog fits most wild animals' image of an enemy—just as, conversely, almost all wild animals fit a dog's prey model. When ground breeders have to leave their clutch too often, for example, because they are put to rout by dogs, the eggs cool down and the breeding success rate drops. Some dog owners think the whole thing is exaggerated, because their dog supposedly does not hunt. But can you say with certainty that your pet would not pursue a startled hare or a deer?

In some of the state and national parks it is standard practice that dogs must wear a leash outside of built-up areas during the entire brooding and breeding season, that is, from the beginning of spring until early summer. When in doubt, inquire in the local community about the regulations that apply in the region.

▷ **In game-rich areas,** even if they are not nature preserves, you should act with similar caution. With more understanding on both sides, many conflicts—some quite serious—between hunters and dog owners could be defused. Then not every dog owner would be literally a "red rag" for many hunters.

By law, you are not required across the board to leash a dog in woods and fields—apart from regional regulations. However, in such areas your dog must obey well and stay more or less on the path. Not infrequently, however, dog owners walk on the path while their canine companions poke around relatively far away in the woods or field, following the scent of game. In addition, quite a few dog owners take a relatively tolerant view of their dog's efforts to pursue a rabbit or a deer. "He won't catch anything anyway," or "He needs to have some fun, after all" can occasionally be heard. As stated above, being hunted causes great stress for the wild game. Especially in winter, when food is scarce and the animals must conserve energy, frequently being on the run can mean, at worst, that the deer or

pheasant will starve to death. And as you read previously, failure is not apt to discourage a dog from hunting; rather, every pursuit only intensifies the desire to hunt.

For her own safety, too, keep an eye on your dog, even though hunters rarely shoot at dogs and usually warn the dog's owner first. Theoretically, however, they are allowed to shoot a dog if they see her in pursuit and she is outside of the owner's range of influence.

What you can do: If your pet has a strong drive to hunt, you should avoid game-rich areas. Instead, take your walks in open country. If your pet's level of obedience is not quite reliable, leash her in appropriate areas as a precaution. Every pursuit will strengthen the dog's determination to try it again at the next opportunity, whether she catches anything or not. For additional information on the subject of chasing and what you can do to prevent or correct it, see page 243. A general-purpose exercise that may be helpful is described on page 104.

The Dog as Helper

Most four-legged companions enrich our free time and our daily routine. But there also are many dogs that have a "real" job and render valuable assistance to their owner in coping with the demands of daily life.

▷ Let's look at guide dogs for the blind, for instance. In a costly, sophisticated training process lasting up to nine months, the dog learns more than 30 commands. For example, a guide dog for the blind must assume what direction to take, indicate or circumnavigate obstacles—ranging from curbs to things that obstruct the blind person's head clearance—lead her owner through the crosswalk to the opposite side of the street, and so forth. Psychological resilience and a good set of nerves are important characteristics in a guide dog for the blind. In addition, she can't allow anything to interfere with her work. Most often Labrador Retrievers are the breed trained for this purpose today. Guide dogs are important to their owners not only because they lead them through town or other areas. The social component is also a major aspect. Guide dogs make social contact with other people easier for their owners.

▷ The situation of service dogs is similar. They too help their handicapped owners through the day, thus giving them more independence and autonomy and facilitating contact with other people. Service dogs also learn quite a lot—they help with undressing, opening and closing doors, turning lights on and off, shopping, picking up whatever their owner drops, and much more.

Guide dogs for the blind and service dogs are placed at the age of approximately eight to twelve weeks with foster families, which socialize them for about one year and are responsible for their early education. Finally they go for further training to a school for guide dogs for the blind or for service dogs. At the end of the process, the appropriate future owner is trained together with the dog for several weeks more.

▷ Dogs have also proven valuable in other

◁ *You can recognize a guide dog for the blind by the special harness she wears. For the dog too, the harness is the sign that she is "at work" now. Don't talk to a guide dog, and don't let your dog go up to her. That would be an unnecessary disturbance.*

areas as co-therapists. Therapy and visitation dogs assist in psychotherapy or in retirement and nursing homes, rehab clinics, and the like, where dog visitation days usually are among the highlights. These dogs usually have no special training, but must pass a temperament test (→ page 274). They must be very even-tempered and have strong nerves; in addition, they must be able to withstand mental and physical stress, and there must be no sign of aggressiveness.

▷ In the meantime, corresponding projects have also been started at some schools. Studies have determined that the presence of a dog is beneficial in problem classes as well. The level of aggression declines, the students are more relaxed, and the educational atmosphere is noticeably improved.

5

From One Dog Owner to Another

Conflicts between non-dog owners and dog owners are nothing new. But problems can arise among dog owners too, and there are ways to avoid them.

THERE IS NO SUCH THING as a typical dog owner. Some people keep a dog as a child substitute, while for others a dog serves as piece of "sports equipment" or something to enhance their own personality. But it's not only the owners who are different; dogs too vary quite widely. The broad spectrum of canines ranges from large to small, from macho types and daredevils to scaredy-cats, from confrontational to playful, from tractable to independent. Because of the great diversity of dogs and owners, frictions and even dangerous situations arise repeatedly. With some foresight, however, they can be easily avoided.

Everyday Encounters

A Word in Advance

One thing right up front—I recommend that every dog owner take out a ⊙ DOG LIABILITY INSURANCE POLICY (page 261), because in spite of all your caution, something can always happen. If your four-legged friend injures another member of his species, for example, you have to pay the veterinarian's bill. The insurance policy, however, will also cover other types of damage possibly caused by your pet.

Most walks with your dog, like most canine encounters, will not be problematic. A certain residual risk always remains, however, no matter whether your own pet is a male or a female, a large dog or a small one, a puppy or a senior citizen. Exaggerated caution is misplaced, however, because it can easily be communicated to your four-legged friend. Many owners of small dogs get into a state of moderate panic when a larger canine approaches. That too is needless. Not infrequently, members of small breeds are rather self-confident, and "big" doesn't automatically mean "dangerous" by any means. If a small dog is picked up every time a bigger dog appears on the scene, or is deliberately kept at a distance, then he often becomes quite aggressive.

But if a puppy meets a large or adult member of his species, my advice is to use a certain caution when dealing with unfamiliar dogs—first, because you don't know how the other dog reacts to puppies; second, because the puppy should not necessarily play with every older dog. If he gets mowed down, or if a larger, heavier dog jumps on him, the puppy can get hurt. When in doubt, the bigger dog at least could be left on leash. With regard to the other rules having to do with encounters between leashed dogs, this is to a certain extent a special case.

Both Dogs Are Leashed

If you have your dog on leash or at *heel* while off leash, then as a general rule you want him to stay near you—even or especially when a distraction is present. And that also includes a leashed dog. If you see such an animal approaching, keep your dog close by, either unleashed or leashed, and make sure that he goes past his conspecific without straining to get nearer. This will also work if you've taught your pet the drills on pages 99, 115, or 116.

Repeatedly we see dog owners stand still, or walk on while allowing their pet to strain at the leash to get closer to another dog. Often this goes on for several feet if the dog is on a retractable leash. This entails the risk of the leash getting wrapped around the legs of the other dog or his owner.

If dogs are allowed to make contact while leashed, the dogs usually strain to get closer, and their owners follow along. This teaches a dog two bad habits. For one thing, straining against the leash is very advantageous, because the dog achieves his objective if he just throws himself into it hard enough. For another, he

◁

To play it safe, this puppy is subordinating itself to the "big dog." You never know how a strange dog will react. "Sucking up" a little can't hurt. If the big dog behaves in a normal way and is not too rough, there's no obstacle to getting better acquainted.

Two dog owners are chatting while out for a walk. In the meantime, the dogs sit nicely in the heel *position. That's how it has to be! You can talk in peace without having to constantly check to see whether a jogger or a cyclist is approaching.*

learns that other dogs are always worth stopping for. With this experience, your pet will have a hard time grasping why he's not allowed to make contact with other dogs in town.

Contacts while on leash actually have no positive aspect at all, just some negative consequences. Imagine the following scene. Two leashed dogs are facing each other and sniffing each other's face. Anything more is hardly possible. They can't act the way they would off leash. They can't circle around each other, or sniff each other everywhere and at great length, or play. If they do try those things while on leash, they quickly get tangled up. Then one can hurt himself or panic and react aggressively. But neither will be able to evade

the other if need be. What both dogs can do, however, is plant themselves in front of each other on their taut leashes and glare. And in the twinkling of an eye, a scuffle is underway.

There are relatively many dogs that react aggressively, when leashed, toward other dogs. If you factor in the information given above, you'll realize that this problem often is man-made. Such encounters teach the dog, for example, that offense is the best defense, because when on leash he can't evade the other dog. Alternatively, he may feel especially strong with his owner available as a back-up and therefore react aggressively.

The right way to react: It's preferable to train with your dog on leash, as well as off leash and heeling, to walk past others in a "normal" way and to ignore other members of his species in such situations. Distract your pet with treats or a toy, and, depending on his level of training, keep far enough away from the other dog. To achieve this goal, you'll find all the exercises "for several dogs" helpful. They are described on pages 99, 114–120, and 146–151.

If you and the other dog owner have agreed that the dogs can get acquainted, unleash them while they are still several yards apart and have plenty of space. Don't wait until they may be already growling and straining against the leashes.

One Dog Is On Leash, the Other Off

This situation can be observed with relative frequency when you're out in public. Experience shows that many dog owners uninhibitedly let their pet go up to leashed dogs, or to dogs that clearly are obeying a command. "My dog just wants to play, she won't do anything bad" or "Can't yours play? Poor dog!" are comments not infrequently heard at such times.

There can be a great many different reasons for keeping a dog leashed. She may be a bitch that is in season at the moment. Or a leashed male may be a bully. The dog may be injured

5

or sick, and for that reason he may be unable to move around freely or may even be forbidden to play. Or the owner and dog may be practicing an exercise at the time.

Basically, when two dogs meet, it's a disadvantage if one is leashed and the other is not. Fights can easily develop, even if neither of the animals is really a rowdy type. An exception, however, is the situation described on page 167, when a puppy encounters a bigger dog. Here you can let the larger animal—leashed at first, to play it safe—initiate contact if he is fundamentally good-natured. First, to see whether his reaction to the puppy is friendly, and second, to see whether he may be too rambunctious after all. Make sure to keep the leash loose.

Recently, I was out with two dogs in a grassy area, about 300 feet off the path. I had downed my bitch roughly 30 feet from me, and I had just gotten a retrieving task ready for my "foster child." It was obvious that neither of the dogs was running free or even playing. Two walkers came along the path with two unleashed dogs. That was completely all right, and no problem at all at this distance. But then the dogs clearly headed in our direction. And neither owner called his dog; both simply stood by and watched. The dogs romped around us and tried get my two to play with them. It took a long time until the two people finally decided to continue on their way and tried to run their dogs down. Apart from the fact that the young dog's concentration was ruined for the time being, a distance of 300 feet between dog and owner is far too great, especially if the dog doesn't come when called.

And what might have happened if the two playing dogs had bumped into an aggressive dog? Or if they had run toward a dog owner whose pet was running along on leash next to a bicycle?

The right reaction:

▷ If an owner with a leashed dog comes toward you, or if it's evident from something else that the other dog isn't running free, then you should recall your pet. The same thing applies in the reverse situation. If you have your dog with you, for whatever reason, and another owner lets his or her pet go up to yours, you should ask the other person to recall the dog. You'll see that over time you'll acquire the requisite "thick skin" and have no problem standing up to the pitying glances at your "poor" dog, which isn't allowed to play and romp. But possibly such encounters will also result in an occasional conversation, and you can explain your reasoning to the other dog owner.

▷ But what if a dog that's running free comes up, and there's no owner anywhere in sight? In this case, it's very hard to give advice across the board. If your pet is not sick, not in heat, and not a fighter by nature, virtually the only thing possible is to unleash him, if you foresee that the strange dog is not going away. If a fight develops, though that is by no means inevitable, there's little you can do—especially

◁

This dog is on leash. Perhaps he or she is ill, doesn't get along well with other dogs, or is in heat. If another dog owner lets his or her pet run up to your leashed pet at this time, the situation is a difficult one—even if it only wants to play.

The dog that is running free is recalled and comes to his owner.
That's right! In this way, conflict situations can be prevented
beforehand. If a little conversation ensues, the owner may
explain why her dog is leashed.

if the other dog is a large one. A malicious little
dog can perhaps be "plucked out" of the fray.
Try to grab him by the back of the neck or
wherever possible.

Sometimes it's advisable in such a situation
to keep your own pet on leash and leave as
quickly as possible, especially if he tends to be
disagreeable. Make an on-the-spot decision,
depending on the lay of the land, but avoid
any risk of injury for yourself.

▷ If you're out in public with your bitch in
heat and have "visitors" for that reason, you
can hold the free-running dog still, if he's
wearing a collar, and wait a little. His owner

may yet come along. If not, things get complicated. Either you try to chase the male away,
or you hold on to his collar and take him
home, if you know where he lives. Otherwise,
all that's left is the animal shelter or simply
taking flight and going back home.

▷ There are dog owners who, for reasons of
convenience, don't take their pet out, but
instead send him out alone. In some circumstances that is not only a problem for other
dogs (see above), but also irresponsible in
general. In our neighborhood, a woman who
was out walking her dog was knocked down
by a "stray" dog that wanted to get close to
her pet. Unfortunately, she suffered a complicated open fracture that required several
operations. It took many months to heal
completely.

If you know who owns a dog that is constantly running free, I suggest that you go and
have a talk with that person. He or she may
not even be aware of what potentially can
happen.

Is It Really a Game?

Are you also one of those people who can watch
for hours while dogs play with each other? It's
really wonderful to see how much fun they have.
They race each other, tussle, carry a stick
together, and do many other things.

But it's not always a game, though at first
glance it may seem like one to some dog owners. And in this case you should intervene and
control things.

▷ **Encounters with lovesick males:** Here, too,
I'd like to offer an example taken from "real"
life. The owner of a bitch not in heat was
walking through a meadow when a male dog
came running up from some distance. He was
very interested in the bitch, and he kept sniffing her rear end and trying to copulate with
her. She kept turning around in circles and
trying to get rid of him by snapping and
barking, which did not dissuade the lovesick
suitor, however. As his owners continued to

stand there doing nothing, the owner of the bitch finally "plucked" the male off her pet and pulled him back. Whereupon his owners, quite upset that their male was not allowed to play with her, asserted that the owner was clueless.

Now, the opposite actually was the case. This behavior has nothing to do with playing; it is merely annoying. In addition, attempting to mount a bitch is potentially even dangerous for her, if she is smaller or weighs substantially less than the male. ◐ HYPERSEXUALITY (page 266) in males, unfortunately, is not at all rare. In such a case, request Romeo's owners to recall their pet.

▷ **Small dog and big dog:** Puppies should have contact with all possible kinds of dogs, but under supervision. As mentioned on page 167, it's too much for a puppy, as well as harmful to his skeletal system, if he is run down by a bigger, heavier dog, however friendly and playful he may be. Some adult dogs, however, will lie down on the ground to play with a puppy at eye level, so to speak. That's just fine, and the puppy will profit from it too.

Unequal relative strength: Puppies can play wonderfully together. If you run into another puppy owner now and then or attend a puppy class, however, you should make sure that the puppies are on an equal footing: sometimes one has the upper hand, sometimes the other. But if one is constantly being picked on or dominated, I suggest that you intervene. This unequal balance of power doesn't have a positive effect on either the one that's getting the worst of it or the one that always feels he's "the boss." The one in the inferior position feels continually in distress, and the "top" dog may tend to have delusions of grandeur. And it's not right to let the puppies work this out themselves, as is often claimed!

Such inequality can exist among adult dogs too, of course. And then too, it makes more sense to find a more suitable playmate for your pet.

When several larger dogs are playing with a smaller one, you also need to pay close attention. Races can quickly degenerate into a real pursuit, if bigger dogs chase a small one. Dogs engage in mobbing as well. If a dog is being deliberately run down or nipped, that has nothing to do with playing. You should put a halt to such goings-on without delay.

◐ **TIP**

"Girl Power"

Some bitches make no bones about putting insistent males in their place. At times they need to resort to very clear "language." Some try to refocus the males' attention by inviting them to play, but this rarely succeeds. Others have no idea what to do. If necessary, provide assistance.

The Cantankerous Dog

Not all dogs are unproblematic in their dealings with other members of their species. The reasons for this are varied: inadequate socialization, fear, and bad experiences are some examples. An excessive interest in sexual activity among males, a pronounced drive to defend toys or food, and a tendency to scuffle based on qualities known as SHARPNESS (page 272) and FIGHTING DRIVE (page 264) may be causes. Aggression can be directed

INFO

Avoiding Scuffles

If there's no love lost between two dogs that encounter each other, their behavior will make that obvious. They will circle one another, growling and trying to impress each other. If you notice your pet and another dog behaving this way, both you and the other owner should quickly walk away in opposite directions. The dogs will follow. But if you corner the dogs or even touch them, the encounter can escalate.

at all dogs, only at dogs of the same gender, or at certain types of dogs. The third category usually is related to prior bad experiences.

Basically, conflicts can't always be avoided; this is quite natural. If the opponents exhibit normal social behavior, they usually will limit themselves to RITUALISTIC FIGHTING (page 272), that is, to conflicts that end relatively quickly and with little or no harm done, even if the situation often looks quite threatening. It can get dangerous, however, if a big

dog and a small one, such as a German Shepherd and a Dachshund, happen to clash. Then the smaller dog can incur serious injuries. The risk that a conflict will turn violent is substantially greater among males than among females. When bitches do come to blows, however, there can be serious fighting, with the objective of harming each other.

If there is a problem with his or her social behavior, a dog may attack another dog with no advance warning. That is especially dangerous, because such an experience can have a very long-lasting effect on the victim. Besides the injuries, there is a threat of other long-term consequences—in the future, such a dog may decide that "offense is the best defense" and in turn react aggressively to other members of the species, or flee in panic because he or she fears other dogs.

Especially long-lasting are the negative effects of such an experience when the "victim" is still a puppy and thus, in the socialization phase. It is not negative, however, if an overly impertinent or "annoying" puppy is put in his place by another dog, using the muzzle grip, a nudge with the muzzle, or "angry" growling.

Out in Public with a Cantankerous Dog

If you know that your pet doesn't exactly get along well with others of his kind, you need to make sure he presents no danger. The basis for this is—once again—reliable obedience, as well as trying to anticipate situations when you go for a walk. Only then is it possible to recall your pet in time if another member of his species approaches. If necessary, ask the other dog's owner to recall his or her pet as well. Alternatively, call out to ask, for example, whether the other animal is a male or a female, in case your pet is aggressive toward other dogs of its own gender. This kind of "preventive care" is appropriate for dogs that react aggressively only to certain types of dogs, or if the free-run area is in a neighborhood with few dogs.

The Muzzle as a Solution

Aggressive dogs that are ready to fight in general, hurl themselves at other dogs with no previous warning, or do not obey reliably should as a matter of principle not run free. Even if they are taken out at times when other dog owners are unlikely to be around, there is always a residual risk. And if worst comes to worst, that can have extremely unpleasant repercussions.

Here a muzzle can provide an extra measure of security. Once a dog is accustomed to it, the muzzle doesn't bother him. And it will save the owner a great deal of stress. The owner will be more relaxed, which in turn can have a favorable impact on his or her pet.

Unfortunately, there are some dog owners who take the view that nothing needs to be done, since their dog liability insurance policy (→ page 261) would pay. And there are others who think it's actually a good thing that their dog "won't take any nonsense." If you know of such an owner in your neighborhood, and if there already have been several incidents, having a talk with the person may help. Completely inconsiderate fellow citizens can be reported to the local regulatory agency.

Solving Problems with Rowdy Dogs

If you keep a few basic things in mind, most conflicts can be prevented in advance. If you are cautious and prudent, many problems will never arise in the first place.

▷ **Food and prey envy:** Put the treats and toys away when another dog approaches (→ photo, page 176). If your pet threatens another dog because he is defending, for example, the food in your jacket pocket, quickly take a few steps away. Then he will no longer have anything to defend. If several dogs meet,

▶ CHECKLIST

Damage Control When Fighting Occurs

Fighting can't always be avoided. Despite the understandable upset, there are a few things that absolutely must be kept in mind:

○ Avoid shouting at the dogs. Your loud, agitated tone of voice is more apt to spur them on than to separate them.

○ If other dogs are running free at the scene, they should be leashed at once, so that they don't get involved.

○ Don't use your hand, the leash, or other objects to strike at the tangle of fighting dogs. They will connect the pain with their opponent and only become more aggressive.

○ Avoid any risk of injury to yourself. Don't try to reach into the tangle to pull your pet out, unless you're certain that you won't be injured. Your dog may not pay attention to what he's trying to bite, and his opponent definitely will not.

○ Don't pull the dogs apart by their hind legs while they still have their teeth sunk into one another; wait until there's a short break in the fighting after you've caught hold of them. Then you can avoid even more serious bites.

5

don't throw a ball or anything else until you know for sure whether the animals can get along when toys are involved. The same thing applies to food. Don't hand out any treats when several dogs are together.

▷ **Hypersexuality** (→ page 266) is, as mentioned earlier, not rare in male dogs. If you own such an animal, you may be irritated when your Romeo goes into a total ecstasy over every urine mark left by a female or at the actual sight of an idolized bitch, regardless of whether she is in heat at the moment or not. Usually you can't get his attention at all at such a time, and his only goal is to mount the female. Not to mention the stress caused when Romeo also thinks he has to eliminate every male rival—which is frequently the case. The consequence is that you constantly have to plan ahead when you're out walking and determine in advance whether an approaching dog is male or female.

A lasting solution is provided only by ◉ NEUTERING (page 269). It spares not only the dog owner, but also the dog, a great deal of stress. It is important, however, to have your male castrated in plenty of time, that is, as soon as this behavior becomes evident. If it has already been going on for some years, the dog may out of habit retain a tendency to get into conflicts even after castration.

▷ **General rowdiness** is not easy to treat and correct. It is essential to seek professional help. Some dog schools offer special groups for rowdy dogs, in which such animals, wearing muzzles, are integrated into a group of dogs whose social behavior is no problem. The muzzle keeps the dog from injuring fellow canines. Over time, he notices that his behavior isn't getting him anywhere. Contact dog schools in your area to ask about such programs (Useful Addresses → page 284).

The dog on the left is quite self-confident—the one on the right isn't sure what to think. Don't intervene. Let the dogs work it out.
▽

Your veterinarian may also be able to give you an address.

If a dog has learned aggression, from a bad experience, from training, or from unwitting encouragement, then the problem can be addressed by systematic training in such a therapy group. The extent to which this type of rowdy behavior can be improved, however, is impossible to predict. It depends on the individual case. But the longer the problem continues, the harder it is to solve. An innate tendency to get into fights is very difficult to influence. Here, as well as with the other forms of rowdiness, reliable obedience is absolutely essential.

▷ **Territorial aggression** means that your dog boldly defends his ◐ TERRITORY (page 275), in this case against other members of his species. You need to be especially cautious when visitors bring a dog along. Give the animals an opportunity to get acquainted on neutral ground, ideally some distance away from your own property. If they aren't getting along even then, it's advisable to put them in separate parts of the house. If both dogs are trained to obey reliably, you also can put them in the *down* position next to their owners, some distance apart.

If your dog also regards certain areas as his territory when you're out walking, a good solution is to frequently choose unfamiliar locations for your walks. In addition, make sure your pet has enough purposeful activity to keep him interested during the walk. Then your four-legged friend has a meaningful outlet for his energy and is successfully distracted.

▷ **Aggressiveness when on leash** was mentioned on page 167. It often is man-made in origin. You can prevent this problem by regularly practicing walking past other dogs, and by consistently avoiding contact with other dogs when your pet is leashed. If you're already having a problem on leash, then the tips on pages 232 and 233 will help you.

◐ WHAT DO I DO IF . . .

. . . dogs start fighting?

In a real "two-fisted" fight, you need to keep your cool! There's no across-the-board recipe for correct action; you need to decide based on the situation.

Solution 1: If all the dog owners are present and spunky enough, you can separate the dogs, with everyone holding their dogs by the hind legs simultaneously and pulling them out of the fight.

Solution 2: It would be very effective to spray the tangle of dogs with a water hose. But how often do you have one right at hand in such a situation?

Solution 3: Fighting dogs can be separated by making a loud noise (bursting plastic bag, firecracker, or the like).

Solution 4: If you throw a blanket or a coat over the antagonists, there's also a chance that they'll briefly stop what they're doing. You need to act right away—in the short pause, get all the "combatants" under control and put them on leash!

5

1 This dog is playing happily with its owner. She has taken its favorite toy along on the walk so that she can play with her dog.

2 An unfamiliar, free-running dog is approaching. To prevent a possible quarrel over "prey," the owner promptly puts the toy out of sight.

If the dog's fear is based on a bad experience, it's good to give him increased contact with good-natured members of his species that visually come close to the type that bit your pet. That is especially important if this happens to a puppy. As you know, experiences in puppyhood make a particularly lasting impression. As soon as possible, get the puppy together again with other dogs in general and with individuals that resemble the "attacker."

If you know that your dog is trying to bite because he's afraid, a muzzle can be helpful (→ page 227). I advise against wild romping in larger groups. That can be stressful even for "normal" dogs, and it is even more so for fearful ones.

Don't Unconsciously Reinforce Aggression

In a situation when your dog reacts aggressively, don't pet him soothingly or talk to him reassuringly. The dog interprets that as praise and turns the aggression up a notch. Painful stimuli, such as a yank on a prong collar (unfortunately still quite common), reinforces the behavior slightly, because the dog links it with his opponent. An angry, excited voice can have the same effect.

Along with the steps listed above, relaxed behavior on your part is helpful in dealing with fear. Other than that, a calm but authoritative word of disapproval or a stop command can be useful as well (→ page 273).

▷ **Fear of other dogs** usually is due to bad experiences or inadequate socialization. Try to get your pet acquainted with individual members of his own species that are calm and thoroughly good-natured. There may be such animals in your circle of friends or in the neighborhood. If not, contact a good dog school.

10 Questions About Behavior in Public

Dog owners often let their leashed dog come up to ours, although my Timo is on leash and doesn't strain to get closer to other dogs. What can I do?

Here your decision should be based on the situation. You can simply keep on going or explain to the other owner that when leashed, your pet isn't allowed to have any contact with other canines. If contact is unavoidable, then at least make sure to keep the leash loose. If you've given Timo a command, cancel it before contact is made.

If there's a leash requirement in an area, can I walk my dog there on a 30-foot leash or a retractable leash too?

Ask your community or municipal authorities about the nuances of the regulation. Usually it refers to normal leashes, but there may be other regulations as well.

Our neighbors' children (10 and 12 years old) would like to take our Hovawart mix and another neighbor's Golden Retriever for a walk. Should we allow this?

I advise against it. Dogs of that size have a lot of strength, and the children can't hold onto

them. Only recently I ran into such a scenario. I was on my bike, with my bitch heeling at my side. One of the other two dogs wanted to go for my bitch and pulled the girl into the street. My pet, frightened, jumped to one side, right into the bicycle.

My Ben hasn't learned the "Stay," but I can still tie him in front of a store without using a command, can't I?

That can be risky. If you tie him to a bike rack or something similar and he doesn't know the "Stay," then he could run away and pull over the bike rack in the process. Ben could get in a real panic and run into the street along with the rack.

Is there actually a muzzle requirement for certain situations?

If the Animal Control Authority determines a dog to be potentially dangerous, they may require that the dog be maintained on the owner's property, only to be removed for medical treatment. When removed from the property, the dog should be under the control of a responsible person, muzzled, and restrained on a lead. The muzzle should be made in a manner that will not cause injury to the dog or interfere with his vision or respiration, but shall prevent him from biting any human being or animal. For further information, contact the city or community authorities directly.

In the area where we go for walks, two bitches are in heat right now. Do I have to keep my male dog leashed at all times, to keep him from harassing the "ladies"?

That depends on his level of obedience. Bitches in heat should be leashed at least during the

If mail carriers, beverage delivery trucks, and the like come to your home regularly, you need to get your pet used to visitors while he is still a puppy. That will spare you and your visitors a great deal of stress.

When children go out for a walk with a dog unaccompanied by adults, dangerous situations can easily develop.

the ability to get along with other dogs and people. SAR dogs are usually the larger working and sporting breeds of dogs. German Shepherds, Dobermans, Rottweilers, Golden Retrievers, and Labradors are among the breeds found on SAR unit rosters. Most handlers prefer to begin training a young puppy. However, an older dog may be suitable if the dog has already developed a good working relationship with his owner.

Are there places where you absolutely can't take dogs with you?

Yes, they include, for example, grocery stores or department stores, as well as bakeries, meat markets, and the like. Dogs also are not allowed in cemeteries and even in some city parks and green areas. Exceptions to this, however, are guide dogs for the blind and service dogs (→ page 165). In addition, cities and communities or store owners can regulate these matters individually.

fertile part of the heat period. If you see a leashed dog, you should be able to recall your dog anyway. But if someone lets a bitch in season run free and you fail to recognize her "condition," then her owner can't expect you to leash your male.

Our white German Shepherd puppy looks so cuddly that everybody wants to pet him, including stroking his head. But he doesn't like that very much. What I can do?

You could tell people that they need to pet the puppy differently, though that's not always easy. You could also practice this kind of touching with your pet, however. Stroke his head from above, and give him a treat at the same time. If he accepts it and lets strangers pet him that way, then you can also give him a treat when that happens. But if he's clearly uncertain or fearful, it's best to avoid such situations.

I'd like to get involved in public service work with my dog and train him as a rescue dog. What do I need to bear in mind?

"Official" rescue dog teams can be contacted through the AKC or organizations such as the Red Cross. Here the dogs are trained by professionals. Requirements for the SAR dog include trainability, agility, endurance, and

Training as a rescue team is time-consuming for both dog and human, and it is not a hobby. It can, however, be very satisfying.

Should I get our young Asterix used to the mail carrier?

You'll definitely spare your carrier plenty of stress if you can keep your pet from acting like one of the Furies when the mail is delivered. Keep some delicious treats on hand, and walk outside with your puppy when the mail is delivered. In the future, let the carrier feed and cuddle him on a frequent basis. Assuming, that is, that your carrier is willing to participate in the familiarization process.

5

Meaningful Play and Activity

Ever since you got involved with your new housemate, playing games and planning activities with the dog have been part of your daily routine. This is important, because your four-legged friend, like almost all dogs, is inherently an active and curious animal. Through play you reinforce his or her trust in you and strengthen the bond between you—and besides, the exercise is something you'll both enjoy!

6

Playing—More Than Just Having Fun

When animals play, this is a sign that they are relatively highly developed. The greatest variety of games is found among animals that live in a social unit.

THAT ALSO INCLUDES THE DOG. Most dogs take great pleasure in playing, especially before the onset of puberty. Depending on their disposition and the encouragement they receive, there are canines that exhibit a more or less pronounced play instinct throughout their entire life. Dogs, like humans, can be divided into different player categories, however. Play is of great importance in a dog's development. But not only playing with other members of her or his species is important; play involving owner and dog plays a special role as well: It is fun for the dog and therefore has a positive effect on the bonding process. Most people play a lot and on a regular basis with a puppy. Here, the puppy's childlike looks obviously exert an influence. With older dogs, the situation is usually different, and the dog is restricted to going for walks and training.

Playing—What's Its Real Purpose?

Playing results from an internal impetus, the ● PLAY INSTINCT (page 270). Play is its own reward. This means that there's no need to reward your dog for playing. You can, however, use play to reward your four-legged companion for a previous desirable behavior, because your pet enjoys playing. For many training courses, such as rescue dog training or agility training, having a strong play instinct is important for the dog.

Playing takes up a large part of puppies' time. When puppies from the same litter are not pressed close to mama's milk bar or in the "Land of Nod," they play continually—both with other puppies and alone. They can also play with themselves, by trying to catch their tail or rolling around on the floor.

Exploring the Surrounding World

When puppies explore their surroundings while playing, they are primarily exhibiting curiosity and an urge to discover things. The little creatures explore the terrain, chew on things that are unfamiliar to them, nudge things, hop around on things, and so forth. They like to toss small objects in the air and then "bring them down" with a leap, as if pouncing on a mouse.

For our puppies, for example, two empty plastic bottles became a real hit. We filled them barely half full with little plastic balls or gravel and closed them tightly. After the pups had rendered an expert opinion on the bottles, they kicked them around enthusiastically and had enormous fun with the moving object and the noise connected with it. The puppies' behavior demonstrates that in this phase they try out everything possible. Depending on the experiences they have in the process, they become increasingly confident, but also learn to be a little more careful in certain situations.

Invitation to Play

To be able to play with other dogs, a dog has to signal that she's in a mood to play and get the other animal interested in participating. An important characteristic of play behavior is the fact that the movements seem exaggerated. The dog hops, runs, or tosses her head in the air. Another popular method is to jostle the other dog with her rear end while hopping around.

▷ **Upper body lowered:** This is a very well-known gesture used as an invitation to play.

TIP

Keep an Eye on the Puppy!

When your little pup is exploring her surroundings—the yard, for example—keep a close eye on her, so that she doesn't play with something that could be dangerous to her. Poisonous plants, snail bait, sharp gardening tools, and the like must not be within the puppy's reach. The garden pond must be surrounded by fencing.

Here, the dog lowers her upper body to the ground. This frequently is followed by racing around.

▷ **Play face:** The dog's face is relaxed. In addition, she opens her mouth wide or bares its teeth. These and other "grimaces," which seem exaggerated in some cases, are used by dogs in other behaviors too, for example, when making a threat.

This brings me to another important matter. When at play, a dog exhibits elements from all possible spheres of behavior—threat behavior,

△

Playing is fun, but it also involves learning important life lessons. Puppies practice many typical behaviors while playing together. In addition, during their romps, they also get exercise that promotes physical fitness.

sexual behavior, prey-capture behavior, and so forth. Their playing, however, lacks the aspect of seriousness: that is, "serious" signals are mixed with play behavior, and the result is not the action that normally follows such a signal. A playful threat, for example, is not followed by a real fight or a genuine sign of submissiveness, but by a game of chase or the like.

Among adult dogs, however, a game can easily turn into a serious confrontation. Alternatively, a serious situation can be defused by playful behavior. Among puppies that tends to

be rare, but here, too, occasionally one will kick over the traces—during a fighting game, perhaps, if the puppy is pugnacious by nature.

In some cases, the playing can get pretty boisterous, with plenty of barking and growling. First-time dog owners occasionally get a little nervous when this happens.

Favorite Games with Other Dogs

▷ **Racing and chasing:** Here the dogs take turns chasing each other and also switch roles. Often the faster dog even runs a little slower, for example, so that the other can catch up to her again. Some dogs especially enjoy this game when the one out in front also is carrying a stick or a toy that can be recovered.

▷ **Mutual stalking** with playful attacks is popular among young dogs in particular, but some adult canines enjoy it too. It may be followed by a game in which the dogs tussle or race each other.

▷ **Tugging:** One dog shows the other that she has a valuable prize and hops to and fro in front of her fellow canine. She moves the "prey" back and forth in her mouth, hoping the other dog will want it. If interest has been aroused, the "owner" of the prize lets the other dog get hold of it. Then an intense tug-of-war game follows.

▷ **Playful fighting:** I've had a good chance to observe this with my bitch's litter. When one of the little puppies (nine months old) runs into her mother, she is mercilessly "played with." To get her to participate, they pull at her flews, neck, or cheeks—but carefully, so that it isn't really unpleasant, except in rare instances. If they are persistent enough, in the end the youngsters usually persuade Mama to play along. Then they "bicker," jostling each other with their muzzles. I'm only astonished that their teeth emerge intact after such a game.

Why Do Dogs Play?

Playing is undeniably lots of fun, but to a great extent it is simultaneously a learning process. By playing, puppies prepare for their life in the years to come.

▷ **Practicing social behavior:** During play, social behavior in particular is learned and practiced, because not all of it is innate. If a dog had no opportunity during puppyhood to play with other dogs of the same age, she may have problems communicating with other members of her species later on. Through play, puppies learn to avoid aggression, and it contributes to formation of a hierarchy and strengthens social cohesion. One important element that puppies learn and practice while playing together is the ◐ BITE INHIBITION (page 260). I saw this clearly with my bitch's litter. After the puppies' little teeth had come in and they were increasingly occupied with one another, we quite often heard fairly piercing squeals every time one nipped another's ear or some other part too hard. Within a few days these cries of pain decreased markedly—the puppies quickly learned how hard they could grab hold of their brothers and sisters without causing them to quit playing. And if a play fight got too wild, their mother would intervene and settle their differences.

▷ **Improving physical fitness:** In the wild, wolf pups develop, through play, the level of physical fitness that will be required as they mature. They enjoy using features of the terrain for their "fitness program." They love scrambling up or through things, exploring anything that wobbles, and then playing with a sibling in "challenging terrain." The varied movements they make when playing improve their conditioning, develop their muscles, and strengthen their entire body without too much strain on any one area. This makes the young wolves fit for long hunting expeditions in later life.

Little dogs, too, train their bodies as they play. Whenever we put another new piece of play equipment in our puppies' run, we usually weren't even finished setting it up before three or four little rascals were eagerly exploring it and trying it out. In this way, they learn to control their bodies, train their motor functions, and have lots of fun!

Playing with Humans

Playing with humans is at least as important as playing with other members of their own species. Playing is fun. If a dog has fun with you, the experience strengthens the bond between you. Since you play the role of the "lead wolf," however, you also need to be dominant in deciding when, how long, and what to play. That underscores your superior status in the hierarchy. As she learns with other members of her species, a puppy also learns when playing with you that she is not allowed to bite you. Ideally, you should plan to play at length with your pet at least once a day—no matter how old she is. The main thing is for the dog to have fun.

◁

An hour of playing and cuddling for two who are fond of each other! Play strengthens the bond between the two-legged human and four-legged friend. In addition, when playing with her owner a dog learns the rules and learns to follow them.

6

Keeping Dogs Occupied —The Basics

Unlike dogs, wolves are constantly kept busy. They have to raise their young, be alert to potential dangers, procure food, and work together in a way that makes good strategic sense.

OUR FOUR-LEGGED FRIENDS don't have anything to worry about. For most dogs, however, a life free of care is not sufficient. Then an under challenged dog will find activities for himself in the house or yard or on "uneventful" walks—and we humans frequently are not enthusiastic about the choices. A dog needs mental exercise, as well as physical activity. Playing is important, but so are exercises that go beyond normal obedience training. Anyone who plays and engages in other activities with his or her dog will notice that the relationship in the human-and-dog team changes for the better.

Adding Variety to Species-Appropriate Play

6

Dogs have different preferences. Some like to fetch things, others would rather test their strength in a tug-of-war, and still others love rolling around on the floor or tussling with other members of their species.

Exciting Toys

The main point of playing with objects is to capture the "prey," the valuable prize—whether it entails a tug-of-war or retrieving something you've thrown. Balls at the end of a cord or durable tug-of-war ropes are suitable for such games. Depending on the overall motivation and the type of dog in question, you will need to be either more or less active yourself, to ensure that your pet has fun, but also to keep him from getting too wound up. Usually, merely holding the toy in front of your pet's nose is not sufficient. But if you "enliven" the object by dragging it back and forth on the ground in front of you, accompanied by a really exciting tone of voice or hissing sounds, you can motivate almost every dog with relative ease to try to "capture" it.

To accomplish that, however, you need a sure instinct. On the one hand, if the dog succeeds too quickly, the game won't be enjoyable enough. And on the other hand, if it takes too long, the dog will lose interest. This means that you have to learn to assess your pet accurately.

If your dog is really hard to motivate or doesn't have much endurance yet, you need to let him succeed more quickly than a dog that is totally involved in the game. If your pet enjoys games of tugging, and if his behavior is normal and playful at these times, then you can tug back and forth on the object for a while with your pet, once he has captured the prize. Most of the time, however, you should be the "winner," and occasionally your four-legged friend can get the prized object. If the dog immediately takes it off to a safe place, however, don't let it be the winner often—that would reinforce the undesirable behavior. But if your pet offers you the toy again right away, you can let him win more frequently. This also applies for very submissive or even somewhat insecure dogs.

If your dog is stronger than you, I advise against tug-of-war games. This is especially true for children!

If your pet prefers to fetch, then you can suddenly throw the toy after first moving it around on the ground for a minute. The dog can race after it and bring it back to you. Then the game can start over again. But keep this in mind as well: It's meant to be a game between the two of you. If your pet runs after the toy but leaves it where it is, runs off with it, or sinks its teeth into it and shakes it until "dead," you need to play something else.

Tussling and Romping

Quite often, dogs play together without using any kind of object. They tussle, nip each other, race each other, lie on the ground, or nibble at

◁

Which cone is the treat hidden under? The dog has to find that out. Games that provide mental exercise are popular with many dogs. Pet stores now offer a variety of games to develop your dog's intelligence. You can always think up some of your own, however.

each other. You can play with your pet in the same way. Important prerequisites here are a good, trusting relationship and a clear hierarchy, to ensure that your dog doesn't misunderstand anything or possibly feel threatened. Find out how your pet likes to play best. Using your hand, you can lightly "nip" at his neck or legs, let him catch your hand, cuddle him when he rolls playfully onto his back, or roll around on the floor together. Only rarely, however, should the dog be on top.

Follow the Rules of the Game!

In all these games, it's necessary for your four-legged friend to adhere to certain rules of play. For example, he must not tug on or clearly nip at your clothing or hands. He may carefully take and hold your hand, but no more. If your pet gets too rough, put him in his place immediately with a stern "No." If need be, grasp his muzzle with your hand. If the dog gets too wild and wound up in general, it's best to stop the game immediately. In the future, plan to make the game more peaceful. This applies especially to children!

▶ CHECKLIST

Games—For Whom?

Not all games are suitable for every dog:

○ **Games involving tugging** are appropriate for dogs that immediately offer the prize to you again or drop it as soon as you say "Out." The dog must not be stronger than the human, and he must not have a strong fighting instinct.

○ **Games of fetch** are good for dogs that enjoy bringing their toy back and relinquish it willingly—at least in exchange for another toy or treat.

○ **Games not involving an object** are fine only if a clear hierarchy exists and there is a good, trusting relationship between human and dog.

How to Keep Toys Interesting

If your dog thinks a certain toy is totally awesome, that has two big advantages. First, it makes you especially interesting to your pet, because he can enjoy this wonderful game and have fun with it only through you. Second, you can easily use such an interesting object to distract your pet's attention from other things—but only if you're his only means of obtaining this marvelous toy.

Think about this. How many toys does your dog have? Many dogs have entire baskets full of toys, with squeak toys, rubber chickens, balls, stuffed animals, and more all in a jumble. This toy collection is available at all times

to most dogs. The animal goes and takes something when he feels like it and possibly invites his owner to play too. And the toy is dropped and forgotten when the dog gets bored with it. Dogs are treated like children. Having too many toys available all the time gets boring over the long run.

The same thing is true when it comes to throwing sticks. They're available wherever you go on your walk. If the dog fails to bring the stick back, you can always throw another. If your pet loses interest, he simply leaves the stick wherever it is. In addition, sticks are dangerous for a dog. When the dog catches a stick, it can easily get jammed in his throat. Quite a few dogs have injured themselves or even died in this way.

By now you surely suspect what I'm getting at. If you're to be able to use a toy correctly, the dog must want it badly and must be eager to play a game with you that involves the toy. But that works only if the toy is not always available to your pet.

Normally, it's enough if the dog has one or two toys that he can occupy himself with alone. He may already have one that he likes especially well, one that's also suitable for use in a game with you: a tug-of-war rope, for example, a ball attached to a cord, or something similar. If not, then look for one that the two of you can play with. And then use only this toy when you play with your pet. He can play with the other toys when he's alone.

The Special Toy

▷ This special toy must not lie around within easy reach; instead, you should put it away every time. When you feel like playing with your four-legged friend, and provided he is not totally worn out or in a deep sleep at the moment, you can invite him to take part in a game together. Get the special toy out and play with it as described on page 187. If you first have to gain your pet's interest, make sure you're feeling energetic enough yourself.

▷ Stop playing while the dog is still playing wholeheartedly; that will keep the toy interesting. If you're still in the phase of getting your pet's interest, or if his attention span leaves a lot to be desired, you may want to cut the playtime quite short. If you play too long and your pet loses interest, then his thoughts go something like this: "My goodness, this is boring, when is he/she finally going to quit." And the next time: "Oh, here comes the boring part again."

But if you end the game at the right time, your pet (in human terms again) will think something like this: "What, over already? Too

1 *The right way to play: The Weimaraner watches his master expectantly. Is he about to pull a favorite toy out of his pocket and start a terrific game?*

2 *The toy is moved seductively back and forth on the ground, and the dog tries to catch it. All he's interested in now is playing with his owner.*

3 *After some time, and before the dog loses interest in the game, his master calls a halt and puts the toy away again. Since the toy is not always available, it doesn't lose its attraction.*

△

Play in such a way that the dog isn't over-taxed and neither you nor your pet can get hurt. Pay attention, for example, to the way you hold the toy.

Give the audible signal in a friendly, motivating tone of voice, however. Then, after some time, the dog will connect it with its play mood, and in almost every situation you'll be able to put it in this mood and invite it to play. You can also use it when you want to distract your pet from something else and aren't sure whether it will react reliably to "Here" or the whistle blow.

You can also connect the end of your game together with an audible signal, such as "Stop" or "End." Say these words, however, in an "emotionless" or muted tone of voice.

Making the Game Safe

When you play with your dog, make sure that:
▷ it doesn't hurt itself.
▷ you don't ask too much of it.
▷ the dog doesn't jump too much or too high; puppies shouldn't jump at all, and young dogs should jump only a little and not very high.
▷ the surface is suitable; a meadow or a grassy area is okay, but asphalt and concrete are too hard.

Requirements for the toy: It must be a special dog toy from a pet store, and the size must be right for your pet. A ball that's too small could get stuck in the dog's throat. The toy also shouldn't be too heavy.

Before you throw a training dummy (→ page 263) or something of the kind, look to see where it will land. Don't throw in the direction of walkers, cyclists, or others.

Whether the game involves tugging or fetching—don't overdo it in any way. You want the dog to have fun, not to cast all his inhibitions aside. Above all, your four-legged friend should give you the object without resisting, when he hears the audible signal "Out."

bad!" and the next time: "Super, that great game again at last! Let's get going!" In this way, playing together acquires a special significance and under some circumstances even becomes more important to the dog than playing with other members of its species.

Again, as a reminder: Once the fun is over, the toy should vanish again into your pocket or, if you're at home, into a cupboard.

Introducing the Audible Signal to Play

While you play with your dog, with or without using an object, it is in a play mood. You can link this positive attitude with an audible signal, such as "Play." Alternatively, of course, you also can name the object you and your pet play with: "Ball," for instance.

THE BEST DOG TOYS

An enormous number of toys, good ones and less sensible ones, are available today. Buy only toys specially made for dogs, because the material and design as a general rule will present no problems for our four-legged companions. Choose the correct size for your particular pet.

6

BALL ON A CORD

Description   Balls attached to a cord are available in various styles.

Comments   They are well suited for fetching and can be thrown a long distance even by less gifted dog owners. In addition, you can use them in little tug-of-war games.

RUBBER ANIMALS

Description   Rubber toys that squeak or make no sound at all.

Comments   They make good toys for the dog to play with alone. Or you can hide them and have your pet search for them. Watch out, since some dogs chew them up quickly, while others get too intense because of the squeaking. Throw away rubber animals that have been seriously gnawed, to keep your pet from eating the pieces.

TUG-OF-WAR ROPE, KONG ON A CORD

Description   Piece of plastic or rubber on a sturdy cord or rope.

Comments   Tug-of-war ropes (below in the photo) with or without a rubber part are wonderful for games involving tugging or also for throwing. The kong, too (above in the photo), is suitable for throwing, and it also will bounce erratically along the ground, which is really fun for the dog. For water enthusiasts: Some kongs will float as well.

TOYS FOR THE BRAIN

Description   For example, a ball with holes that can be filled.

Comments   For gifted dogs, there are special toys like the food ball. When the dog rolls it by pushing with his muzzle, the treats fall out. On the same principle, there are games made of wood, where the dog has to push a kind of drawer, among other things, to get at the tidbits.

STUFFED ANIMALS

Description   Washable figures made of soft fabric.

Comments   For some dogs, stuffed animals are a real highlight. They can be thrown or used in games of hide-and-seek. They usually stand up less well to games involving tugging. When you purchase one, make sure no small parts can come off.

Up-to-date: Clicker Training

For some years now, this method of training dogs has enjoyed widespread popularity. For the training, all you need is a clicker, a kind of small plastic box. The device, which works on the same principle as a toy frog clicker, contains a thin metal plate that makes a "click" sound when pressed. Clicker training originated in the U.S., where it is used in training a great many kinds of animals, including whales and dolphins. With these aquatic species the technique has proved invaluable, because no leashes or reins can be used as training aids. Immediate rewards involving petting or treats are also not feasible, for example, if the whale or dolphin has managed to perform a wonderful leap. The click stands in for the treat—as a reward from a distance, so to speak.

In the material below, I would like to give you a short introduction to this training process, as well as a few suggestions for using it yourself. If you want to read more on this subject, see the list on page 285.

How Clicker Training Works

Actually, it is "click and treat" training. This method relies exclusively on positive reinforcement. First, through classical operant conditioning (→ page 26), the dog learns to connect the clicker sound with food (PRIMARY REINFORCER, page 271). Thus, the initially neutral clicker noise becomes a SECONDARY REINFORCER (page 272). Theoretically you could also use another sound, such as your voice, by saying "Good"

Once the dog is conditioned to the clicker, lying on his back is only one of the lessons he can learn. The clicker is in plain view here only for the photograph.
▽

or "Nice." The clicker has certain advantages, however:

▷ It is an exclusive sound that the dog does not hear frequently; moreover, it always sounds the same. Your voice, on the other hand, usually is used too much anyway and without enough differentiation. A dog whistle would be less satisfactory in this context, because it often serves as a command to come or stop. It would only confuse the dog if you now start to use the whistle as a form of praise too. There is also no need for the sound to be really loud, because generally the dog is not as far away from his trainer as a dolphin would be, for instance (→ page 192).

▷ The clicker is so small that it can be taken along everywhere without any problem.

▷ The timing works especially well. That is, the clicker can be used with great precision, especially in situations where you can't give the dog a treat at the right moment (→ below).

With clicker training, the conditioned sound becomes the dog's only affirmation. Neither verbal praise nor petting is used in addition. The acknowledgement is made only once, and always at the end of an exercise. The dog himself must find out what he has to do to get this acknowledgement. He is never corrected; if misconduct occurs, there simply is no reward.

The individual steps: A desired behavior is molded systematically; this is known as "shaping." First, even the tiniest, accidental steps in the right direction are reinforced. With increasing progress in learning, the demands on the dog increase as well. Then only the more advanced steps are reinforced. Only when a dog has reliably mastered a behavior does the trainer add an audible or visual signal. Gradually, the animal is praised only when he responds to a signal (audible or visual) with the correct behavior. Then the praise is increasingly variable (→ page 83).

Basically, the procedures for clicker training and "normal" training are quite similar. There too, the simple forms of an exercise are rewarded at first: for example, "Sit" at the moment the dog actually sits. Then, increasingly, only the enhanced demands—such as a longer *sit*—are rewarded. And the treat, too, is provided only at the end of the exercise.

What Is the Clicker Used For?

The clicker has multiple uses. True fans of this method make it the basis for the entire training process. A great deal of patience is needed for this, however, because you can work on only one behavior at a time, as I've pointed out. In addition, generally the dog is not encouraged to take a certain position, as is the practice in normal training. Instead, the owner waits for the dog to exhibit a certain behavior, or early stages of it, by pure chance. You can, however, urge him to do so nonetheless.

Above all, in basic training there's no need, I believe, to work exclusively with the clicker, because the exercises are easy and you can practice several things in parallel (such as the *sit* and *heel*). The clicker, however, can be used for certain special exercises such as tricks or feats, or for exercises in which you aren't having any real success otherwise. An example is getting the dog to fetch. If your pet has no prey instinct and no interest in fetching, you frequently can use clicker training to positively motivate him to fetch nonetheless. In addition, training with a clicker can help all those who find it hard to communicate with their pet "in a natural way," that is, through body language and certain tones of voice. For clicker training, however, very exact timing is required; otherwise, you quickly will find yourself reinforcing the wrong thing.

Which Dogs Is This Method Best For?

If you want the clicker, together with the food for the dog, to become an extremely attractive reinforcer, then the treats you use must be very appealing indeed. In addition, your dog has to be hungry.

Problems can arise with very fussy or very noise-sensitive dogs. The clicker sound may produce anxiety reactions in such animals. Sometimes slow, gradual adjustment is helpful. Often dogs that were previously trained through avoidance techniques (→ page 26) or negative reinforcement (→ page 28) will respond poorly to clicker training. They have not learned that trying something independently leads to success, but that "mistakes" have negative consequences.

Making the Click = Food Connection

Get an adequate helping of tiny, tasty morsels ready. The dog must be able to swallow them quickly and without having to chew a lot. And I'll repeat—he has to be hungry. A good time for a training session, therefore, would be before mealtime. If your pet tends to be picky, normal chunks of food probably will not suffice. In advance, try to find out what your four-legged friend is especially fond of. Cooked turkey or chicken can work miracles.

△

Many different models of clickers are now available. Use one that makes a crisp, clear clicking sound.

Train in a quiet room and with no distraction of any kind.

Time to get started: Put the food within easy reach—on the kitchen counter, for example. Now take the clicker. Click it about 20 times in succession, immediately after each click (not before) taking a treat in your other hand and giving it to your pet. You also can hold several treats in your hand at once. To make the connection as clear as possible, no more than half a second should elapse between the click and the treat. After every click, the dog immediately gets a bite. Go through this procedure twice in one day, repeating it the following day if necessary. By then most dogs will have connected the click with the treat.

First Exercise

There is an exercise that will tell you quickly and unmistakably whether the dog has made the right connection between the click and the food. The exercise is not primarily intended to be a "test," but it lends itself well to this purpose.

▷ Equip yourself with a pointer, or use the handle of a flyswatter or the like as a substitute. Hold the tip of the pointer in front of the dog's nose. Your objective is for the dog, of his own accord, to touch the tip of the pointer with his nose.

▷ If your four-legged companion is not interested in the pointer, you can move it back and forth in front of the dog, but without touching the dog's nose. At some point your pet will start sniffing it. At the exact moment when the dog's nose touches the tip of the pointer, make a click. Then give your pet the treat.

▷ Now hold the pointer in front of the dog's face again. You'll probably see by your pet's face that the wheels in his brain are starting to turn: "Now what did I do to make that clicking noise?" Once his nose returns to the pointer—click, and then another treat follows.

▷ For the next three days, do this three to four times daily, for a few minutes at a time. By then, if not sooner, your pet will deliberately be poking at the pointer with his nose and collecting a treat from you after the click.

▷ Now you can hold the pointer some distance away from you, and later on even stick it in the ground or lay it in an open drawer in the room. Your dog will go to the pointer, nudge it—click, and he will come back to you to get his reward. Now you can be quite sure that your pet has understood what's going on.

▷ As the next step, you can introduce an audible signal such as "Touch" or "Nudge" for touching the pointer. Say it at the moment the dog touches the pointer. As time passes, reward the dog only when he touches the pointer on command, not when he does so voluntarily.

More Click Exercises

▷ **Turning the light on and off:** I used the exercise with the pointer (replacing "Touch" with a different audible signal) to teach my bitch, among other things, to turn a light switch on and off. To accomplish that, I put the tip of the pointer on a switch plate. She stood up on her hind legs and tapped it— click. With increasing certainty, I clicked only when she had really flipped the switch. Gradually I dispensed with the pointer. After she was operating the light switch reliably, I introduced the audible signal—in this case, "Light"—as described above. As the next level, I practiced with her on different light switches.

▷ **Closing the door:** Every dog can push open a door that's slightly ajar. But what if

△

With the clicker's help, this dog has learned to push the door closed with his nose. Once the "trick" has been mastered, you can add an audible signal, such as "Door."

you're sitting comfortably in the sofa in your warm living room and your dog comes in and leaves the door wide open—and you get cold? One option is to get up and shut the door. It's more practical, however, if the dog does that himself on command. In principle, this is just like the exercise with the light switch. You touch the pointer to the door, the dog nudges the pointer—click, treat. Over time, reinforce your pet only when he pushes so hard at the door that it is only slightly ajar or, later on, completely shut. Once the dog has grasped the exercise, introduce the audible sign "Door," and omit the pointer.

Learning to Fetch Properly

By ◐ FETCHING (page 264), we mean bringing or retrieving objects. This is also a meaningful way to keep your pet active. You can practically "kill three birds with one stone":

▷ The dog can engage in mental activity.

▷ He gets physical exercise.

▷ Simultaneously you reinforce his obedience.

Fetching, of course, entails far more than just running after a ball.

Encouraging a Puppy to Carry

If your puppy displays the right predisposition by taking pleasure in carrying things, it's a good idea to keep fostering this behavior. Praise him every time he carries something, and coax him to come to you. If the little creature tends to carry his "prey" to his bed or basket, you can sit down on the floor so that he has to pass you. Praise him lavishly as he comes toward you and again when he reaches you, and pet him as long as he holds the object in his little mouth. After some time, say "Out," for example, and gently take the object away, but give it back a few moments later. The puppy mustn't feel that he loses its "prey" as soon as he comes to you! Even if he's carrying something he really shouldn't have, praise him anyway and coax him to come. Then give him something else in exchange.

If the puppy comes to you but drops the object, stop praising him and end the exercise by picking up the object without comment.

If your pet doesn't like relinquishing his "prey," under no circumstances should you run after him. It will only learn over and over that he is the "winner." Depending on the way you assess your pet, you have four possible ways to react here:

▷ Ignore the dog when he tries to get you to run after him.

▷ Walk decisively in another direction, or ostentatiously give your full attention to something else.

▷ When he brings a toy to you or at least near you, offer the dog another favorite toy or a delicious tidbit in exchange.

Some puppies or young dogs will come if you make yourself look small by squatting down or even lying down on the floor. If your pet falls into this category, don't take the "prey" away from him right away. Put your arms around his chest and hold him still for a minute, lavishing him with affection as long as he has the object in his mouth. With a dog of this type, relinquishing the object also should be rewarded with praise and the occasional treat.

Helping is fun! If your dog enjoys fetching, you can teach him to pick up almost everything and put it in your hand.

▷

First Systematic Fetch

If there is an object, such as a training dummy (→ page 198), stuffed animal, or ball on a cord, that your four-legged friend enjoys bringing, then you should treat it the same way as an interesting toy (→ page 189). Keep it out of sight and use it for this specific purpose. Depending on how easy your pet is to distract, practice in your home, in the yard, or while out walking. Hold the puppy—or older dog, if he's a beginner—firmly and throw the fetch object. If your pet is a laid-back type, make this really exciting and use your tone of voice to motivate. Have him run after the object as soon as possible. Once the dog picks up the object, show that you're glad and run in the opposite direction. If he has reliably mastered the *come* command ("Here," for example, or the whistle blow), call him to *come* at the same time.

If your dog is full of pep, wait a few quiet moments before you let him set off. You can also start this way, however. Hold the fetch object in your hand and call the dog. When he comes, let him hold the object. Keep your pet close and praise him amply while he holds the object. After some time, quietly say "Out" or give some other audible signal, and take the object away. Only if the dog willingly stays with you and holds the dummy should you start to lay it out or throw it, and then tell the dog to fetch it.

Fetching with the Clicker

If your pet is not a passionate retriever by nature but is interested in objects, the clicker may prove helpful. First, condition the dog as outlined on page 194. Practice at home and without distractions at first. Place the fetch object on the ground. Your goal is to teach the dog to pick it up and hold it until you take it away by saying "Out."

Exact timing is especially important here, to really reinforce the holding and not the dropping, for instance. The procedure you choose depends on your pet:

▷ If he picks up the fetch object right away, click once the object is in his mouth. Now the dog drops the object and collects his reward. As time goes by, click a bit later each time, so that the dog gradually has to hold the object longer and longer before hearing the click. If he drops the object before the click, don't do anything. Wait until he picks it up again, and click at the right time: that is, while the object is still in the dog's mouth.

▷ If your pet is not especially interested in the motionless fetch object, for the time being you should acknowledge any kind of movement in the object's direction. Increase your demands slowly. For example, if the dog focuses in that direction after several attempts, don't click for that anymore; wait until your pet has moved a little farther toward it. If you think this is taking too long, make it more interesting by giving the object a little kick. Or use some other method to make it so interesting that your pet grabs it or at least nudges the object. Click as soon as the object is in the dog's mouth. With a good bond and a little natural inclination, your pet may pick up the fetch object right away and bring it back to you. If you click at the right time—when the dog is near you and before it has dropped the object—you can reinforce the *hold* and possibly also the *come* at the same time.

If the dog has learned to hold the object in his mouth in front of you for a longer time, you can introduce an audible signal, such as "Bring" or "Fetch." If the dog has made the connection, run away from him while he's still holding the object, and call him. Click when he reaches you. Gradually lengthen the time between the *come* and the click. If your pet has understood everything after a suitable amount of training, omit the clicker, and the dog should put the fetch object in your hand when you give the audible signal "Out." Before the "Out," however, you can praise your pet for the *hold* by saying "Bravo" or "Good dog."

The ideal end result: The dog sits next to you, and you walk several yards or more away to lay out the fetch object. Go back to the dog and send him off by saying "Fetch" or "Bring." The dog runs off, brings it, and sits or stands in front of you, holding it until you say "Out" to indicate that it's time to put the object in your hand.

You can also use this exercise to teach your pet to pick up all kinds of objects on command and bring them to you. That can definitely come in handy around the house.

Fetch with the Food Pouch

If your four-legged friend is reluctant to give up the "prey," or if "normal" fetch objects are less interesting for him, you can try using a food pouch. Special pouches or holders are now available in pet stores, but sturdy pencil cases or pouches from a store that sells school supplies are a good alternative. The point of all this is that the dog must learn that he is fed from the pouch if he brings it and, if at all possible, places it in your hand. To do that, the dog has to be hungry, of course.

Let your pet watch as you fill the pouch with delicious treats. Then proceed exactly as outlined in "First Systematic Fetch" (→ page 196). All of the exercises described after that section could also be done with a food pouch.

Combining Fetching with Obedience

If your pet has learned the fundamentals and enjoys fetching, you now can combine this activity with obedience exercises. This is important, since you don't want the dog running uninhibitedly after everything that moves. If possible, always use the same objects for the fetch training. Highly suitable are special ⦿ TRAINING DUMMIES (page 263). These are oblong objects, not too heavy, and available from pet stores. They are sold in various colors, and dummies that will float are also available for water-loving dogs.

The extent to which you incorporate obedience exercises as part of fetch training depends on the dog. You need to avoid boring a dog that is not totally crazy about fetching, or else his motivation will decrease even further. From time to time, also let such a pet immediately race after a dummy that is thrown in an enticing way—that is, accompanied by an inviting tone of voice and plenty of "action." Dogs that adore fetching, on the other hand, should sit longer before they're allowed to start, to keep them from getting caught up in the activity.

Delayed Start

This is also a drill for a dog's brain! Tell your dog to *sit/stay*, and place or throw the dummy some distance away. Go back to the dog. Alternatively, you can take the dog with you to place or throw the dummy, and then go with him a few yards away from the dummy. Now wait a few seconds before you send the dog to fetch. During this time, he has to remember where you put the dummy. You can turn this up a notch. After putting the dummy in place, do a few more exercises with your pet—such as the *heel*, *down*, and *stay*. Then return to your original starting point and send the dog with the audible signal "Fetch." The more time there is between the dummy placement and the order to fetch, the harder it will be for him.

You can take this to yet another level by giving the fetch order at a place other than your original starting point. At first, there should be less time between placement and fetch order, but then you can gradually lengthen the interval.

▷ **Variation for Very Advanced Dogs:** Lay two or more training dummies in place. Then your four-legged companion has to note and remember several sites. The first time, lay them at wide angles of at least 90°, and somewhat closer to you than normal. Before you send the dog, make sure he is sitting next to you, facing in the exact direction of the dummy you want him to fetch. It's best to offer some support in the form of a hand sign indicating the right direction. For more on this topic, see "Sending the Dog in Front" on page 200.

Fetching in Different Types of Terrain

You have several possibilities for variation when you combine fetch training with obedience drills. At first, the dog should find his fetch object quickly. For this training, a field that has been mowed fairly close to the ground is best. You will make it even easier for the dog if you also lay or throw the object in a prominent spot—right in front of the only bush, for example.

With increasing skill, or if you notice that your dog enjoys using his nose to hunt for the dummy, you can lay or throw it in higher grass or stubble—depending on your pet's level of training. Then he has to look a little harder in the area where the training dummy is—even if he could see ahead of time where you placed the dummy.

You can also add variety to the exercise by having the dog master a "terrain change" on the way to the dummy. For example, ask him to cross a track between fields or to make his

△

A helper initially throws the dummy with an easily visible trajectory, into a field or into a path. The dog stays sitting at heel until you give it "clearance for takeoff."

way across a narrow stream or even a wider one, from a mown field into higher grass, from a wooded area into a meadow or vice versa. You need to match the level of difficulty to your dog's abilities, however. He should always be successful.

When you start training in more challenging terrain, you should reduce the distances again at first.

For Variety: You Fetch

This type of exercise will do a lot for your physical fitness as well!

▷ Dogs that enjoy retrieving often find it hard to sit still and not take off right away when something flies through the air. You can take advantage of this and teach your pet that not every dummy in the air or on the ground is intended for him. Structure the exercise exactly as if you were going to send the dog (→ below). But instead of being allowed to go and retrieve, he has to sit still while you "fetch."

▷ This exercise is also exciting: You stand across from the sitting dog at a distance of several feet. Now throw the dummy a little to one side, wait a moment, and then get it yourself. You can also throw two or more fetch objects, but at the beginning always in such a way that you can reach the dummy faster than your pet, should he make a "false start."

▷ At the highest level of this exercise, you throw the dummies relatively near the dog or even behind him, and then call him to come to you, ignoring the dummies. Then gather up the dummies yourself.

▷ With a water-loving dog that adores retrieving, you can do exercises of this kind next to a body of water as well. Fasten a long cord to a dummy that will float. Tie the cord, for example, to a tree on the shore. Then you can toss the dummy in the water and let it float there while the dog has to do a few exercises. Then pull the dummy out of the water. Sometimes you can also let the dog retrieve the dummy—but in this case, don't fasten the cord to anything, because your pet could get tangled in it.

Sending the Dog in Front

For this exercise, you first need to choose a field or meadow that has been mowed. At the beginning, use only a dummy in the training, so that the dog can succeed quickly. Lay the dummy in place as described on page 199. Next, stand next to the dog again and, always using the same arm and holding it roughly parallel to your pet's head, point in the direction of the fetch object. Wait until the dog is concentrating on looking in the right direction. Now give the signal "In front"—with more sedate dogs, using a markedly enticing tone of voice and waving your arm out in front or leaning forward; with livelier dogs, using less motivation and movement. Your four-legged friend runs off and brings back his dummy.

After some period of training, if the dog has grasped the principle, you can try the exercise with two dummies. At first, put them far apart again, ideally at a 180° angle.

If your pet isn't passionate about retrieving, you can also use food bowls instead of the dummy for this exercise and the one that follows. Then your four-legged friend can eat his reward and then come back to you, or learn to sit there after he has finished eating.

Sending the Dog to One Side

You can also teach the dog to run to the left and right. Tell your dog to *sit/stay*. Place a dummy about 6 feet away, to the dog's right. Now, you should stand a few yards from your pet, raise your right arm, and give one blow on the whistle (→ page 137). Now the dog, as he has learned to do, will give you his attention.

Next, stretch your arm out to the right and give the audible signal "Right" or "Over"—and the dog takes off. As soon as he has picked up the dummy, recall him. Once things are working on the right side, practice the same thing on the left.

Once you've practiced both sides separately for a time, you can combine the two, provided your dog can be sent to the right or left without hesitating. Tell your dog to *sit* and *stay*, and then place a dummy on both the right and left sides. Now send the dog to one side, specifically to the side where you first placed an object. Mostly, dogs tend to go to the side where something was placed last, but he must learn to go where you send him.

If this works when the dummies are at shorter distances, you can increase the distance first, and then you can also decrease your own distance from your pet, step by step.

6

He Who Seeks Finds

The dog, with his well-developed olfactory sense, greatly enjoys activities in which he can use his nose in a purposeful way. Retrieving, therefore, can also be combined with seeking.

You can practice in your home or yard at first. Tell your pet to sit on the patio indoors. Next, hide one or two favorite objects, but they mustn't be too heavy. It's all right if your pet watches. Then go back to the dog, say "Seek" to encourage him, and go with him to one of the places where something is hidden. If he finds the object, show how happy you are and run back to the starting position with your dog now carrying his fetch object. Once there, take the object away from your pet. If anything else is hidden, go through these steps once more. You'll see that after the first few times there's no need to go with the dog; "Seek" will be sufficient. Once he finds and brings the object, reward him with a treat.

Once your four-legged friend has come this far, don't let him watch anymore when you hide an object. The number of things you hide depends on the dog. A persistent dog can seek more often than one that is harder to motivate.

If your pet is fully attentive, you can practice seeking outdoors—for example, in a spot with a few trees or in a grassy area with relatively low bushes. At first, let the dog watch from the edge of the area while you hide the objects. Place them so that your pet doesn't have to seek too long before he finds something. Then continue the steps of the exercise as described above.

Keep an eye on your four-legged companion. If he seeks in an experienced way and shows eagerness, then you can hide the objects in more difficult spots—for example, right behind a tree or in some undergrowth. Depending on his staying power, you can increase the number of hidden objects—but don't ask too much of your pet.

1 *Sending out in front: With your hand, indicate the direction you want the dog to take. Don't send him until he has focused on that area for a few seconds.*
2 *If you want to send the dog to one side, use your arm to clearly indicate whether he should go to the right or the left. Keep your arm outstretched while the dog is underway.*

Popular: Obedience and Agility

Nowadays, there are a relatively large number of widely varied, meaningful kinds of sports for dogs. I would like to briefly introduce two of the most popular types to you: obedience trials and dog agility. They now are offered in quite a few clubs and dog schools. Both types of sports are frequently part of the gala program at the big dog shows sponsored by the AKC. Another well-known sport is ◐ FLY-BALL (page 264).

Obedience and agility both originated in England, and for some years now they have been increasing in popularity in this country as well. Both can be pursued as recreation or as competitive activities. To participate in competitive events, a dog is required to pass a Companion Dog Test. If you're interested, you can contact appropriate clubs or dog schools. Make sure the trainers have plenty of experience with these sports—ideally, a trainer's certificate—and also participate with some degree of success in competitions with their own dog.

Obedience

The dog sport known as Obedience includes far more than the "normal" exercises like walking at *heel*, the *sit*, or the *stay*. It also applies to exercises such as retrieving a metal object, sending the dog in front, picking out a certain object from many others, commands like *sit*, *down*, or *stand* at a distance, and much more. The point of the exercises is perfect execution, as well as harmony between dog and handler and elegance of movement. Obedience has nothing to do with military-style drill and bellowed commands. On the contrary, great value is placed on seeing that the dog takes pleasure in cooperating and forms a team with his two-legged partner. Unlike most

One category of obedience trials is retrieval of a metal object. Many dogs find it unpleasant to carry metal, so this is a rather demanding exercise. It is required only once a dog reaches the second level of competition.

The weave poles are one of the most difficult obstacles in the agility course. The obstacle consists of several poles placed relatively close together. Since this places great stress on the dog's spine, don't train your dog specifically for this until he is fully grown.

Look out, here comes a ball! In flyball, the dog uses his paws to trigger a mechanism that launches a ball from a box. The dog has to catch the ball and quickly bring it to his owner—this is enormous fun.

traditional ◐ WORKING DOG TESTS (page 277), Obedience has no fixed procedures. Right before the trial, the judge determines how the team should execute the particular tasks. There are rules governing what is tested and how the exercises should look, but the sequence is open. This lends added interest to the event, because dog and human can't get a fixed routine down pat: they have to stay flexible.

There are four performance categories: First comes the Novice Class A & B, followed by Companion Dog, Companion Dog Excellent, and Utility Dog. In each class, a number of subject areas are tested. In addition to the exercises listed above, the judges score other things as well, such as a dog's behavior with other members of his species and the way the handler deals with his or her dog.

Obedience basically is appropriate for all dogs, whether large or small, purebred or mixed breed. Dogs that are very eager to work and biddable are especially well suited. Since no jumping is involved and time is not a factor, Obedience is also appropriate for older dogs or dogs that are not in the best of health.

Agility

In this sport, the emphasis is not only on obedience, but also on the dog's ability to move quickly and nimbly and negotiate obstacles. An agility course consists of 12 to 20 different obstacles, which are laid out in a different sequence each time. Thus, the dog and his handler have no opportunity to practice a certain pattern ahead of time.

What you need to know:
▷ The handler and the dog go through the course together. Using voice and hand signals, the handler directs the dog through the course and runs along next to the obstacles.
▷ The dog wears neither a collar nor a leash. This requires close cooperation and clear body language on the handler's part.

▷ The course has to be completed not only in a certain order, but also within a limited time. Moreover, the obstacles must be correctly negotiated.
▷ With some obstacles, such as the dog walk, A-frame, or seesaw, there are so-called contact zones (zones painted a bright color at the beginning and end of the obstacles), onto which the dog must place at least one paw while ascending and descending.
▷ There are also jumps, including the tire jump, broad jump, and panel jump. Other obstacles include the weave poles, a type of slalom (→ photo, page 202), a table, and tunnels made of vinyl and cloth. There are also different classes that can be played on the agility field. For example, depending on the dog's height at the shoulders, agility can be played in mini, midi, or standard classes. In each of these classes, there are three levels of difficulty: A1, A2, and A3. Faults can include the following: missed contact zone, knocked or dropped bar, missing an obstacle, and refusal to attempt an obstacle.

Agility, too, is basically suitable for all dogs. For competitive events, however, the animal should not be too large and bulky. In addition, because of the hurdles and rapid movements, he must not be overweight or have skeletal problems. For these reasons, a thorough examination by the veterinarian is recommended before participation in agility. A dog also needs to be full-grown—that is, at least one year old—before starting agility.

If you want to participate in agility on a purely recreational basis, you can adapt the requirements to your pet and eliminate the hurdles, for example. Most dogs thoroughly enjoy agility. Many run through the course so quickly that your eyes can barely keep up with them.

Skilled Trackers

As I've frequently mentioned, dogs have strong olfactory capabilities. You'll notice this again and again on your walks with your pet when he reads the latest "news" from the ground with rapt attention.

You can use this inclination as a meaningful activity and have your dog work a ○ TRACK (page 275) laid in advance. For one thing, he can act on his natural inclination in a purposeful way. For another, concentrated tracking is tiring, and it will keep your pet occupied appropriately. Since tracking is done predominantly on leash, it is also a good type of activity for dogs that can't always run free, whatever the reasons. In the section below, I would like to suggest ways to do tracking for "domestic use." If you want your dog to track and search as a competitive sport, you need to contact a working-dog club.

Good to Know

When you start with an older dog, it must reliably obey all the basic commands. You can train your pet while he is still a puppy, but the track must be no more than a few yards long at first. You need these items of equipment: a roughly 30-foot-long leash for tracking and a wide collar or harness for the dog. In addition, you need a food bowl with something in it, as well as a respectable portion of treats to lie along the track. Put the bowl at the end of the track. If you want the dog to search eagerly, he has to be hungry.

The scent on a track is created primarily when the ground surface is disturbed. Plant parts are crushed, and bacteria begin their work there. The atmospheric conditions are quite important—there must be very little or no rain, and it can't be too hot or too cold. In addition, it must be a windless day so that the scent is not dissipated. Fall and spring are good times of year. In summer, training early in the morning is best. It's not a good idea to start training in winter, because little scent is created in cold weather.

To start, look for a field that has been mowed and is largely free of other traces and scents. Lay the first tracks in a straight line, but later on you can incorporate corners and terrain changes. At first, lay plenty of treats such as sausage or pieces of cooked meat on

○ TIP

The Efficient Canine Nose

A dog's olfactory mucous membrane has a heavily wrinkled wall. Spread out flat, it is roughly thirty times the size of the human equivalent. Olfactory sensitivity, however, is dependent on the dog's breed and anatomy. A pug, with its short skull, has a poorer sense of smell than a bloodhound, for example.

the track. They should be small enough for the dog to swallow without chewing, to keep from having to interrupt the search.

If your dog is a novice, wait only a few minutes after laying the track to let him begin the search. As his skill increases, increase the "age" of the track (the time that elapses between laying and seeking) to several hours or even overnight. Gradually discontinue the treats, and lengthen the track to 300 or 600 feet or more, depending on your pet's ability.

Calmly, and with your pet on a short leash, show him the beginning of the track. If he follows the scent attentively, praise him and lengthen the leash a bit.

How to Lay a Track

Put your dog in the *down* position in the mowed field, possibly where he can watch you lay the track. I say "possibly" deliberately, because some dogs are smart cookies and don't follow the scent but head straight for the place where you put the food bowl.

Now pick a starting place, and wipe your feet on the spot a few times. Put a little stake in the ground to mark the beginning of the track, and lay several treats next to it. Now, walk out with relatively small, firm steps so that you leave an impression on the ground surface. As you go, put a treat down on the track about every four inches. At the same time, mark the line of the track with several stakes, putting them in the ground at one side of the track. At the beginning, about 60 feet is long enough. At the end, set the food bowl down or lay a few treats on a raised area. Next, take a big step away from the track and go back to the dog, moving in a wide arc. Wait a few minutes to let the scent develop. Finally, put your dog in *heel* position and return to the starting point. Call your pet's attention to the scent by squatting down and pointing to the starting point, speaking in an inviting tone of voice.

If the dog starts to search and eat, praise him and say "Seek" or "Track," for example. Once he has the scent in his nose, give him a little more leash, but not too much. If he loses the scent, shorten the leash and show him the line of the track, once more making your voice enticing.

Repeatedly praise the dog while he works the track, that is, follows the track, using your voice and repeating the command "Seek." Once he reaches the end, let him empty the bowl. Finally, lead him away from the track.

Variation for Dogs That Like to Fetch

If your canine companion obeys really reliably, and if you've already taught him to fetch, you can also place his favorite fetch object at the end of the track. When laying the track, you can drag the object behind you on a rope. In advance, rub it with a piece of meat.

At first, teach your pet this variation on leash. As soon as you reach the end of the track, run with your dog—now carrying his fetch object—back to the starting point. If the leashed dog doesn't lose the scent and seeks in a concentrated way, you can show him the starting point as described above and then let him work off leash. At the end of the track, he must pick up the object and bring it back to you. Practice this only in open terrain where there is no wild game, however, and don't make the tracks too long.

Research & Practice

Dogs: The Quintessential Good Noses

Since we humans are no matches for dogs when it comes to the sense of smell, we can take advantage of this ability in our canine friends to train them for various tasks.

▷ **Avalanche search dogs:** Despite all of our modern technology, they are unexcelled when it comes to finding people who have been buried in or under snow after an avalanche. Since avalanche search dogs work in the mountains and in deep snow, this is a very demanding and dangerous job, not only for the dog.

▷ **Search and rescue dogs:** They also perform valuable services in finding missing persons. They are used to search large areas, for example, if someone is missing in a wooded area. After catastrophes like earthquakes, gas explosions, and the like, they search through the rubble, looking for missing persons in collapsed buildings and under other debris. This is quite exhausting for dogs, because they often work here in unaccustomed climatic conditions and have to move carefully and deliberately through the rubble.

▷ **Corpse-sniffing dogs:** They are employed when the search for victims includes dead bodies. These dogs can also tell if a corpse has been transported in the trunk of a car, and—after additional training—can detect gases rising from corpses under water, thus, making the work of the police easier.

▷ **Searching for diseases:** Dogs that are very sensitive and live in very close contact with their caretaker can, in some instances, detect a drop in the blood sugar of a diabetic owner or recognize an approaching seizure in an epileptic owner. Great attention was aroused by a study in the United States, in which three

Labradors and two Portuguese Water Dogs, after special training, could tell whether someone had a tumor. The dogs obviously smell certain scents exuded by tumors. The dogs were told to sniff breath samples of healthy

◁ *A search and rescue dog looking through rubble. Here dogs can put their keen sense of smell to good use. In spite of dust, heat, and odors, a dog can smell human scents even when buried under debris and will indicate the spot by barking.*

and diseased test subjects. With lung cancer and breast cancer, their success rate was 99% and 88%, respectively.

▷ **Bark-beetle search dogs:** Recently two dogs in Germany were trained to search for bark-beetle infestation. They search through spruce forests and detect the infestation even before the trees exhibit any external damage caused by the beetles.

▷ **Additional applications:** In addition, dogs are used to search for drugs, explosives, and weapons. They can find truffles under the soil or leaks in pipelines. Now there are two dogs in England that can sniff out DVDs and were trained to search for pirated copies.

10 Questions About Play and Activity

Can I teach Chico to rub his eyes with one paw when I say "Tired?"
You can condition Chico by using the clicker (→ page 192). Stick a small piece of Scotch tape on one of his eyebrows. He'll try to get rid of the pesky thing by moving a paw across his eyes. Click at that moment, and then give him a treat. But click only once, even if he keeps wiping his eye because the tape is still there. If he does this reliably after a few days without the strip of tape, you can introduce the audible signal.

My Tinca works a track fairly quickly. How can I get her to slow down?
Give her a chance to let off some steam beforehand. She may slow down once she has used up a little of her energy. Or lay down more treats, and then she'll have to work slower to keep from missing any. Maybe the track is too easy for Tinca, and she needs something more demanding. Do your track lying on more difficult ground, or incorporate more corners.

My dog isn't interested in toys. What's the explanation for this?
Usually this means that the human is using the toy too passively. Get some real action going (→ page 187). Depending on the dog, you may need to get really involved. Not everyone finds that easy to do. Your canine companion may also be too "saturated," for example, because the children have been romping with him all afternoon. Or is something distracting him when you want to play? If none of these suggestions solve the problem, then your dog probably does have a low play drive.

Is it true that fetching encourages a dog's hunting instinct?
If you throw everything possible—balls, sticks, and the like—to a dog, indiscriminately and in excessive amounts, and reward him when he bites the "prey" or tears it to pieces, then the hunting instinct may have gotten out of control. But if you use only a certain fetch object (which must be retrieved unharmed!) when working with your pet, it is apt to become "standardized." Some ball-crazy dogs become oblivious to everything else at the sight of their ball. Combining fetching with obedience exercises also has a positive effect.

When your dog comes out of the water with the training dummy, run away from him. He will try to reestablish contact with you and will run after you without even stopping to shake off the water.

When Enny brings me her dummy, she's so high-spirited that she first runs right past me. What can I do about this?
Stand in front of a wall or a hedge, and then there's no way Enny can run past you. Coax her to come to you. Or turn around just before Enny reaches you and say "Heel." If she has a good level of obedience, she will assume the heel position. Then let her put the dummy in your hand.

6

△

Little tricks let your dog shine! An assistant and a treat help your pet jump through a hoop formed by your arms.

Puppies really shouldn't get too much exercise. Isn't playing harmful too?

Puppies and young dogs shouldn't take excessively long walks, since walking or running for an extended period can cause repetitive stress at this age. But when the puppy plays with you or other canines of similar age and body build, it moves in many different ways. At times it hops, at other times it races around, and then it rolls on the ground, and so forth. These highly diverse procedures do not produce repetitive stress.

My Nando loves searching for his toy balls. What do I need to keep in mind if I hide them from him on our walks?

At first, don't choose terrain that is too difficult, and let him watch you hide them for the time being. Be sure to avoid areas that may contain wild game. A long search is real work for a dog, and your pet may well get thirsty. When you're done, provide him with water, and don't train in hot weather.

How can I provide our active dog with some variety at home?

Go through the garage or basement to look for "obstacles." A large cardboard box, for example, is wonderful for crawling through. You can make a hurdle by putting a broom-

stick across two chairs and hanging an old towel on it. You can also make a slalom course yourself. Stick a few tomato stakes in the ground at proper intervals (in the living room, bottles will work), and use treats to get your dog to weave through the poles. Keep your pet's size in mind when setting up the course, however.

Our puppy regularly gets an urge to run around and play every evening. Should we play with him then?

No, because he would learn that such actions get your attention. Simply ignore him. If he's making too much commotion for that to work, then give him a time-out in his crate, or tie him to the table leg with his leash and then ignore him. You also can take the initiative and invite him to play before he gets in such high spirits.

◁

Don't always give in to your puppy's regular invitations to play. Instead, you issue the invitation.

Our dog loves the water. Can we teach her to retrieve something from the water?

To do so, she must have learned to fetch on dry land first. Take her to the bank and throw a dummy that floats into standing water with a little slope at the edge. Have the dog wait briefly, and then send her. As soon as she has the dummy in her mouth, run in the opposite direction and call her. The correct response is to bring you the dummy immediately, without first stopping to shake off the water.

Solving Problems, Mastering Specific Situations

▶ By now you're surely aware that a dog is not a pet that just "goes along with" your daily routine. You have to methodically devote attention to your canine companion and train her systematically, to make the human-dog relationship harmonious and prevent unpleasant incidents. Now and again, however, situations occur that can negatively influence your life together. To solve problems, big and little, it's important to know as much as possible about their cause. Then many problems can be corrected without a great deal of trouble.

7

All You Need to Know About Living Together

Dogs are well known for their adaptability. In most "human-and-dog packs," therefore, life together usually is smooth and free of friction.

BUT ON THE WAY from puppyhood to canine "adulthood," you may well have to overcome some difficulties. Similarly, if the owner and the dog are an ill-suited match, daily life may be more or less negatively affected. Various factors can cloud the relationship: treating the dog like a human; a breed that doesn't fit the owner's lifestyle; or simply two very different human and canine personalities. Acquiring more than one dog in a moment of rashness or adopting someone else's dog can have the same effect.

The Wrong Dog

If the owner and the dog are not a good fit, minor or major difficulties usually crop up.

Two Different Personalities

If the personalities of the two-legged and four-legged partners are too different, the arrangement will not be especially successful. For example, if the owner finds it difficult to be dominant and radiate authority, and if he or she tends to be a softer, less assertive person, it will be very hard to handle a strong-willed, self-confident canine companion. In addition, it is not helpful if the owner is small and slight in stature and the dog is bursting with strength.

Conversely, a soft, sensitive dog also can be disconcerted and intimidated if her owner behaves too authoritatively and forcefully. Keep this in mind when selecting a breed and a particular puppy.

Choose the Breed Thoughtfully

There are still people who think that dog breeds differ only in terms of appearance. That's way off the mark. There are pronounced differences, especially in the essential features of their temperament. Even though, for example, a Golden Retriever may look like a Hovawart, they are fundamentally different breeds. The Golden Retriever has been bred, obviously, as a retriever. Any kind of fighting instinct is undesirable in this breed; friendliness is a much-prized quality. In contrast, the Hovawart is a protection and guard dog, meant to protect its owner and to be quite reserved toward strangers.

Not infrequently, however, people are dazzled by the appearance of a puppy. Little herding dogs, for instance, look exceptionally cuddly and resemble stuffed animals. But they grow up to be large, powerful dogs, which were bred to independently and firmly defend all their owner's possessions in isolated regions and to be wary of strangers. They retain these essential characteristics in our homes as well.

Or let's take a trendy dog like the Jack Russell Terrier, for example. It looks cute and perky, and its size is practical—well suited for an apartment. But these terriers are usually strong-willed, feisty, and fearless hunting dogs bred for work in vermin hunting holes, and they place high demands on their owner's persistence and determination.

Never buy a dog without thinking it over very carefully!

A Dog to Keep You Healthy?

Dogs have a good influence on their owners' health, and they can make social contacts easier for older people in particular—but only if owner and dog are well matched. If they don't get along well, the positive effects quickly turn into negative ones.

◁
Let's get out of here! Not a rare scene—a dog owner calls her dog, and she turns around again but doesn't really take her seriously. In the end she does as she wishes, and thinks, "The human will come with me anyway."

Puberty and Adolescent Phases

Depending on the breed, it may take two years or more for a dog to reach her full growth and fully develop her character. Smaller breeds usually reach adulthood faster than larger ones. Sexual maturity, however, is reached by most dogs between the ages of six months and one year. You can recognize this stage by your pet's increasing tendency to "read" the scent messages left by other members of its

 INFO

Growing Up

Today we suspect that puberty also entails "structural alterations" in the brain. The young dog reacts more strongly to stimuli and has to learn to control herself.
Pay attention to your adolescent dog's body language, and deliberately reward her for calm, relaxed behavior—even in the face of distractions. Once she is fully-grown, at the age of approximately two years, you'll see a certain "maturity" and poise in your pet.

species. Bitches go into heat for the first time in this phase, and males start lifting their leg and marking. After puppyhood, however, it takes a few months to get to that point, and in the interim all kinds of things are happening.

Many dog owners are really enthusiastic about their puppy because she's "already behaving so well." It would be more accurate to say "still behaving so well." As you know by now, a puppy instinctively tries to keep in contact as closely as possible. Her "pack" is still the most important thing at this stage. As she grows older, she becomes more autonomous, however, and is no longer dependent on the pack's protection to the same extent as when she was a more or less helpless puppy.

Thus, many owners of a four-legged youngster realize toward the end of puppyhood that their dog seems to have forgotten some things that she once knew perfectly well, and that what you say seems to go in one ear and out the other. Your young dog may even try to question the rules that apply to your life together and test you, to see whether she can get away with sleeping on the sofa or being fed at the dinner table. Particularly during puberty, in the second six months of life, such awkward adolescent phases are common. In addition, you may notice an excess of testosterone (→ hypersexuality, page 266) in males at this time.

Avoid Undesirable Successes

If your four-legged companion is in such a phase, you need to stick to your guns. These "little problems" unfortunately will not go away on their own just because the dogs get older. That would be very practical, of course. Thus, you need to look ahead and plan how to deal with your pet.

▷ Don't ask too much of your dog, but insist that she continue to correctly execute the exercises it had already learned well.

▷ Don't give a command until you're sure that the dog will obey it, or until you can enforce it if necessary. If you know, for example, that your pet always tunes out when she sees another dog, leash her promptly and do a few exercises on leash, or play exuberantly with her. If it's already too late for that and your dog has already headed off, walk away quickly, but without wasting your time on the special recall signal.

▷ Continue to insist that the dog observe rules governing what she should and should not do in your daily life together. Don't ever give in! If your pet sees that she can just as easily ignore you or your signals, she won't take you seriously anymore. Even after puberty, that will have a detrimental effect on your relationship and on the dog's obedience.

Training pays off: There are some dogs that develop in a completely "unobtrusive" way. This means that whether adolescence and puberty are noticeable and to what extent doesn't depend exclusively on the dog—even though the dog's personality plays a partial role. In strong-willed or more autonomous animals, you'll notice more signs than in very compliant dogs that readily accept a subordinate role.

To a great extent, however, problems of this kind depend on the previous training. If the puppy learned that her human didn't always mean everything so seriously and that she could certainly carry out her own ideas, then the adolescent phases will be more obvious than if the little dog had been systematically trained. Remember—what puppies learn makes a lasting impression, and what they experience has a lifelong effect.

Patience with "Overly Sensitive" Dogs

Quite apart from their training, many dogs now enter a phase in which they react somewhat sensitively to external stimuli for a time. They may be mistrustful of optical stimuli such as statues or fluttering ribbons, or even of individual persons—just as small children are temporarily afraid of strangers—and bark loudly at them. Dogs that basically tend to be cautious or insecure usually exhibit such behavior at this stage to a greater extent than dogs that rarely lose their cool. Good socialization during puppyhood has a positive effect here as well, since the dog will already have seen on a frequent basis that she can successfully cope with unfamiliar situations (→ page 74).

△

In puberty, obedience problems are increasingly common. Don't let up on the training process. In addition, interest in the opposite sex also increases, especially among males. This male is sniffing at a bitch with intense interest.

Treat such a young dog as if she were a puppy. If she's mistrustful, encourage her to explore the scary object together with you. Depending on the situation, you can arrange to see this object more often in the near future.

In dealings with humans, this touchiness often takes the form of eyeing individual passersby suspiciously or barking loudly at them. Distract your pet promptly with a toy or a treat, and calmly walk past the people.

More Than One Dog—Less Work?

Some dog lovers aren't satisfied for long with just one dog—soon a second four-legged friend, perhaps even more, joins the household. There are many different reasons for this. One often-mentioned reason is that the first dog will have a playmate. Now, as you already know, a dog—unlike a parakeet or a guinea pig—does not necessarily need another member of her species as a companion. You, the dog's owner, are her most important social partner. But it's undoubtedly lots of fun to have two dogs and to watch them interact. You can almost do without the TV!

But owning more than one dog also means more work. If several canines live together, they form a real little pack. Therefore, in many situations—when they meet strange dogs or detect the presence of wild game, for example—they often behave differently from a single dog. If their bond and training aren't all they should be, they tend to focus on each other rather than on their human partner. Moreover, a young dog learns a great deal from an older dog: negative as well as positive things. But if you have a "pack" that is not under control, an outing can quickly become highly stressful.

 TIP

More Than One Dog— Which Signals?

You can use the same signals for all the dogs. So that they know which one you're addressing, always state the dog's name before the signal—for example, say "Timmy, down." Practice at first with each dog separately. After some time, include the second dog, and then any others.

Consider This in Advance

Before you acquire a second dog, you need to think about a few basic things. This is quite important.

▷ **Will two or more dogs fit into your life?** More dogs need more room, both in your household and in your car. You not only need twice as much food, but you also have to dispose of twice as many droppings. A single dog generally is easy to take along, whether you're going out to town, on vacation, or to visit friends. With several dogs, however, things start to look different, especially if the breeds in question are large. Finding vacation accommodations that allow several dogs can be difficult. And other plans, too, may be difficult to carry out. If necessary, you have to ask yourself whether you need to leave one or both dogs at home or to board them, or whether it might be better to cancel some of your plans entirely.
▷ **Male or female?** If you keep both genders together, you need to house them separately about twice a year while the bitch is in heat, at least for part of this time. Another option is to have one or both of them neutered.

The "reproduction problem" doesn't arise if you keep two dogs of the same sex. If both get along with other members of their species and if the hierarchy is clear, there usually are no problems here.

Upholding the First Dog's Rights

The inclusion of another canine in the household may not necessarily meet with an enthusiastic response from the other dog at first. Many dogs will initially ignore or be cool toward the newcomer. Some seem to hope that the troublemaker has moved into their home only temporarily.

Usually the first dog is joined by a puppy. A puppy naturally looks cuddly, and it's understandable that you want to look after her constantly. In the interest of your first dog—please don't do that. Under no circumstances must your first pet feel discriminated against. She has longer-standing rights, and that's how things should stay. For you, this means that the senior dog is the first to be fed and greeted (by visitors too), she has exclusive rights to her chew bone or toy, she can declare her favorite spots a ◑ TABOO ZONE (page 274) for the puppy, and so forth. All this applies if the senior pet exhibits normal social behavior toward other members of her species. If not, I advise against getting a second dog. Alternatively, consult an expert who will come to your home and look into the situation.

You'll make the adjustment period for the newcomer easier for all concerned by choosing a puppy that is not necessarily the most self-confident in her litter, but shows some willingness to play a subordinate role.

This also applies if the second dog is not a puppy, but already a full-grown dog when she moves in. It is better, however, if the new pet is distinctly younger than the first one, because she will be more likely to acknowledge the other dog as dominate.

Please note: No matter what constellation you choose—you should always be the "top dog" in the pack.

△

Each individual dog must obey well. Then there will be fewer difficulties when you're out with the two together. These two dogs come cheerfully and immediately when their owner calls.

Giving the Dogs Attention Separately

If a puppy is the second dog in your household, it's advisable to treat her like a single dog—at least until she has mastered the lessons of basic obedience. This means regular walks for bonding (→ page 78) and excursions for socialization (→ pages 74, 80, 81) alone with the puppy. Play with the little pup a great deal and train with her alone. Once the basic obedience commands have been reliably learned and the bond between you and the second dog is firm, you can occasionally take both pets out, but continue going out with the young one alone from time to time. This assumes, of course, that the first dog also has a good bond with you and obeys basic commands reliably.

The puppy takes a lot of time, but the older dog should get her fair share of attention nonetheless. Your plans must include sufficient time for the first dog and her activities.

If the second dog is older, proceed as described above.

A Secondhand Dog

When planning to acquire a dog, many people think of getting one from an animal shelter or from another owner. There are different reasons for this. Some people prefer an older dog to a puppy. Others want to give a home to an unfortunate animal. Still others would rather have a dog from a shelter for financial reasons, since purebred dogs from a breeder are more expensive.

In principle, there is no objection to a dog from another owner or from an animal shelter. But here too, there are a number of things to be considered in advance.

Important: The Prehistory

As you now know, during puppyhood and adolescence every dog has experiences that continue to influence her throughout her life. If you acquire a full-grown dog, she already has a certain prior history. The more you can learn about her previous life, the better you can gauge whether problems are to be expected, and if so, which ones. For example, if the dog has had bad experiences (or none at all) with humans or has experienced other negative things, problems can arise in situations that she connects with what she has undergone. Specifically what those situations are, however, frequently can't be predicted; often they are detected only in the course of living together. Sometimes the causes can no longer be determined, and in some cases the problems respond to therapy only to a limited extent or not at all.

And if the prehistory is completely unknown (as in the case of feral street dogs or strays that have been picked up), you have no way to estimate what problems could occur. Some animals may have a hard time adjusting, be fearful of many things, and need a long time to become somewhat accustomed to their new environment.

Naturally, there are also totally uncomplicated dogs that are acquired secondhand or from an animal shelter. Some dogs, for example, lose their home for family reasons (such as divorce or death) or health reasons (such as an allergy to animal hair) and up to this point have led a "normal" canine life. If such an animal is placed in a similar environment, there are unlikely to be any real difficulties. Ask as many detailed questions as possible to learn why the dog is being given away or why she has ended up in an animal shelter.

▶ INFO

Get Better Acquainted First

With secondhand dogs, there is often an opportunity to get better acquainted in advance, before you decide whether the animal is right for you. You can go out for walks a few times or take the dog home for a few days on a trial basis. A well-considered decision benefits the dog too, after all.

Knowledge Is Essential

If you bring into your home a dog that may possibly have problems, you need to know as much as you can about canine behavior in order to deal with the situation satisfactorily. Loving animals is not enough. You also must be prepared to cope with problems, because ultimately you don't do the dog a service if she has to be given away again after a few weeks or months.

Certain basic qualities can be more or less predicted if you're dealing with a specific breed,

△

Have you taken in a dog whose previous owner didn't want her anymore? Even if you feel sorry for her—don't coddle her too much. Dogs need clear rules in order to feel safe and secure.

because these traits are genetically determined. This applies only if the dog in question is a typical representative of her breed.

For mixed-breed dogs, this applies with certain restrictions, if at all. Usually we can't determine both parents of such a dog or know that both of them were also mixed breeds. Appearance alone is not enough to tell us which breeds were involved. Labrador mongrels are a good example of this. In the 1970s, many Labradors were available, but there were already a good many "Lab mixes." Almost every mix that was black or yellow and had

drooping ears ended up being called that—no matter where she came from, and whether one of the parents was really a Labrador, or not. This is even truer today.

Assignment to a certain breed, therefore, is problematic, because then the owner frequently expects to see certain characteristics of the parents' temperament, but they often are not apparent in the mixed-breed dog. That does not mean, of course, that mixes are problematic. On the contrary, there are decidedly successful mixes. But in a certain way, what you have is a Cracker Jack prize—you're never sure what you'll get.

A Particular Case: The Family

If you have children, my best advice is to get a puppy. They too are available at pet shelters. But even in this case, it's important to know where the little pups come from and where they have lived until now, that is, how they have been socialized thus far.

An adult dog, especially one of a larger breed, is less well suited for families with children. That is especially true if the prehistory is unknown or disappointing, or if the dog basically has exacting characteristics, such as a strong instinct to protect and guard, a pronounced degree of self-confidence, mistrust, or the like. Even if the animal has lived with children before, she may not accept children whom she doesn't know or who are clearly younger. A full-grown dog is a "finished" personality, and it can take a good while for her to become attached to her new owner, accept rules, and be under control.

Research & Practice

Not All Aggression Is the Same

7

Aggressiveness is part of the dog's social behavior and is not synonymous with dominance, or with fear. In the wild, aggressive behavior frequently is ritualized (threat signals) and thus, serves to prevent conflicts from "coming to blows." Whether this is also the case with a dog depends on her or his socialization, as well as on selective breeding. In addition, the individual human-dog relationship is important.

There are various forms of aggression:
▷ **Territorial aggression** is the readiness to defend one's own territory. How pronounced it is depends on the dog's disposition, on a conscious or unconscious reward, or on the degree of control exerted by the dog's owner. The human decides who enters the house, not the dog.
▷ **Aggression toward sexual rivals** is displayed by males when they're around a bitch in season. Depending on their testosterone level and disposition, however, even the presence of a bitch not in season may be sufficient. Some bitches are aggressive toward other bitches when in season.
▷ **Fear-based aggression** is exhibited by a dog that sees herself in a dead-end situation. This might be, for example, a group of people in an elevator. The dog's experiences and her (inadequate) socialization, as well as her disposition, are the factors that determine when a dog feels this way about a situation. This type of aggression is typical for dogs that bite when frightened. Such a dog has no way to withdraw from the situation that she finds threatening, and therefore, she bites—trying to assault rather than wait or retreat while under threat.

▷ **Aggression as a reaction to schock** or pain can also be exhibited by a dog, for example, if she has been startled awake or if a child has yanked her ear. Whether the dog ulimately bites in such a situation depends on her intrinsic emotional state and her threshold.

◁
Watch out—this dog is issuing a threat, largely as a defensive measure. She has made herself look smaller, her ears are laid back, and her teeth are slightly bared. A defensively threatening dog may, without warning, snap at the air or bite deliberately.

▷ **Aggression due to** ○ **FRUSTRATION** (page 265) is a possible reaction when a dog doesn't get what she wants. A dog owner wanted to use treats to motivate her almost full-grown canine companion to lie down. She was unwilling to obey, but she wanted the treat. The owner closed her hand, and the treat was unreachable—so the dog snapped out of frustration.
▷ **Playful aggressiveness** is displayed by some puppies when they deliberately snap at a hand or a piece of clothing. This little fuss absolutely must be taken seriously, to keep from raising a tyrant. Put the little pup in her place (→ page 29).

Training Aids

If there are problems during a dog's training, it usually is necessary for the animal's owner to change his or her behavior. However, sometimes training aids are also helpful.

SOMETIMES THE USE of special training aids is required to solve problems—at times temporarily, at times permanently. On the following pages, I'll present a few recommended aids for you to consider.

The use of training aids requires a certain technical effort and, in part, also more perseverance on the part of the handler. To achieve the desired training effect, the Halti, muzzle, and other aids must be properly used. The best solution is to visit a dog school and have an experienced trainer show you how to handle the aids.

The Right Way to Use the Halti

Basically, the Halti dog harness resembles a harness or headcollar for a horse (→ photo, below). The head harness is available in various sizes. It should not be too loose, however; otherwise, the dog can slip it off. This means that you should take your pet along when you're buying the Halti.

How It Works

The strap across the bridge of the nose creates a slight pressure that resembles the muzzle grip (→ page 30). This pressure alone has a positive effect on some "ill-mannered" dogs. It gives insecure dogs a greater sense of safety and security.

The major effect is that you can steer the dog's gaze and thus, her concentration in your direction without applying any force. The leash hangs through the head harness at the dog's front end. If your pet pulls in a certain direction or wants to head toward another dog, you merely have to put up a slight resistance. That automatically guides the dog's head toward you. Thus, the dog can't pull at the Halti the way she would with a collar or, usually even more strongly, with a regular harness.

When and How to Use the Halti

This training is especially recommended if your dog pulls hard at her leash, does not heel attentively, and can't be motivated in any other way to give you its attention. It is also helpful with dogs that exhibit on-leash aggression. There is no other method that lets you turn a dog away from her "opponent" so systematically. As soon as the dog is concentrating on you again, praise her.

Keep in mind that you should never use a tug to correct a dog wearing a Halti. You would jerk the dog's head around. Basically,

the leash must be loosely connected to the Halti; it becomes taut only when you offer a little resistance whenever the dog pulls.

You can use the Halti either for specific situations or all the time, temporarily or permanently. If the dog fails to walk properly on leash only when you're downtown, but in other places is fine, then you can use the Halti only in town. If the dog reacts aggressively on leash, you have to use the Halti at all times until your Rambo has "unlearned" this behavior. If the dog is off leash, remove the Halti to prevent any risk of getting hurt.

Getting the Dog Used to the Halti

Before you can walk your dog with the Halti, she must become completely accustomed to wearing it. If she tries to slip it off, for the time being put it on your pet for eating and playing (with you). Remove it at a moment when the dog isn't trying to slip it off. Simply distract her again with a treat or her favorite toy. It can take several days or sometimes even longer for the dog to accept it completely.

◁

This is the right way to wear the Halti, and it's also the right size. While wearing it, the dog is steered in two ways—by the Halti and by the collar. In this way, you still have your pet under control if she should try to slip off the headcollar.

Using the Long Leash

It is used instead of the short leash, in case the free-running dog (once past puppyhood) makes overly large circles and fails to focus on you—in short, whenever she ignores you while you're out together. This can happen during puberty, for example. For this purpose, use a 9–30-foot-long tracking leash, not too thin, and a relatively wide collar that doesn't tighten in any way.

When and How to Use the Long Leash

Your goal is for the dog to pay better attention to you and stay near you. She learns to do so by having a negative experience whenever she gets too far from you and doesn't focus on where you're headed. The principle actually is the same one followed in your bonding walks with the puppy (→ page 78). If unannounced changes of direction aren't sufficient to increase her attention, help your pet along by using the long leash.

How it works: Look for a large, open expanse of ground, such as a field or a meadow. Bushes and undergrowth should be avoided; the leash could get tangled in them. There should be no distractions in the area.

▷ Fasten the leash to the collar and roll it up with your hand. With the other hand, hold the loop tightly. With strong, powerful dogs, it's best to wear a glove.

▷ Start walking without giving a command. If the dog starts pulling, drop the rolled-up part of the leash on the ground and quickly head off in the opposite direction without saying a word, regardless of what the dog does. If you and your dog now continue moving in opposite directions, at some point the leash will become taut. The dog will feel a jerk—an "aha" experience, so to speak—and notice that you're already somewhere else. Don't stand still!

▷ If the dog is moving along close to you again, say a few words of praise, but keep on going. Now the leash, no longer rolled up, is dragging on the ground between you and your pet. As soon as the dog drifts off again, repeat the procedure.

Over time, you'll see that the leash no longer grows taut; the dog will promptly turn in your direction on her own. If you stop without a word, the dog will stop too. If she already knows a recall signal (such as a whistle blow or "Here"), you can use it at the moment the dog heads toward you of her own accord. Make sure, however, that she comes all the way to you, not just near you, and reward her with a treat. If she hasn't learned a signal of that kind yet, you should first practice it thoroughly at home (→ page 85).

Duration of the exercise: It's a good idea to practice twice a day for a week, about 15 minutes each time, with the long leash. That alone may be enough to get the dog to focus on you correctly again. This is quite possible, if she's still relatively young and the problem is not a long-standing one.

▷

Training on the long leash is helpful with many problems. Potentially, however, the leash must be used for weeks or months on every outing. Use only a normal collar that does not pull in any way.

If you have bigger problems and a very independent-minded dog, you'll have to work longer with the leash, possibly for a period of months, and with a gradually increasing distraction level. As soon as the dog concentrates on you, let the leash drag along the ground, and step on it at the first hint of undesirable behavior. Don't let her succeed under any circumstances and head toward another dog without your permission, for example. Don't stop using the long leash until there has been no need for quite a while to use it as an "emergency brake" and the dog is responding reliably to your call or whistle blow. Every week, cut off a piece of the leash until it's completely gone.

Good to Know

Handling the long leash is not so easy at first, and you also need a suitable location. Consider in advance whether you are willing and able to undertake this. During this time, you can't let the dog run free at all, to keep her from experiencing any success with undesirable behavior in the meantime. In "serious" cases, this applies even to your yard at home. Only if the dog wears the leash long enough and every time she's outdoors, will she get so used to it that she finally "forgets" it. She will switch to the new way of behaving because she has no alternative. But if she wears the leash only occasionally, she will learn when she can take some liberties and when she can't. Then the leash won't teach the desired lesson, and all your efforts will be wasted.

Also keep in mind that with a strong dog, a really powerful jerk can be created when the leash gets taut. Ask yourself whether you're strong enough to hold onto the dog during this exercise.

If the dog has progressed to the point where she's dragging the leash on the ground behind her, you can let it play with one other

△

As long as you have to keep stepping on the long leash as an "emergency brake" for a dog that's running away, you need to use the leash every time you're out together. Otherwise, all your effort will have been in vain.

dog at most; otherwise, the dogs and their leashes could get seriously tangled.

Variation

You can use this type of correction with the normal leash as well when your pet is at *heel*, if no other correction is working. Then, however, you should reverse direction—again, without comment—if your four-legged friend even hints at leaving the correct *heel* position at your side.

Dog Training Discs

These are thin, saucer-shaped metal discs that are linked together and make a rattling sound when shaken or thrown. Once the dog is conditioned, you can use them to bring undesirable behavior to a halt.

Conditioning the Dog

There are two options for the conditioning (→ page 261): outside conditioning (that is, by someone else) or the do-it-yourself method.

 TIP

Looking for an Experienced Trainer

If you're unsure whether this method or a different one is right for your dog, contact an experienced trainer before taking a shot at something yourself. This is important with outside conditioning, but it can also be helpful if you're interested in behavior modification through the startle effect.

▷ **Outside conditioning:** It is more highly recommended, but should be performed by an experienced professional trainer. The trainer should be unknown to the dog, because the method involves a negative experience. Training can be done outdoors or indoors; the only crucial element is a hard surface. The unfamiliar person lets the dog take several treats, one after another, from his or her hand, and then throws one on the ground. As soon as the dog tries to take it, the discs fall on the ground next to her, making a clanging noise. The dog is not allowed to get the treat! She is scared and frustrated (→ frustration, page 264)—after all, she was allowed to take the treats before—and

runs anxiously to her owner. The owner now commiserates, consoles, and lavishly praises the dog. Usually one "session" is sufficient.

If the dog now displays undesirable behavior outdoors—for example, if she wants to pick up trash off the ground, keeps on sniffing although you've recalled her, or growls on leash at other dogs—rattle the discs immediately. The dog will stop what she's doing, react in an anxious way, and come to you. And again you commiserate with your pet and praise her lavishly.

▷ **Do-it-yourself conditioning:** If you condition the dog yourself, you will need to rely on the startle effect alone. Suppose the dog wants to eat something off the floor. Even before she picks up the food, call out "No" or "Phooey" in a stern voice and throw the discs next to the dog. You can also use a throwing chain (available in pet stores) for this purpose. It's important not to let your pet see that you've thrown the discs. She is startled and looks up at you. Immediately, in an especially friendly tone of voice, you coax her to come and comfort her at length. At the very end, quietly pick up the chain or discs, unobserved by the dog, and put them in your jacket pocket.

Not Right for Every Dog

The throwing chain and the discs in particular are not a universal remedy and should be employed only with adult dogs. In the case of outside conditioning in particular, caution is required with dogs that react to humans aggressively or with mistrust. These training aids are also not suitable for dogs that are highly sensitive to noise.

There are, however, some especially thick-skinned dogs that are not influenced at all by these techniques.

My best advice is to contact a professional trainer who has experience with this method.

These saucer-shaped discs hang from a ring that is attached to a cord. If you shake them or throw them on the ground, they make a unique clanging sound.

Wearing such a muzzle, a dog can pant, drink, and even be given treats. It may not look decorative, but it helps prevent dangerous situations.

7

Training with a Muzzle

Admittedly, a dog wearing a muzzle looks like it needs to be domesticated. In some situations (→ below), however, the muzzle is an important tool that enhances safety. Use a basket muzzle, because it allows the dog to pant and drink, and it also lets you give your pet a treat.

When Does a Muzzle Make Sense?

If a dog is threatening humans or other members of its species or shows aggression toward them, danger can be avoided with a muzzle. Since the dog no longer can do any harm, the owner's stress level drops as well. Nevertheless, you should never leave a muzzled dog alone with people or other dogs.

The muzzle is not a substitute for any other kind of therapy, but it does teach the dog something: She sees that she has little or no success when she tries to bite.

Getting the Dog Used to It

Before you use the muzzle, you have to get the dog accustomed to it, as in the case of the Halti harness. If the dog presents a serious threat, she must wear the muzzle for several days at a stretch, without any adaptation period.

Introducing the muzzle: For several days, place edible treats at the bottom of the muzzle, and let your pet thrust her nose inside to retrieve the morsels. You can also rub some spreadable sausage or something similar inside the muzzle and let the dog lick it out. After a few such feedings, fasten the neck strap while your pet is eating, and then remove it again. The next step is to put the muzzle on the dog and then feed her. Gradually she will wear the muzzle for increasingly long periods.

Depending on the area of use, don't muzzle the dog right before the problem situation, but far enough in advance that she can't draw a connection. If the dog is aggressive when you have visitors at home, for example, don't wait for the sound of the doorbell to put the muzzle on; instead, muzzle your pet appreciably sooner.

What to Do When Problems Arise?

Many problems, though not all, are of your own making. Often, we hear that the problem is never the dog but always the human—that is, the owner. I don't think that's true in all conditions and instances.

DOGS HAVE different characteristics, and in some cases this makes their training quite challenging. All owners make some mistakes in training their pets. Whether and to what extent potential consequences become noticeable, however, also depends on the animal's temperament. An example: Your four-legged friend barks a few times because the doorbell rings. If he lacks a pronounced instinct to guard and protect, your attempts to calm him may, in the circumstances, be less problematic than with a pet whose guard-dog instinct is strongly marked, because the latter is even more vigilant.

Looking for the Cause

The causes of problems are manifold, as are the means of solving them. One thing right up front: Not all problems can be eliminated permanently. With some, improvement is possible, but for others there is no solution at all. Socialization and training don't automatically make every type of dog into a trouble-free companion in daily life. Innate shortcomings and breed-specific characteristics can't be trained away, but perhaps they can be managed to some extent through obedience training.

Causes of Bad Behavior

▷ **The wrong living environment:** Even if a breed looks amazingly decorative or impressive—if its prominent breed-related characteristics aren't a good fit for the dog's living environment, problems frequently are the result. If the animal has, for example, a strong guard-dog instinct like that of a Rottweiler or a German Shepherd, or if it is leery of strangers by nature, as ◐ HERD PROTECTION DOGS (page 265) such as the Great Pyrenees or Komondor are, and is kept in an apartment building, serious problems can result. A dog with a well-developed hunting instinct—such as a Weimaraner or a Greyhound—probably will pick up every scent of wild game on your walks or also chase joggers, cars, and the like.

▷ **Lack of activity:** Most dogs are active animals that want both physical and mental exercise. If a dog constantly has too little to do, a surplus of energy builds up, and at some point he needs an outlet. Nervousness, destructiveness, digging in the garden, increased aggressiveness, and similar behaviors can be the result of not having enough to do. This applies especially to dog breeds in whose development special emphasis was placed on high performance and ◐ PASSION FOR WORK (page 270). This category includes many

hunting breeds and guard- and protection-dog breeds as well as ◐ HERDING DOGS (page 265). Unless they are employed for their intended purposes, these dogs need purposeful alternative activities. More physical exercise alone is not enough. For suggestions, see Chapter 6, beginning on page 192.

If a dog's caloric intake exceeds his needs, this can also result in ◐ HYPERACTIVITY (page 266). A dog that gets a lot of exercise doesn't automatically need a diet resembling that of a four-legged high-performance athlete, such as a sled dog during the racing season.

▷ **Things neglected during training:** The causes of many minor and major problems fall into this category. Frequently, a lack of consistency on the part of the pet owner is one reason for difficulties, but failure to understand how a dog "thinks" is also a common cause. The latter aspect in particular is frequently responsible for the dog's being unwittingly rewarded at the wrong moment for what actually is undesirable behavior, or punished for desirable behavior. An unclear or improper hierarchy, treating the dog like a

◁

Lack of physical exercise and mental activity is a possible cause of problems, especially with active breeds like the Jack Russell Terrier, which are bred for performance. Then the excess of energy often looks for an outlet— and this shoe shows the result.

7

Hello world, we're curious about you! If puppies grow up in a nondescript environment with few opportunities to explore and make contacts, developmental problems can appear. Often these are virtually impossible to correct at a later date.

human, and spending too little time on training are additional reasons. If the family members can't agree about the way they want to raise the dog, and each one forbids or allows the dog to do different things, this can be another cause of difficulties. Anti-authoritarian rearing can lead to problems, as can too much pressure and the use of methods involving overt physical force.

▷ **Poor socialization:** This topic was covered in some detail in the first chapter. Deficiencies during the socialization phase lead to insecurity and anxiety. Frequently they can be overcome only with difficulty and only to a limited extent.

▷ **Inherent** ◐ **TEMPERAMENT FLAWS** (page 274): Insecurities and anxieties, however, can appear even if dogs have been reared and socialized in a normal way. Then it has to be assumed that the traits in question are innate and genetically determined. This can happen if the breeder has not paid careful enough attention to the temperament of the dam and sire, for example, because he or she valued appearance more highly or chose quantity over quality. There are also breeds that fundamentally are considered "sensitive," and here sensitivity often deteriorates into insecurity or fearfulness, unfortunately.

▷ **Changes at home:** Sudden changes in the domestic setting can cause behavioral changes in many dogs. It may be the birth of a baby, the arrival of a new life partner, or serious changes in the daily routine: for example, you may have been at home all day in the past, but now you're taking a job. The behavioral changes can become especially glaring if something also changes for the dog. If he has been a child substitute and the focus of your attention, and then a baby enters the scene, the dog may now be banished from certain rooms and get little attention. That can lead to dangerous situations.

▷ **Illnesses:** Organic diseases also can result in altered behavior. Serious pain from hip dysplasia, injuries, as well as brain tumors, loss of hearing, and other health problems, can give rise to unexpected reactions in a dog.

Approaches to Solutions

There are various approaches to solving problems. Some can be solved with relatively little effort. Others, however, require systematic work for an extended time. Frequently there are various ways to reach your goal, and you can try out several methods to see which one you personally can best implement. It must also be suitable for your particular pet.

Basic training: Without good basic obedience → page 259), many problems are very

7

difficult to influence. In any event, the dog must learn to come reliably when called, walk correctly on leash, relinquish an object, sit, lie down, and also stay alone in the *sit* or *down* position at an assigned spot. Gradually, these exercises should also be successful in the face of distractions. Basic obedience was discussed in greater detail in the third chapter.

Clear hierarchy: This is an additional prerequisite for a good relationship between owner and pet. If your dog doesn't acknowledge your authority, that will hinder your efforts to solve many problems.

Make sure that the dog basically looks to you for guidance. Don't try to justify everything to your pet from a human point of view! Remember the first chapter: In most cases, you should be the one to make the opening move.

Avoidance of problem situations: Your goal is to anticipate events in advance and keep your dog from getting away with bad behavior. Any inadvertent success on your pet's part will only serve as reinforcement. For example, if your dog likes to engage in skirmishes with certain other dogs that yap from behind their fences while you're out for a walk together, leash him ahead of time. If your pet isn't calm and obedient enough, don't wait to see whether he will run over to the fence or not, or come when called or not.

Reinforcing alternative behavior: Here the dog learns that it's more advantageous to do what you want instead of what he wants. If your pet jumps up on you, for example, when you see him getting ready to jump you can say "Sit" (if he has learned the *sit*) and reward him for complying.

Redirecting his attention: If your dog has learned to maintain eye contact with you, you can combine this with the previous suggestion, "Reinforcing alternative behavior." If your pet wants to run after someone on a bike, for example, have him sit next to you and ask him for eye contact. Both actions must be rewarded with a special acknowledgment to make obedience worthwhile for the dog.

Ignoring: This method is also extremely useful in dealing with many problems. Actually, it's quite easy as well, if only emotions didn't keep getting in the way. Many dog owners find it difficult to adamantly ignore their pet and to simply do nothing. But don't worry; your dog won't be harmed if you refuse to pay attention to him, quite the opposite! Go back to page 31 to read more on this subject.

Habituation to situations: You can gradually get a fearful dog accustomed to irksome situations. At first, keep your distance from sources of noise or the like, and gradually get a little closer. Depending on the dog, it can take a few minutes or even several weeks or months to overcome his fear.

To motivate your pet to go over a grating or a narrow footbridge, for example, hunger often is very helpful. You can also reward the dog if he has relaxed near a noise that makes him uneasy. A coveted toy can help as well. If his hunger or his pleasure in the toy is greater than his fear, the dog can overcome quite a lot of things.

There are, however, some dogs whose fear is so great that you just can't do anything with them. Here, in addition to the methods listed above, I recommend considering the use of a medication with a calming effect. Ask your veterinarian to suggest an appropriate preparation.

Problem Situations from A to Z

In the section that follows you'll be directed to methods and approaches to help you solve or improve specific problems with your four-legged friend. Since every human-and-dog team is different, I can't say across the board which procedure is best suited for which individuals. I suggest that you select the tips that apply to you, that you can implement easily, and that are most appropriate for your dog. If you can't handle a problem alone, you should promptly seek competent and practical support from a veterinarian with training in behavioral therapy, a good dog school, or the like.

 TIP

Jotting Down Details

Keeping a daily diary of your pet's actions can help determine the possible causes of troublesome behavior. When problems arise, write down what happened where and when, a description of the exact situation, when the problem first appeared, and whether there were any particular noises, people, or visual impressions at the time.

Aggressive Behavior on Leash

Does your four-legged friend start sending out alarm signals when another dog approaches? If so, many of your undertakings quickly become stressful.

Possible causes

▷ When your dog showed the first indications of aggression, such as glaring at an opponent or growling, you tried to soothe him by petting him, thereby reinforcing the behavior.

▷ The dog has developed the aggressive behavior through regular on-leash contact with other dogs. That taught him that he could ultimately get where he wanted to go by pulling, yowling, or barking and getting really worked up about it.

▷ When leashed, another dog attacked him, and this experience led him to adopt a strategy of employing offense as his best defense.

▷ You yourself fear such encounters. Your own tension and the tautening of the leash give your four-legged friend an alarm signal when other dogs appear, "Look out, here we go."

Possible solutions

▷ Try to stay as relaxed as possible yourself when another dog turns up.

▷ When your pet is on leash, don't let him have any contact with other dogs (→ pages 101, 114).

▷ Divert your dog's attention to you whenever such an encounter looms. Act promptly, and motivate your pet with your tone of voice and a toy or treat; then walk rapidly past the other dog, giving it a wide berth.

What else you can do:

▷ At the very first signs, such as tensing or glaring at the opponent, give your dog a stop signal, or spray his ears with a water pistol.

▷ Get your pet accustomed to a Halti dog harness (→ page 223), and use it to get his attention. Use the Halti in addition to treats or a toy, especially when these temptations and your voice commands fail to work in such a situation.

▷ If a free-running dog comes toward you and it obviously is not going to be leashed, and if your leashed pet behaves normally, you should unleash him promptly—before he can stare angrily at the other animal or show signs of aggressiveness (→ pages 168 and 176).

▷ Don't attempt to "calm" your dog by petting him or giving him any other consolation—this will be interpreted as praise.

Aggressive Behavior Toward Humans

Problematic behavior toward humans must be taken very seriously. Don't take any risks. Because problems of this nature are generally difficult to resolve on your own, you need to seek expert help without delay. The extent to which this aggressive behavior can be completely eliminated is impossible to predict. Sometimes it may be advisable to part with such a dog.

Possible causes

▷ The dog is afraid or insecure because he has had bad experiences, has been poorly socialized, or has an innate temperament flaw.
▷ The dog has an excessive instinct to guard and protect.
▷ He is defending his territory.
▷ He is defending his food.
▷ You have consciously or unconsciously (perhaps by trying to "calm" your pet) reinforced aggressive behaviors such as barking or growling.
▷ The dog has learned that by making threats (by growling, for example) he gets his way and can impress people or keep them at a distance. This may be due to fear, but it can also be a way of defending his cozy little spot on the sofa. There's something wrong with the hierarchy here.
▷ If the problems are occurring within the family, the hierarchy may not be right, or the dog may be insecure because each family member deals with him in a different way.

Possible solutions

▷ If you can bank on the fact that your dog will snap at or bite you or others, you absolutely must use a muzzle. In addition, leash your pet in situations of this kind.
▷ Step up your pet's level of obedience with appropriate exercises (→ Chapter 3) so that you have the dog securely under control if his instinct to guard and protect causes problems.

A dog that behaves so aggressively toward humans must not be taken out in public. Someone with experience needs to intervene quickly here.
▽

△

This dog wants to get up on the sofa—he is pestering his owner and staring at her fixedly. She is behaving correctly by staying in her seat and ignoring her pet. This may be enough to get the dog to stop his attempts at dominance.

If the dog is accustomed to lying down near your front door, at the top or foot of staircases, or in main traffic paths in your home, you need to move him farther away. For one thing, you will be depriving the dog of his sentry position as "boss," and for another, you will keep him from being the first one at the door when visitors arrive. Don't store any food near the entrance; this is a strategically important area from the canine point of view.
▷ You can interrupt aggressive behavior toward visitors by calling out a stop command (→ page 273) or using the throw chain or another loud noise (→ page 226).

If the behavior is less pronounced, put the dog in the *sit* position as an alternative. If it stays quiet for a few moments, the visitor can hand him a reward.
▷ If the dog has a tendency to bark at passersby when you're out together, recall him promptly and distract him with something that's more important to him, such as his favorite toy or some food.
▷ If the dog's aggressive behavior toward humans is due to fear (watch his body language), he should be ignored, not pressed, by people such as visitors or passersby. Allow contact to be made only if the dog himself indicates an interest in it. However, the person must not seem threatening and must not bend over the dog (→ photo, page 52). You should treat the other persons in a decidedly casual and friendly way. If the dog has a tendency to attack visitors out of fear, *down* him within sight of all the activity (don't lock him in another room) and far away from the front door area, or tie him up.
▷ If the dog reacts aggressively to family members, you need to make the hierarchy stable (→ page 36).

If you're doubtful about the dog, then the muzzle will help. It's important not to show any fear or uncertainty, because the dog will be aware of it. He will evaluate even a tiny flinch as a success.
▷ If the dog perhaps has eked out some privileges for himself over time, it's advisable to rescind them. If your four-legged friend defends the sofa, for example, put a longer lead on him at home as well. You can use it to pull your pet down from elevated spots without saying a word or making eye contact, but with determination. Make such places unusable by putting bulky or awkward objects, such as a broom, on them.
▷ Make sure that all members of the family are dealing with the dog in the same way. Don't let your pet lie in strategically significant spots (→ left), and practice obedience

△

Excessive barking at the fence is unnecessary and frequently leads to problems with the neighbors. Don't leave such a dog alone in the yard.

exercises with him on a regular basis. In addition, you can declare rooms of strategic importance, such as the kitchen (where the pack leader's food is) or the bedroom (where the pack leader sleeps), off limits for your pet.

Barking

If the dog barks two or three times when the doorbell rings, or when somebody walks past your car or fence, that's okay. But a dog that barks more than that or won't stop barking, can be nerve-racking, and he can scare passersby.

Possible causes

▷ The tendency to bark is innate. This applies, for example, to guard-dog breeds and many gundog breeds. But many mixed-breed dogs also bark untiringly.

▷ Your four-legged friend has a pronounced instinct to guard.

▷ You have unconsciously rewarded the barking by petting the dog "comfortingly," or by running to the door excitedly, trying to beat your pet to it, or even by giving in to the dog when he was barking to demand something of you.

Possible solutions …

… for barking in the car: Put the dog in a crate and lay a blanket over it, so that there's no visual contact with the outside world.

… for barking at the fence: This is basically normal, but if people walk by frequently or if the dog overdoes things, you might have problems with the neighbors. Apart from that, passersby often get a real scare when they unsuspectingly walk down the street and a barking dog races up to the fence. In the dog's eyes, this is a success, because he has "driven off" the intruder.

▷ Put up a privacy screen.

▷ At an appropriate distance from the fence, put up an additional fence, so that the dog no longer can go all the way to the property line.

▷ Don't leave the dog alone or for an extended period in the yard.

▷ Never leaving him alone in the yard will prevent the dog from potentially being annoyed by someone on the other side of the fence.

▷ By staying in the yard yourself, you also prevent the dog from accepting tidbits from neighbors or passersby while he's barking which would only reward such behavior.

… for barking in the house

▷ Where appropriate, move your four-legged friend's bed away from the front door area into a strategically insignificant part of your home.

▶ TIP

Barking Out of Insecurity

If your dog barks out of insecurity, perhaps because a statue or a person in a hooded jacket is upsetting him, forbidding him to bark is no help at all. First try to distract your pet. If he calms down, explore the situation with him or, if possible, initiate contact with the unfamiliar person.

▷ Tell him to sit or lie down; in these positions, many dogs bark little or not at all.
▷ If your pet can fetch, give him something to hold. As we all know, it's hard to talk with your mouth full.

What else you can do:
▷ Keep the dog busy enough. The less excess energy he has, the less he will "wait" for opportunities to really let loose.
▷ Work on strengthening his level of obedience. Then you can recall the dog if the situation requires and have him execute an alternative command, for which it then gets a reward.
▷ Sometimes it's helpful to link the barking with an audible signal, so that the dog barks only on command, but stops again in response to a prohibitory word. If he doesn't bark again, he has earned a tasty reward, of course.
▷ Interrupt his behavior with a stream of water from a water pistol aimed at his ears. But don't let the dog see that you did the squirting.
▷ If you've conditioned your dog to the clicker (→ page 192), or if you use a throw chain (→ page 226) in connection with a ▶ STOP COMMAND (page 273) such as "No," then you can also use these aids to prevent the barking.

△

If a dog defends his toy this aggressively, something is wrong. If you feel insecure around your pet, seek professional advice for the dog without delay.

▷ Employ the muzzle grip, along with a growled "No" (→ page 30).
▷ Don't give in when the dog barks to get you to do as he wishes. Steadfastly ignore him until he has been quiet for a few moments. After that, you can reward him.

Defending Food and Toys

If your dog defends his food or toys, things can get to the point where he bites when you try to take them away. The best solution is to try the suggestions given below as soon as you see even slight indications of such behavior. If the problem has already developed, lengthy

7

training is required to correct the behavior again. In addition to the following tips, you can consult a behavioral therapist if you feel unable to cope with the problem alone.

Possible causes

▷ The puppy is simply testing to see whether he can make an impression.

▷ Your dog, while still a puppy, already had some success with growling next to his food bowl or toy, because then you left him alone.

▷ In other situations, the dog has already seen that his threats make an impression.

▷ A dog that grew up as a feral animal usually had to forage for his own food until joining your household, and in some cases he also had to defend his food from other dogs. Therefore he becomes aggressive when he believes his food may be taken away.

▷ A generally unclear or faulty hierarchy can also be the cause.

▷ From the outset, all kinds of things were taken away from the dog frequently and in a rude way.

▷ The dog is always allowed to dig into his food immediately; he hasn't learned to wait for permission.

▷ The tendency to defend food or toys can also be innate.

▷ If a bitch obviously is experiencing pseudo-pregnancy, she may be building a cave-like place for her litter and gathering puppy substitutes there—usually, toys and other objects, which she then defends because of her parental instinct.

Possible solutions

▷ If the puppy growls when next to his bowl, take the bowl away from him, in combination with a prohibitory word. Whether you also use the muzzle grip (→ page 30) or pick up the little rascal by the scruff of his neck depends on the dog and on your own courage. You should behave with great authoritativeness and decisiveness, without seeming nervous or frantic in any way. If the little puppy's reaction is friendly again, set the bowl back down.

Often, a single correction will fix the problem. If not, repeat the procedure.

▷ Alternatively, sit down on the floor next to the food bowl and, using your hand, put a few morsels at a time into the bowl. When the puppy has eaten this little portion, add the next morsels. If he growls, that means the meal is over, possibly after only a few bites. Stand up again. The rascal doesn't get another chance until the next mealtime rolls around. You can try this procedure with an older dog too, provided he does nothing more than growl and doesn't go too far in defending his bowl.

▷ Have your pet sit before you put the bowl on the floor or give him a bone to chew. After a few moments, use a fixed audible signal (such as "Take it") or your normal finish signal (→ page 85) to grant permission for the dog to go to his bowl or take the bone. If you happen to be training the come at mealtime, first reward the dog for obeying by offering him a few treats from your hand, and then let him wait next to his bowl.

If you're not sure whether your pet will react aggressively, tie him so firmly that he can't get to the bowl unless you push it over to the dog. If he growls while you're pushing the bowl to him, move the bowl away again. If he growls while he's eating, push the bowl far enough away, using a broom or something similar if need be.

▷ If the dog defends his food very vigorously, feed him only from your hand for a considerable time. If necessary, he should wear a muzzle at these times, but be sure to put the muzzle on long before feeding time (→ page 227).

▷ Stop feeding the dog in the kitchen. Instead, choose a spot that he doesn't connect with food.

▷ Your pet, of course, should be given no food at the table or in between meals and he must "earn" every morsel by executing some exercise first.

▷ If he boldly defends a certain toy or chew bone, put these things away. Don't give your

△
If the dog demolishes the furnishings, that's not very pleas[e]
Possible causes of this behavior are boredom and protest.

pet access to them for a considerable time. Use less important things in the training process. As soon as your pet does the exercise, he should get some tasty treats in exchange for the less important objects.

▷ Work on reinforcing the obedience training, and take a close look at the hierarchy.

▷ With a pseudopregnant bitch, it's best to take the puppy substitutes away from her and distract her with various activities. Treatment with medications is also an option.

Demanding Behavior

Giving in once or twice when the dog wants something from you is generally not a problem. But if you keep doing it, and if you have a strong-willed pet that systematically takes advantage of these gains and keeps pushing for more, you can easily raise a domestic

tyrant. He will scratch at the door and bark because a bird he dislikes is sitting in the yard. When he wants to play, he will nip your leg, and as soon as it's time for dinner or a walk, he will act up. The same thing will happen when you're making a phone call or otherwise not devoting yourself to the dog.

Possible causes

▷ Probably you have unconsciously rewarded the undesirable behavior.

▷ You're treating your dog like a human.

▷ The hierarchy is unclear or incorrect.

▷ You have failed to ignore your pet persistently enough, so he has learned that if he keeps it up long enough and adds some emphasis, perhaps by scratching at the door, he gets his way in the end.

Possible solutions

▷ Ignore the dog's demands. Remember: Ignoring means no eye contact, no talking, and no movement in the dog's direction until he stops the undesirable behavior!

This means that you can continue with your phone call (it can even be a staged call) or sit down in your favorite armchair and read the newspaper or a book when it's time for your pet's meal or walk, despite his urging.

▷ Keep it up, even if the undesirable behavior may escalate at first. This happens because the dog has repeatedly seen that the more he pushes, the more often he succeeds.

▷ Don't take your pet out for a walk or fix his meal until he has behaved in a calm, "normal" way for some time beforehand.

▷ To keep the dog from ruining anything when he scratches at the door, you can apply protective masking or put something in front of the door.

Destructiveness

If your pet tends to chew on objects, you may frequently be in for some bad surprises. If the dog also happens to eat inedible items, there may be a health risk.

Possible causes

▷ The young dog is teething at the moment.

▷ The dog is bored.

▷ This is the dog's way of protesting against being left alone.

▷ This is an individual tendency—some dogs simply are more inclined than others to behave this way from an early age, but many never are destructive at all.

Possible solutions

▷ Prevent opportunities for such behavior. If the dog is staying home alone, don't give him access to every room. The hallway or a spacious vestibule will be sufficient. Put things that are at risk—shoes, chairs, rugs, and the like—out of the dog's reach.

▷ If your children's toys are the favored objects of his destructive actions, you need to make sure that these playthings are in the children's rooms, with the doors closed.

▷ If your pet always chews on the same piece of furniture, block access to it with a large flowerpot or the like. Pet stores sell products (bitters) that can be applied to such objects to discourage the dog from chewing. That does not work with every dog, however.

▷ On a regular basis, give your pet cowhide strips, rawhide bones, or the like to chew. That will keep him occupied and help keep his teeth healthy and strong. During the teething period in particular, there is an increased need to chew.

▷ Destructiveness is frequently a sign that a dog has too little to do. Take time at least once a day to play extensively with your pet. In addition, depending on the breed, he needs a chance at least once a day to really work off some energy outdoors—at times by playing with other dogs, at times together with you, perhaps jogging together or, depending on the dog, also biking. Provide plenty of mental challenge as well. With a little skill, for example, you can construct a little obstacle course in the yard or the hallway. Fetching and tracking, depending on the dog, are also suitable activities. Regular obedience training, too, helps keep the dog fully occupied. Frequently, we underestimate the extent to which working with the dog provides an outlet for his energy. For example, if I don't have much time for a walk, then I do half an hour of intense training with my bitch. That's at least the equivalent of a long walk.

Digging

Some four-legged companions make it their hobby to redesign the yard—not always to the delight of their two-legged partners.

△

If you want your dog to learn not to eat garbage, you have to react very quickly. This dog has seen something inedible and is concentrating on it, but doesn't have anything in his mouth yet.

Possible causes

▷ Natural tendency—some dogs simply can't help it.

▷ Boredom: If your dog is left to his own devices too often or has too little mental and physical exercise, digging is a popular alternative activity.

Possible solutions

If your dog digs only in certain places (the flowerbed, a certain plant), you can surround these areas with fencing for one or two summers. Deprived of his success, the dog may "unlearn" the habit of digging. Fence in such inviting areas at the time the puppy joins the household, and then your little rascal won't acquire a taste for digging in the first place.

▷ Provide plenty of exercise and activity, so that the dog has a meaningful outlet for his energy.

▷ Don't leave the dog alone in the yard. If you can prevent the digging only through disciplinary measures while you're in the yard with your pet, and if he can resume digging once he's alone again, your efforts quite likely were in vain—unless you have an exceptionally compliant dog.

Please note: A yard is no substitute for spending time or going for walks with your canine friend. If he gets bored, he will look for some diversion that suits his taste.

▷ In intractable cases, I recommend putting a sandbox in your yard, where the dog can dig

7

to his heart's content—but nowhere else. Go to the spot with your pet and show him that he can dig there. To make things more fun, you can bury toys or bits of food for him there and let him search for them.

Eating or Rolling in Garbage

If the dog enjoys rolling around in things that are unfit for consumption, or if he eats everything he comes across while outdoors, this is understandably a horror for most dog owners. Besides, many of the things the dog ingests in this way can be harmful to his health.

Possible causes

▷ Rolling around is an inborn behavior; wolves also roll on the ground. Some dogs, however, really get very involved and roll in all kinds of refuse, sewage, and so forth. Others, in turn, only have a craving to roll in the remains of animals that have just been run over by a car or the like. But there are also dogs that have no urge at all to behave like that. Researchers still haven't figured out the real meaning of this behavior.

▷ Young dogs often have quite a pronounced tendency to eat garbage. This usually disappears as they get older. But unfortunately not always.

▷ Sometimes a nutritional deficiency is the cause, but usually an individual inclination is at the bottom of it all. Whether training procedures yield results depends on the dog and on the timing of the corrective action.

Possible solutions

When you're out for a walk, watch your dog closely but unobtrusively. If he's about to lie on the ground, or if he starts to eat something off the ground, you need to take action at

A sudden noise may briefly startle the dog. But if he reacts to all noises with fear and avoidance behavior (page 259), the result will be a great deal of stress.
▽

▶ TIP

Excessive Fear

Some dogs' level of fear is so high that even after various attempts to reduce it, no improvement is in sight. In such cases, the only alternative is to spare the dog the burdensome situation and thus, a great deal of stress.

once—that is, before he's on the ground or has something in his mouth.

▷ If he doesn't obey reliably, run excitedly in the opposite direction, or start investigating the ground next to you, talking in an interest-arousing tone of voice. If the dog comes to you out of curiosity, there must be rewards for him in the form of treats or a toy.

▷ Work on reinforcing your pet's basic obedience, so that you can recall him promptly (→ above) or tell him to sit from a distance. This alternative behavior must be generously rewarded.

▷ Introduce a *stop* command (→ page 273). If that's not enough, try to condition your pet with a prohibitory word, combined with a negative action such as using a throw chain (→ page 226).

▷ You can use the following training recommendation to influence a dog that eats garbage. Put a Halti on your pet. Then, deliberately walk up to different kinds of "bait" that you have put in place beforehand. As soon as the dog has noticed the bait, instruct him to sit. Don't forget the reward! The goal of this exercise is to eventually have the dog sit of his own accord as soon as he notices garbage, even if it's running free at the time.

Very greedy dogs must wear a muzzle when they're outdoors, also to prevent any harm to their health from eating rocks or similar things. At the same time, it's advisable to have the dog execute an alternative command ("Here" or "Sit") and reward him for obeying.

Fear of Noises

If everyday noises like those made by cars, trains, thunderstorms, and vacuum cleaners scare your pet, there will be a high level of stress in his life. The extent to which the dog can adjust to them depends on his disposition. A naturally sensitive and noise-sensitive dog will make less progress here than a phlegmatic dog with nerves of steel that has grown up in a low-stimulus environment. If the dog reacts this way only to a certain sound, this usually is easier to influence than a fundamental fear of noises.

Possible causes

▷ The dog connects a certain noise with a negative experience.

▷ It had too little exposure to noises while he was a puppy.

▷ If you consciously reward a slight insecurity, by "consoling" your pet this feeling may develop into anxiety.

▷ The dog is fearful and insecure by nature.

Possible solutions …

… for fear of noises: Using hunger as a tool, gradually accustom the dog to the noise that scares him. If he is hungry enough and if the noise begins at a relatively low level while he's eating, the dog can gradually store it in his memory bank as something positive.

▷ At first, select a noise intensity that causes the dog no more than slight discomfort. For example, leave the vacuum cleaner running on a low setting in another room, or keep sufficient distance between you and a street or rail line.

▷ As your pet grows more composed, gradually lessen the distance from the noise source or raise the volume. Depending on the dog and the magnitude of fear "gradually" may mean weeks or even months.

... for fear of firecrackers and the like: First try to put the dog in a relaxed ⊙ MOOD (page 268) at home, by playing with him or feeding him. When you can plan ahead for events, such as New Year's Eve, don't feed the dog during the day; give him something to eat only after the midnight commotion is over. Stay at home with your pet during this time.
▷ If nothing seems to distract the dog from his fear, at least make sure your own behavior stays in the range between cheerful and completely relaxed.

... for fear of thunderstorms and other noises that you can't deliberately bring about: In such a situation, CDs with nature sounds are sometimes helpful. They are available in music stores. Here too, proceed as described above; that is, play the CD with the thunderstorm mood at low volume while the dog is eating. Gradually turn up the volume.

Fear of Visual Stimuli

Some dogs are insecure or fearful in the face of optical stimuli, including such things as a fluttering piece of foil, a barrel that normally stands elsewhere, and the like.

Possible causes
▷ The dog was inadequately socialized as a puppy.
▷ You "comforted" the dog when he showed the first tiny signs of insecurity and thus unconsciously rewarded him for this behavior.
▷ Insecurity or fear is part of the dog's nature.

Possible solutions
▷ If the dog's reaction is not one of total panic, encourage him to explore the object with you. If need be, leave him on leash, but keep it loose. Your behavior should be cheerful and relaxed. If the dog relaxes and goes up to the object with you, praise him and give him some treats.
▷ If you can't persuade your pet to get any closer to the object, or if he becomes panicky and wants to run away, you should stay in the

vicinity of the object at least until the (leashed) dog has relaxed to some extent. If necessary, increase the distance between you and the frightening object. Then, in the next few days, return to this spot several times, trying each time to get a little closer. Make sure the dog is really hungry at these times. If you can plan this procedure in advance, let the dog fast the day before if necessary. Don't worry, he won't starve. If his hunger exceeds his fear, a dog often succeeds in overcoming the latter.
▷ To the extent that this is feasible, try laying a few tasty tidbits on top of the "sinister" object. Encourage your pet to go up and get them. If you can't place a few morsels on the object, give your pet the treats as soon as he has relaxed in the vicinity of the scary object. Don't let him go away from the object while he is still exhibiting fear.

Hunting

In every dog there slumbers the legacy of its ancestor, the wolf: a ⊙ HUNTING INSTINCT (page 266). It is not equally pronounced in all dogs, however. There are breed-specific differences. Some breeds were bred specifi-

◁

Your dog isn't listening, so you run after him. That only shows him your "powerlessness." He won't let you catch him, and he may see the whole thing as just a nice game of chase. Or he may think, "My owner wants to go where I'm going, so let's get started."

△

If the dog ignores your recall command, it's high time to make some changes. Usually, the underlying cause is not an unresolved problem, but several "imbalances" in your life together, for example, in the hierarchy.

cally for use in hunting. Moreover, there are great differences within a breed. Often, breeds that on the one hand have a strong hunting instinct, but on the other hand were not bred for working closely with a human—such as hounds (like beagles) or Nordic breeds like Huskies—are especially hard to control. Hunting is a very slippery matter, and in "hard" cases it is virtually impossible to gain reliable control of. Hunting is its own reward; it gives the dog a great deal of pleasure, whether he has any success or not.

Every hunt, therefore, ultimately reinforces his behavior. This applies to pursuing wild game, as well as to chasing cars, bike riders,

joggers, and so forth. If the dog succeeds and kills a chicken, a deer, or other game, problems are made worse.

Possible causes

▷ The dog has a very pronounced hunting instinct and prey drive (→ page 270).

▷ He doesn't have enough to do.

▷ His obedience lessons have not been learned thoroughly.

▷ As a puppy and adolescent, the dog had positive experiences with hunting, perhaps while flushing birds or chasing cats.

Possible solutions

▷ Reinforce his obedience lessons and systematically practice the *come* in response to a signal (→ page 85) once more, as well as the *come* in the face of distractions (→ page 111). Reliable basic obedience is one of the most important prerequisites for being able to control dogs that love to hunt.

▷ If your dog frequently ignores the *come* command, choose a new one. Ideally, use a dog whistle, which is far more penetrating (two short whistle blows in succession are best), and redo the exercise (→ pages 85–86).

▷ In addition, teach the dog to sit or lie down at a distance in response to a long whistle blow (also using the dog whistle). Frequently, it is easier to stop the dog than to get him to turn around (→ page 138).

▷ For an extended period, walk the dog only on the long leash, and practice as outlined on page 224.

▷ If wild game or some other favorite "hunting object" (a jogger, a flock of birds) is in sight, call the dog immediately, if necessary by influencing him with the long leash (→ page 224). Have him sit next to you and use especially tasty treats to get his full attention until the "prey" is far enough away.

▷ If he reliably obeys basic commands in the face of "normal" distractions, you can deliberately train in situations that tempt your dog to hunt. For example, if he likes chasing joggers, you can train at a popular jogging area with your dog on leash, practicing all kinds of

244

○▶ **TIP**

Accidents with Children

Children attract many dogs—unfortunately, not always in a positive way. Because of their body size and the way they move, children obviously trigger prey-capture behavior in some dogs. The crying of a baby also can arouse the hunting instinct. In these cases, dogs primarily direct their attacks at the head.

△

When a dog jumps up on someone, every movement in his direction—like the arm movement seen here—is a form of attention and reinforces the behavior, even if you don't look at the animal. Simply turn away.

commands, including the *heel, sit/down, stay,* and *recall.* Motivate him with delicious morsels (such as cheese or cooked chicken or turkey). If he prefers to chase animals, you might train near free roaming chickens or ducks or next to a sheep paddock. If your pet gets too excited at first, start the training session at a greater distance and gradually move closer over time (→ page 104).

What else you can do:

▷ When training, make sure your dog really is quite hungry and is concentrating enthusiastically on your treats.

▷ Using the clicker (→ page 192) is very helpful with some dogs.

▷ Some dogs can be allowed to run free only when wearing a Halti (→ page 223).

▷ Until your dog can be reliably recalled or brought to a stop, you shouldn't let him run free in applicable areas. For some dogs, this means a lifelong ban on running free.

Independence, Too Much

A dog that is too independent does not take his cue from his owner, may even ignore him or her, does not obey signals outdoors, and goes too far away. If the dog does what he wants, by and large, this will cause problems in many everyday situations. Not infrequently, the dog will have to stay on a leash almost all of the time as a result.

Possible causes

▷ In puppyhood and adolescence, bonding was encouraged too little or not at all. Life together is not interesting enough for the dog.

▷ General training and obedience training have been neglected.

▷ The dog is overly spoiled and coddled. That leads him to think he merits a higher social position within the "pack."

▷ The owner plays by the dog's rules instead of the reverse and gives in to the dog's demands.

▷ The dog is inherently disinclined to take a subordinate role.

▷ He had too little contact with humans and may have lived on his own for an extended period. This is the case with many stray dogs.

Possible solutions

▷ Do obedience exercises with the dog on a regular basis.

▷ Make the dog really earn every morsel.

▷ Ignore all the dog's demands, even if this is hard for you at first. Systematically invite him to play, be petted, go for a walk, and so forth.

▷ Make sure you display your authority.

▷ While you're out walking, incorporate frequent changes of direction (→ page 101).

▷ Make your walks interesting, so that the dog has fun. Find out what he likes, that is, how he likes to play, and consciously develop the bond between the two of you. For more on this topic, see the section beginning on page 182.

▷ If all that is insufficient, training with the long leash should help (→ page 224).

Jumping up on People

Suppose your four-legged friend has a tendency to jump up on you or other people every time an opportunity presents itself. Scarcely anyone enjoys this, because people aren't always wearing their "dog clothes." Besides, a large, powerful dog can easily knock a person down in this way.

Possible causes

▷ The dog is very fond of humans and would like to say hello to everybody.

▷ The dog is very high-spirited.

▷ He is nervous, under stress, or insecure and is jumping up to get "help" from you.

▷ He was unconsciously rewarded for jumping up.

Possible solutions

▷ When you're out with your pet and a potential "victim" is approaching, recall your dog promptly and leash him. In this way you prevent the situation from occurring at all and keep the dog from experiencing any undesirable success as a consequence.

▷ All the family members and/or visitors should silently turn away and completely ignore the dog whenever he starts to jump up. As time passes, he will learn that jumping up doesn't get him any attention, and the behavior will cease. When he stops and stays calm for a while, praise him, but in an equally calm fashion. This procedure is especially important for nervous, stressed, and insecure dogs. If the visitor fails to ignore the dog, it's better to leash him.

▷ If your dog has the appropriate obedience training and the requisite composure, you can ask for an alternative behavior—such as the *sit*—before he jumps up, and then praise him.

△

Obviously, the dog is embarrassed by his accident. Under no circumstances should you scold your pet; that will only make the problem worse.

Lapses in Housetraining

Problems with housebreaking lapses are unpleasant. With puppies, however, it's impossible to predict how long the housetraining process will take. There can be various reasons for that. Even dogs that have been housebroken can experience relapses.

Possible causes

▷ If the dog has already been housebroken, an illness may be causing him to do his business

▷ It's not too early for a puppy to learn that biting and nipping are not allowed, even in a game. If your pet gets out of hand, distract him by playing with a toy, stop playing altogether, or employ the muzzle grip. You'll find out what works best with your dog.

indoors again. He may possibly have cystitis or an intestinal infection. A change in food or a food allergy can also lead to digestive problems.

▷ Older dogs may become incontinent; that is, they may release urine involuntarily.

▷ Bitches may become incontinent after they have been spayed.

▷ The dog is relieving himself indoors as a form of "protest" (hierarchy problem), for example, because he doesn't want to stay home alone. Or there may have been drastic changes in his environment, such as a change in the family constellation (baby, new partner) or your acquisition of a second dog.

▷ Wrong correlation with housetraining during training: Perhaps you scolded or even punished the dog after he relieved himself in the house, but he connected "going to the potty" with "causes trouble." Therefore he hides in remote corners of the house or in the basement to urinate or defecate.

▷ The puppy is forced to relieve himself indoors because you don't take him out often enough. Possibly you're also leaving him alone too long.

▷ The breeder failed to give the puppy enough space, and he couldn't satisfy his natural need

to relieve himself at a good distance from his bed. Now, therefore, he never goes far from his bed to do his business.

▷ At the breeding facility, the puppy was familiar only with stone or concrete floors. Therefore he tends to relieve himself exclusively on such surfaces—that is, at home instead of outdoors on the grass or on a path in a wooded area.

▷ If you take the puppy outdoors when he has to go in the daytime but not at night, then he will relieve himself in the house. The house-training process will take longer in this case.

▷ When you're outdoors, the puppy is so distracted by all the new impressions that he "remembers" that he needed to go only after he's back at home.

Possible solutions

▷ If you suspect the presence of a disease, consult the veterinarian without delay. Hormones can be helpful in cases of incontinence among neutered bitches.

▷ Take a close look at the hierarchy in your human-dog team. If you decide that your "would-be boss" is the center of attention too much of the time, change the way you deal with the dog where appropriate. In addition, do more work on obedience training (→ page 82).

▷ If your puppy would rather go to the potty indoors than outdoors, for whatever reason, I suggest that you stay outside with your pet until he no longer has a choice: he has to go, however long it takes.

▷ For nighttime problems, you can restrict the puppy's radius of action by putting him in a crate. Then you'll know when he gets restless, and you can take him outdoors.

▷ Prevent improper correlations on the dog's part by removing any accidents you come across without saying a word. Punishment of any kind is counterproductive, since your four-legged friend will relate them to doing his business in general, rather than to the ban on doing it indoors. If you suspect that your pet has drawn the wrong conclusion, repair

TIP

Connecting objects

If your dog chases cars, people riding bikes, and so forth, the "punishment" also can spring from the object directly. For example, the cyclist may have some tin cans tied together or filled with stones that he or she throws in front of the approaching dog's legs. Or someone can pour a bucket of water out of the car window onto the dog.

the relationship of trust by providing plenty of positive attention. Praise the dog lavishly when he relieves himself outdoors. If his anxiety is really pronounced, you need to consult a behavioral therapist.

Playing Too Rough

Does your canine companion play so rough that some of your clothing shows the effects and his teeth have left clear marks on your hands? Then it's high time to get his behavior back on the right track.

Possible causes

▷ This behavior is innate, in part also breed-related. Spunky breeds and breeds with an inborn fighting instinct are more likely to "kick over the traces" now and then.

▷ Your dog has too little respect for you. This can be the case if your other dealings with him also announce that he's the hub of your world. Or your pet may be a very self-confident dog.

▷ You or your children are playing too rough with the dog.

▷ The dog doesn't have enough to keep him busy and has a surplus of energy

▷ He's testing you to see how far he can go.

Possible solutions

▷ Interrupt the game immediately and without a word if it's getting too wild, and ignore the dog. That alone is sufficient with some dogs.

▷ If that's not enough, you need to put a stop to the behavior at once by calmly using a more or less firm muzzle grip (→ page 30) on your pet, along with a very assertive but quiet "No." If the dog licks your hand afterwards or goes away, you've reacted correctly.

▷ If you're not confident enough to use the muzzle grip, or if the muzzle grip makes no impression on your pet, give the dog a time-out in a crate or briefly in another room. Do this in a businesslike manner, with no show of emotion.

▷ Take a close look at the way you deal with the dog. Is it your pet that usually calls the tune? If so, I suggest that you make some changes.

▷ Don't play directly with the dog; instead, use an object such as a tug rope, which is suitable for games of tug-of-war, seek, and fetch. Play games involving tugging only if the dog doesn't get worked up and play uninhibitedly, while growling extensively. In addition, the hierarchy must be clear, and your pet should let go at once when you give the signal.

▷ In general, make sure your dog gets enough mental and physical activity.

Restless Behavior

Some dogs love being the center of attention, especially when you have company or are visiting a friend's home—they want everything to revolve around them. They tug in various directions, pester people, or yowl. This can be annoying—and not only for the owner.

Possible causes

▷ The dog is basically used to having everything revolve around him.

▷ He has often seen that such behavior gets him more attention.

▷ If you have guests or if you're visiting, use your pet's normal leash to tie him to the table or chair (both need to be heavy enough, depending on your dog's size). You and every-one else should ignore the dog. At some point he will lie down, once he notices that he isn't getting anywhere with his behavior.

▶ TIP

No "Down" or "Stay"

When you leave home, don't *down* your pet in some spot with a command. He would have to stay there the entire time, for several hours. For one thing, that would be asking too much of the dog; for another, you have no way to ensure that he complies with the standards of the exercise.

▷ He is excessively friendly toward humans.
▷ His basic training was neglected or omitted altogether.
▷ His socialization was inadequate or nonex-istent, and in such situations he comes under stress.
▷ He is inherently unable to cope, despite socialization.
▷ The dog is reacting to insecurity and anxi-ety by being restless.
▷ The dog can't stay quiet because he had too little opportunity to blow off steam before-hand.
▷ The dog misses his customary resting place.
▷ General restlessness can also be disease-related (for example, thyroid hyperfunction).

Possible solutions

▷ Basically, don't yield to your pet's efforts to "suck up" to you and get your attention. Ignore the dog, and also prevent him from having any success with other people.
▷ Take a close look at the hierarchy and your demeanor toward the dog. Make corrections where appropriate.
▷ Intensify the obedience training, so that you can keep your dog in the *down* position longer in such situations, at least with you in sight. Structure the training systematically, and gradually increase the distraction level (→ page 83).

If he "acts up" seriously, I recommend that you first practice ignoring him at home or in the home of friends.
▷ Make sure that your pet has a chance to let off sufficient steam and get tired before such outings. Use the training exercises to provide him with mental activity.
▷ Take his blanket along when you're away from home, and put him under the table or, when you're visiting friends, in a quiet corner. Then he will make a better connection between such a situation and the need to be quiet.
▷ If your pet is insecure, this stressful situa-tion may cause him to become restless. If so, you must slowly accustom him to such situa-tions. For the time being, don't take the dog along when a lot of people will be together in a small space and where it may be noisy as well.
▷ If the insecurity is innate, even slow habit-uation will not help much. Then, the only

◁

Luckily this dog stays alone without an ensuing reign of terror. Often, it's difficult to correct problems with being alone, especially if you simply have to leave at certain times. A dog sitter, at least on a temporary basis, would be helpful here.

alternative is to spare the dog such irksome situations entirely, by always leaving him at home or putting him in another room when you have guests.

▷ If you suspect that illness may be the cause, take your pet to the veterinarian.

Staying Alone

Staying alone is rather abnormal for the dog, a pack animal. Nevertheless, every dog should be able to stay without his caretaker for a few hours without any problems.

How problems with staying alone express themselves:

▷ If the dog has separation anxiety, he will feel stress every time he is left alone. He will whimper, yowl, or bark and possibly expel urine. These symptoms often appear even before you've left the house.

▷ If the dog doesn't have enough to do and the hierarchy is unclear, he also will protest loudly, but more often by barking or chewing on objects.

▷ If the hierarchy is unclear, the dog may deliberately mark places with urine: his owner's bed, for example. Both males and females do this.

A protest or a reaction caused by boredom need not occur every time the dog is left alone, however.

Possible causes

▷ The dog has not been systematically taught to stay alone.

▷ He doesn't have enough activity.

▷ The dog sees himself as high-ranking; he behaves assertively in daily life in general and usually gets away with it. Such a dog understandably will not accept the idea of his "pack" going somewhere without him.

▷ The dog was left alone too young. He connects this with a negative experience because something frightened him while he was alone.

This may have been, for example, a heavy thunderstorm or the sound of low-flying aircraft.

▷ He has separation anxiety, because the bond with his owner is too close or because he is basically insecure.

Possible solutions

Especially if you're already having problems with neighbors, you need to find someone to look after your dog while you're away, until you can get him accustomed to staying alone.

With separation anxiety: The dog, like the puppy, first has to learn to stay some distance from you inside your home.

▷ If he stays alone in the car with no problems while you're doing some quick shopping, always say "Wait" when you get out of the vehicle. At home, don't let your pet follow you wherever you go. For example, close the door when you go into the bathroom, and say "Wait" at this time too.

▷ If you use a crate in the car and the dog is accustomed to it, you can use it at home too. Leave the dog alone in the crate while you're home.

▷ You can still use the crate to train your pet to stay alone, however, even if the crate is new to him. You have to help him adjust to the crate in advance, of course (→ page 76): At first, stay in the same room where the dog is sitting in his crate. If your four-legged friend accepts this after appropriate training, leave the room and go to another part of the house. Practice only for brief periods at first, gradually extending them over time. Always end an exercise before the dog starts showing symptoms of stress, such as restlessness or heavy panting.

▷ If your pet gets nervous the second you pick up your key or put on certain items of clothing, you first will have to get him accustomed to this. Dress accordingly, take the keys, and then sit down at your table and read something. Ignore the dog consistently. Remember what ignoring means to a dog (→ page 31).

Once he has calmed down and relaxed, take off the items of clothing and act "normally" again. Don't pay your pet any special attention at this point either. If this is working all the time, then you can keep practicing as described above, but always in your "going-out outfit." That is, first go to another room and when that works, leave the house.

Unclear hierarchy and boredom:

▷ Provide more mental and physical activity (→ Chapter 6).

▷ Train basic obedience commands systematically, both indoors and outdoors.

▷ Take a look at the hierarchy. To do so, you can repeatedly leave the dog in his crate for a certain time. Without the crate, you should *down* your pet on his blanket for longer and longer periods, assuming he has learned this lesson. That "forces" the insubordinate animal to let you go to another room.

▷ Practice daily. Once the dog has learned to tolerate your presence in another room for awhile—indoors, while you're home, and without protest—you can start leaving the house for brief periods of time. If this is working, gradually prolong your absences.

Important with protests as well as separation anxiety: no dramatic goodbye and hello scenes! The dog mustn't feel that staying alone is something special, rather than something quite normal.

What else you can do:

▷ When you leave the house, you can also leave the dog in his crate if need be. The feeling of being in a cave often gives insecure dogs a sense of safety. Personally, I do not advocate leaving the dog in it for hours on end.

▷ Never go back to him if he yowls! That would teach him that somebody will come if he's just loud enough. Always wait until he has been quiet for at least a few moments, so that he no longer connects your return with his complaints.

△

Opportunity makes a thief! If your dog has a tendency to snitch food, avoiding the situation is essential. Otherwise he will repeatedly experience the success you want to deny him.

▷ If he scratches at the door while you're away, a crate can help again. But you can also cover the door with scratch-proof foil or the like. Pet stores carry special dog shoes that can help temporarily. If your four-legged friend is one if those dogs that enjoy "stripping," combine the shoes with a muzzle.

Stealing Food

Almost every dog, sooner or later, seizes the opportunity to help himself from the kitchen counter or even from the table. That leads to

△
A leap into freedom! If your dog strays, make sure he can't escape from your yard, and give him plenty of mental and physical exercise. Then he will enjoy staying at home again.

quite a few disagreeable surprises. The solution that works in this case depends on your dog.

Possible causes

▷ The dog has little or no respect for his owner.

▷ The dog frequently has been fed at the table.

▷ He grew up as a feral animal and thus, was used to finding its own supplies of food.

▷ The dog is motivated by sheer greed.

Possible solutions

▷ Close the doors to rooms such as the kitchen or pantry, especially when you're going out.

▷ Opportunity makes a thief—don't leave anything edible lying around when you're not home.

▷ Tie cans filled with rocks, pot lids, or similar objects to some type of "bait" that the dog can't swallow in a single gulp (a large sausage, hard rolls or bread). Place this bait on the dining table or work surface without letting the dog see you. The cans or pot lids should not be visible to the dog, so that he doesn't connect these objects with the effect produced. If the dog takes the bait, his ⬤ PUNISHMENT (page 271) will follow like a bolt from the blue—everything will fall to the floor with a huge clang. Immediately take the bait away from your pet—if he manages to eat it, this still could be interpreted as a success! Otherwise, do nothing.

7

▷ With some dogs, it's sufficient to catch them "red-handed" and storm into the room with a loud "No" and a lot of bluster, before the dog has the morsel in his mouth.

▷ If the dog begs for food at the table, ignore him. You can *down* him in his place while you eat—assuming he has learned this lesson.

Don't forget to release your pet again after your meal is over.

▷ Growl at your four-legged friend the way dogs do, if his nose gets too close to your plate. That is helpful in some cases.

▷ If your pet does not obey reliably and the hierarchy is not quite right, you should intensify and improve the obedience training (→ Chapter 3 and page 36).

Straying

Straying can have serious consequences. The roaming dog may cause an accident, for example; in addition, he will become too independent. Even if he "only" goes over to play with the neighbor's dog, he will learn that he can have fun without you. Some dog owners may think this is practical, but by now you know that going off on his own has a negative effect on the bond between dog and human.

Possible causes

▷ The dog is bored.

▷ The bond with you is flawed.

▷ The dog sees the "outings" as something positive.

▷ Your dog is a male and is on his way to a female in heat.

Possible solutions

▷ Don't leave the dog alone or for a long while in the yard.

▷ Don't let your dog have the experience of succeeding. Make your property escape-proof.

▷ If the dog has to stay alone, lock him up in the house.

▷ If your yard can't be fenced in completely, at least enclose part of it. That way you can restrict the dog's radius of operation.

▷ Leash your pet before you open the door or the garden gate. If one of the doors has to stay open longer, then you should shut the dog in a separate room in the meantime.

▷ Banish any hint of boredom by systematically playing with your dog, keeping it occupied during your walks, and practicing obedience exercises regularly. Everything the dog enjoys, he should experience with you. Then the bond between you will be intact again.

▷ If your male suffers from an unusually strong reproductive drive, neutering ( HYPERSEXUALITY, page 266) will help.

10 Questions About Problems

Our Sammy, even on leash, goes after other dogs. If he stays seated on occasion, can I praise him for it?
If you want to praise a dog for not engaging in undesirable behavior, you always have to take a close look at what he does instead. If Sammy continues to sit but glares fixedly at his "opponent," possibly also growling softly, and you praise him for this, then you're actually validating him again for incipient aggressive behavior. You can praise him if he concentrates on you rather than on the other dog, or if he stays relaxed and walks past the other dog without glaring.

When I want to train with my Ricky, he often bites the leash and jumps around. Can I get him to stop this?
Stand still, keep the leash in your hand, and ignore Ricky. If he gets no attention (since that's what he wants), he'll give up sooner or later. If you're authoritative enough, then he may also react to a familiar stop command (→ page 85). Asking for an alternative behavior would be another option.

What do I do when our dog "clings" to my leg?
Unless your dog is hypersexual, trying to mount your leg is an effort to establish dominance. If necessary, use the muzzle grip to discourage this behavior. Then reward your pet for an alternative behavior (such as a *sit*).

We're expecting an addition to the family soon, and we've noticed that our Pete tenses up when he hears a crying baby at our friends' house and tries to snap at her. What can we do?
Take this very seriously. Intensify your obedience training, so that you have Pete under control at all times. Take a close look at the hierarchy. The baby's room and your bedroom must immediately be declared off limits for Pete. Start now to get him used to a muzzle. Purchase a doll that "cries," put baby clothes on it, and treat it like a real baby. When the doll cries, put a stop to undesirable behavior with a stop command, and reward Pete for alternative behavior (such as a *sit* or a *down*). Never leave the dog and the child unsupervised! You may have to find another home for your dog.

At the moment, our two four-legged friends keep tangling with each other. Should we let them work it out themselves?
That's not advisable, since such encounters can always escalate. Here, you should take the role of "top dog" and set some limits. Interrupt any impending conflicts and give the rivals a timeout in their beds. Think about what might be causing the conflicts. Are you possibly granting the lower-ranking dog privileges that he wouldn't be rightfully entitled to?

▷
If a dog tries to mount the back of another, this is usually a dominance play. It happens not only between male and female, but also between dogs of the same gender.

7

△
To prevent such a situation from arising in the first place, promptly get your dog to give you his attention.

directly up to him, or look directly at him. Then the dog will learn that your spouse won't do anything to him. If your pet relaxes and perhaps voluntarily decreases the distance over time, your husband can feed him from his hand, but without looking at him.

Our 14-week-old Amy likes to lie in an armchair in the yard. When I try to pick her up, she bares her teeth and growls. Should I just let her lie where she is?
Starting now, Amy will not lie in an armchair in the yard again. Firmly take her out and set her on the ground. In general, pay more attention to setting limits for the puppy. Even though Amy looks cuddly and cute, she's already a "real" dog!

I have a dog from a pet shelter and I don't know which commands he was already familiar with. What can I do?
Simply try the common terms and visual signals used in this book. Praise the dog if he reacts to them. If you can't determine which signals he may have learned, just start afresh and teach the dog the commands you choose.

We took in our dog as an adult, from a bad breeding facility. Now he's afraid of my husband, who visually resembles the breeder, and also growls at him. My husband has been scolding the dog when that happens. Was that the right thing?
No, it means that the dog is also being punished for his fear-related reaction—and his mistrust increases. Your husband should cease to pay the dog any attention at all, walk

My Rocco recently growled at me in an aggressive way. What's the best way to act here?
If the hierarchy is basically all right and the threat is not severe, then a pat under the chin and a stern glance may be sufficient in some cases. If you feel insecure around the dog and if the hierarchy is unclear, however, then you should avoid direct confrontations. Either pretend that you didn't notice anything, or ask for an alternative behavior. For example, call the dog and walk some distance with him at *heel*, having him sit from time to time. Praise him for this.

◁
Most dogs like riding in a car. Some, however, despite slow habituation and an empty stomach, don't tolerate it well.

On her first trips in our car, our dog threw up. She no longer does this, but she's still afraid of riding in a car. What can we do?
For the time being, feed the dog in the car while she's not moving, and stay there until your pet has relaxed. Once this has succeeded a few times, do the same thing with the motor running. If your pet remains relaxed in this situation too, you can take short drives, making sure you drive slowly and carefully. Each trip should end with a highlight for the dog.

Quickfinder
from A to Z

▶ The Quickfinder section provides you with an easy-to-reference alphabetical listing of all the terms you'll want to know when training your four-legged friend. Each entry contains basic facts based on practical experience, as well as fascinating background information. If you want more details, the references to related chapters and sections will take you immediately to what you need.

▶ **STOP COMMAND**   Quickfinder term

⑦ Barking, *Page 235*   Numbers in a circle, titles, and page numbers refer to chapters and places in the text that deal with the Quickfinder term.

▶ **SIGNAL** (page 272)   Cross-reference to related Quickfinder terms

● ABILITY TO CONCENTRATE

A dog's ability to concentrate depends on her age, the level of training she has reached and on her general type. Practice with your four-legged friend only while she is still concentrating and attentive. Otherwise, whatever you're trying to teach her will not be learned. Puppies can concentrate for only a few minutes. Well-trained and systematically developed dogs can concentrate for several hours, if need be. This is essential, for example, on long hunts with dogs trained for hunting.

③ **Three-Step Lesson Planning,** *page 83*

● AKC

The American Kennel Club (AKC) is the largest and second oldest purebred dog registry in the world. Founded in 1884, the AKC was formed as a "club of clubs" to promote the sport of purebred dogs and breeding for type and function (● BREED, page 260). Today, the AKC comprises over 580 member clubs and over 4,000 licensed and affiliated clubs. The AKC currently registers 155 dog breeds representing a wide variety of size, color, coat, temperament, and heritage. A dog that has full registration with the AKC is eligible to participate in many of the over 18,000 events offered by the AKC and its affiliated clubs each year (some events are breed-specific). The AKC is the only purebred dog registry in the U.S. that conducts kennel inspections to ensure the health, safety, and welfare of AKC-registered dogs. The AKC inspects breeders who register seven or more litters per year, and randomly selects some breeders who register between four and six litters a year for inspection. Inspectors verify that breeders are maintaining accurate records, which must be maintained for at least five years. Nearly 5,000 kennel inspections are conducted each year. DNA testing is conducted during inspections as a way to verify the parentage of a litter of puppies. Employing this technology confirms that breeders are maintaining accurate pedigrees and maintains the integrity of the AKC registry. The AKC Public Education Network is designed to help educate the general public about responsible dog ownership. Note that owners of a particular breed, wishing to have that breed registered, must establish an organized National Breed Club.

① **Where to Learn about Breeders,** *page 18*

● ALTRICIAL SPECIES

Altricial young are completely dependent on their mother during the period following their birth. They cannot search for food independently or move far from their nest. Puppies are born deaf and blind. The mother dog removes their umbilical cord, cleans them, nurses them, and tends them. That is quite important, since the neonates initially can release feces and urine only when the dam intensely licks their abdomen and rear end. Puppies can grow up and be healthy, therefore, only if their mother has a strong brood-care (parental) instinct. This factor must also be considered by breeders in

selecting bitches for breeding. The opposite of altricial is "precocial."

① The Neonatal Phase, *page 25*

▶ APPEASEMENT GESTURES

This term applies to all the signals sent out by the dog to have a calming effect on her opponent's ▶ DOMINANCE GESTURES (page 263). It also applies to signals of active and passive submission. These include averting the eyes, evasion, yawning, licking, offering a paw, sniffing at the ground, scratching, and so forth. Appeasement gestures are also used when a dog feels an internal conflict or is under stress or is worried and do not always require an addressee. To interpret the gestures correctly and avoid overemphasizing them, you always must consider the situation and the rest of the dog's body language as well. By no means does every sniff at the ground or lick of the muzzle have a deeper significance.

② Signals of Conflict and Appeasement, *page 62*

▶ AVOIDANCE BEHAVIOR

Through avoidance behavior, a dog attempts to withdraw from an unpleasant situation or influence. For example, a dog exhibits avoidance behavior toward cows or sheep if she has made the acquaintance of an electric fence when she had the animals in her sights and tried to run into the pasture. If a dog is trained with ▶ STRONG-ARM METHODS (page 273), she will execute the commands in order to avoid the effect of the overt physical force, but she will appear visibly stressed or frightened.

① Positive Motivation and Reinforcement, *page 26*

▶ BASIC OBEDIENCE

Basic obedience includes the exercises that every dog that is taken out in public must master as a minimum. These include coming reliably in response to a call or whistle blow, walking on a loose leash at *heel*, staying quietly in the *sit* and *down* positions for a few minutes next to the dog owner, and sitting or lying tranquilly in a certain spot and at some distance from the owner until released upon the owner's return. In addition to its practical purpose, diversified obedience training that is related to daily life also provides mental activity for your four-legged friend. Usually the basic exercises will not meet that objective for long, however.

③ Meaningful Training—with a System, *page 83*

▶ BIDDABLE

When a dog is biddable, this means that she is more or less anxious to do everything correctly and reacts to relatively slight signals from her human partner. Biddability is present above all in breeds that are bred to work closely with humans. Many hunting dogs and ▶ HERDING DOGS (page 265) breeds fall into this category. If traits such as the instinct to guard and protect, the prey drive, and the hunting instinct are highly pronounced, a high level of biddability makes the dog easier to control. If, however, pronounced instincts are combined with stubbornness—a low level of biddability—many things become more difficult. Examples are herd-protection dogs and terrier breeds, as well as breeds such as the beagle. These and similar breeds are bred to perform guard duties or hunting-related tasks untiringly, attentively, and independently.

① Indirect Assignment of Rank, *page 36*

◐ BITE INHIBITION

Many dog owners assume that dogs have an innate inhibition when it comes to biting other members of their species and humans. The bite inhibition, however—that is, the disinclination of dogs under normal circumstances to bite either other dogs or humans—must first be learned during the course of socialization. Dogs learn this by seeing that overly rude behavior on their part gets a negative reaction (for example, the ◐ MUZZLE GRIP, page 268), or that their playmate won't play any more. The only innate inhibition, however, is the one that restrains dogs from biting their own young.

⑥ Why Do Dogs Play? *page 185*

◐ BOND

This is the basis for the relationship between human and dog. The bond between the two-legged and four-legged partners is made solid and stable through play and physical contact, among other things. Basically the dog is very willing to bond, since her species is reliant on a social community. The bond must not be so close that the dog is completely helpless without her caretaker, but strong enough for the animal to look trustingly to her human partner for guidance.

③ Establishing a Positive Bond, *page 78*

◐ BREED

Worldwide, there are approximately 400 recognized dog breeds, in all possible sizes

and phenotypes. Some are so dissimilar in appearance that at first glance you can hardly believe that they belong to the same species. In the United States the accepted registry for all breeds is the American Kennel Club (AKC). In Canada, the accepted registry is the Canadian Kennel Club, which is a government-run organization. If you would like to see the multitude of breeds first-hand, I recommend attending one of the large dog shows sponsored by the ◐ AKC (page 258). Several of these events are held in various cities each year.

① Is There a Really Child-Friendly Dog? *page 21*

◐ COERCION

People frequently argue about whether "coercion" is necessary in training a dog, and if so, how much. Catch phrases such as "non-coercive" training for dogs are fashionable today. But it all depends on what you mean by the term. Strictly speaking, you are using coercion by motivating a dog (positively or negatively) to exhibit a certain behavior (such as the *sit*) or to stop a behavior (such as chewing the rug) and insisting that the animal obey. The dog would not simply do that of her own accord. Seen in this light, training a dog without some type of coercion is impossible. Colloquially, however, it's generally accepted that coercion refers to ◐ STRONG-ARM METHODS (page 273) involving overt physical force.

① "Dog-Appropriate" Reprimands, *page 29*

◐ CONDITIONED STIMULUS

A noise or something similar (such as a ring tone) that initially has a neutral meaning for the dog is regularly combined with an ◐ UNCONDITIONED STIMULUS (page 276), such as food: that is, with a stimulus that basically triggers a certain reaction (such as salivation). After a certain time, the previously neutral stimulus, even without the unconditioned stimulus, produces the reaction; that is, it becomes a conditioned stimulus. The dog is conditioned to the conditioned stimulus. An example from daily life illustrates this. You put on your "dog-walking jacket," and your four-legged friend immediately knows that it's time to go out, and is delighted.

① How Does a Dog Learn? *page 26*

CONDITIONING

The principle of conditioning has its origin in the discipline of psychology. It describes the learning of a certain stimulus, which then triggers a certain pattern of behavior. We distinguish between classical conditioning and operant or instrumental conditioning. In the classical form, an initially neutral stimulus (sound of a spoon in an almost-empty yogurt container) is combined with an unconditioned reaction (salivation before licking out the container) to produce a CONDITIONED STIMULUS (page 260). The noise made by the spoon alone triggers salivation. In operant conditioning, the dog learns that a certain behavior that she volunteers leads to success or failure.

① How Does a Dog Learn? *page 26*

CRATE

Crates are available in many models, made of plastic or metal. When selecting one, decide whether you want it only for puppyhood or for use with the adult dog later on. You'll also need to determine whether the crate will only be used indoors or used in the car as well. The crate should be large enough for the dog to both comfortably lie down and sit upright. A slanted front will make it easier to fit in the rear of the car.

③ Use the Crate for Training, *page 75*

DISPLACEMENT ACTIVITY

Displacement activities are behaviors exhibited when an animal or a person is torn between two conflicting instincts or actions. In humans, scratching one's head out of embarrassment is an example of a displacement activity. You might, for example, urgently need to take care of a few things, but you can't decide where to start—so you first scratch your head. Dogs exhibit similar behavior. Your male is determined to get close to a bitch, but you tell him to sit. He may indeed sit, but also scratch itself at the same time.

In dogs, displacement activities are classified as APPEASEMENT GESTURES (page 259). They don't necessarily serve to calm the other animal, however. In the example, the male isn't trying to calm either the bitch or you by scratching himself.

② Signals of Conflict and Appeasement, *page 62*

DOG LIABILITY INSURANCE POLICY

Every dog owner should get such a policy as soon as the dog joins the household. Then

any damage caused by the dog will be covered. The animal could cause an accident, for example, in which people are harmed; she might injure another member of her species; or she might break or ruin something in the home of friends. The rates and scope of coverage vary, so it pays to make some comparisons.

⑤ A Word in Advance, *page 167*

● DOG SCHOOL

There are increasing numbers of dog schools, since in principle, anybody can open one. It is not always easy for the average dog owner to determine the quality of the school. The offerings are varied—puppy classes, basic training, preparation for the Obedience Training, clicker training, agility, and so forth—and they are open to owners of all breeds, including mixed breeds. Usually, the training provided by dog schools focuses on everyday matters rather than on dog sports.

③ Attending a Puppy Class and a Dog School, *page 124*

● DOG WHISTLE

These are available in a wide range of styles. The important thing is to be able to hear whether the whistle works. Each whistle has a tone of its own, and it is best to buy two at once, to have one in reserve. The dog whistle should be made of sturdy plastic or of stag or buffalo horn, and the frequency must not change, or at least not change on its own. Remember: The dog has to be trained to respond to the whistle just as to every other signal.

① The Right Equipment, *page 40*

● DOMESTICATION

The word comes from Latin *domus*, meaning house and refers to adaptation to intimate association with human beings. This describes the development of a wild animal into a house pet. We can't say exactly when the domestication of the wolf began and when the domestic dog came into being, since many remains are difficult to identify firmly as being the bones of wolves or of dogs. The oldest bones that clearly are those of a dog are approximately 14,000 years old and were discovered in North Germany in a grave from the last Ice Age. Domestication resulted in numerous differences between wolf and dog. This is most evident in their physical appearance. For one, the dog's teeth and bones are smaller than the wolf's. Breeding behavior is also accelerated in the dog. Wolves (both females and males) are ready to mate only once a year and reach sexual maturity only at the age of two; dogs, however, usually mature sexually in their second six months of life. Males are always ready to mate, and bitches are in season about twice a year.

① Why Training Is Important, *page 13*

● DOMINANCE

The word comes from Latin *dominare*, meaning to rule. In dogs, a diagnosis of "dominant" is often made prematurely. There

certainly are dogs that tend more in that direction than others, but a dog can become "dominant" only if she or he has someone whom she or he can dominate or who allows him/herself to be dominated. A dog that has no rules or boundaries and no leadership has no choice, ultimately, but to do what it thinks is right. That doesn't automatically mean that it is a "dominant" dog. The behavioral researcher Dorit Feddersen-Petersen interprets dominant behavior as meaning that one individual restricts the freedom of another and grants him/herself a great deal of freedom, without the other one doing anything to oppose it.

② A Few Words about Dominance, *page 56*

⊙ DOMINANCE GESTURES

These are to be contrasted with
⊙ APPEASEMENT GESTURES (page 259). They include, for example, fixedly staring at another dog, pushing her away, blocking her path, mounting her back, laying her own head on the other's back (in the "T position," with the lower-ranking dog forming the crossbar, and the higher-ranking dog, the upright bar of the T), or failing to maintain individual distance. These signals must always be seen

in the context of overall body language and the general situation. Not every instance of eye contact, for example, has a "dominant" effect, and not every laying of a head on another dog's back is intended as a dominance gesture.

② Communicating by Body Contact, *page 47*

⊙ DUMMY

Originally developed in England as a substitute for wild game so that retrievers had something to do in the off-season and didn't get out of practice, dummies are used to train dogs to fetch. They now are available in different sizes and shapes, and their use is no longer restricted to retriever training. The dog is supposed to maintain "soft mouth" when carrying them, like real wild game—that is, she mustn't grip too firmly. This objective is easier to attain with the dummies, which are made from pliable materials, than with the so-called training bucks made of wood.

⑥ Combining Fetching with Obedience, *page 198*

⊙ EXPRESSIVE BEHAVIOR

This refers to all of the dog's means of communication—body language (optical communication), vocalization (acoustic communication), leaving scent messages (olfactory communication), and touch (tactile communication). The world of scents, however, probably will never be fully accessible to humans.

② The Dog's Body Language, *page 45*

⊙ FAMILY DOG

The endorsement "good family dog" is applied to almost all breeds. There is really no dog that would not become attached to her family—the dog is a pack animal by nature. But if we interpret "family dog" as one that shares the normal daily life of a family in our society, that is, deals with noise and a great variety of people and environments, then certain requirements for such a dog begin to crystallize. These include a liking for humans, a low level of aggressiveness (that is, a high threshold), composure, and dependability in everyday situations such as daily walks, hustle and bustle, and crowds of people. Other prerequisites are little or no ○ INSTINCT TO GUARD AND PROTECT (page 267), no ○ PREY DRIVE (page 270) in combination with a fighting instinct, and a good level of trainability.

① Is There a Really Child-Friendly Dog? *page 21*

○ FETCHING

To fetch means to go after something and bring it back, or to retrieve killed game. Fetching is actually an advanced form of obedience, since in the wild it is usual to carry prey, but not to bring it to someone and relinquish it (apart from feeding the young). In the case of many hunting breeds in particular, the "retriever drive" is deliberately encouraged by breeders, since these dogs must find downed game— ducks, foxes, or hares—and bring it to the hunter.

⑥ Learning to Fetch Properly, *page 196*

○ FCI

The Fédération Cynologique Internationale is the international umbrella organization for officially recognized purebred dog associations in Europe (except Britain), Asia, and South America. It is headquartered in Thuin, Belgium. It sets breed standards, establishes parameters for showing, breeding, and training, and issues kennel names for breeders associated with its member countries. Today the FCI has 80 member countries worldwide. The purebred dog registry in the United States is the AKC (page 258).

○ FIGHTING DRIVE

This expression comes from the world of working dogs. "Fighting drive" is desirable in the ○ WORKING-DOG BREEDS (page 277); it is fostered by breeders and is one of the qualities needed for training as a protection dog. The dog must display willingness to confront her opponent fearlessly and combatively, using her teeth. This is necessary, for example, when prey must be caught or when the dog is beset, but she must not let herself be deterred by anything or anyone except her handler. If a dog shows indifference or friendliness here or even retreats, that is considered a flaw. On the other hand, there are breeds, such as the Labrador and Golden Retriever, in which the fighting drive is emphatically undesirable. It is not necessary for normal daily activities with a dog, and if an animal with such a drive is improperly raised and trained, there can be problems with both humans and other dogs.

⑤ The Cantankerous Dog, *page 172*

○ FLOOR AND GROUND SURFACES

Since our domestic dogs have to cope with a great variety of unnatural surfaces like smooth wood and stone floors, all types of stairs, and so forth, they should become familiar with many of them while they are still puppies. Once a dog can walk without fear across all kinds of floors, you should practice the obedience exercises that are working well at home on many floors and ground surfaces. Then the dog will be safe and obedient in any kind of terrain.

③ Familiarizing the Puppy with Different Surfaces, *page 73*

○ FLYBALL

In this dog sport, which originated in the U.S., a dog races across four hurdles to a machine, which she activates with her paws. The machine then releases a ball, which the dog catches and carries at top speed back over the hurdles to her owner.

⑥ Popular: Obedience and Agility, *page 202*

⏵ FRUSTRATION

If an action can't be completed as intended, frustration is created—the dog interrupts what she is doing. We take advantage of this, for example, when we use frustration in conditioning our pet to a ⏵ STOP COMMAND (page 273), such as the discs or a verbal signal such as "Stop," in order to interrupt an undesirable behavior. If the dog reacts with frustration and bewilderment and stops what she's doing, we reinforce this reaction with praise, "consoling" and "commiserating with" her because of the "bad thing" that happened to her. Depending on the dog's type, sometimes frustration can turn into aggression. For example, a dog fervently wishes to go after the neighbor's cat, but you stop her by grabbing her collar, and out of frustration she tries to bite your hand.

⑦ Not All Aggression Is the Same, *page 221*

⏵ HEAT (Estrus)

Bitches are in heat about twice a year. The cycle can vary widely among individuals. Some bitches are in heat every six months, others only every nine months. The time of the first heat, or estrus, also varies greatly; in some females, it can occur as early as the age of seven months, while in others it begins only after the age of one year.

Heat lasts for about three weeks. During this time, never leave your bitch unsupervised. When she is in heat, she will not only wait for a male to come to her, but will also be on the lookout for one of her own accord.

② Scent Messages, *page 49*

⏵ HERD PROTECTION DOGS

This group of breeds, also known as "shepherd dogs," is often wrongly equated with ⏵ HERDING DOGS (page 265). Most herd protection breeds, such as the Kuvasz, Anatolian Shepherd, and Great Pyrenees, are deliberately bred to guard the herded animals independently and single-mindedly and to defend them against predators or rustlers. These are large, heavy dogs with a long, dense coat. From a young age they are socialized with the animals they later will protect, and they practically live in the herd. Herd protection dogs are highly territorial and wary and act independently. They are reserved to mistrustful in regard to everything that is strange, and are sometimes unpredictable. Therefore, it is not easy to keep them as pets.

⑦ Causes of Bad Behavior, *page 229*

⏵ HERDING DOGS

The job of herding dogs is to keep the flock or herd together and to move the animals wherever the herdsman wishes: perhaps to another pasture or from one pen into another. They usually work very closely with the herdsman and react sensitively to signals such as whistle blows, words, or visual signs. Herding breeds include the Collie breeds, Australian Shepherd, and others. One of the best-known herding breeds is the Border Collie.

Herding dogs often are real workaholics and need purposeful activity. They are slight, agile, and untiring, usually biddable and quick to learn.

⑦ Causes of Bad Behavior, *page 229*

⏵ HEREDITARY DISEASES

A whole series of genetically determined diseases have now been identified in dogs, and they are equally likely to appear in mixed-breed dogs and in purebreds. Some breeds or breeding lines, however, are especially prone to develop certain disorders. There are, for example, disorders of the musculoskeletal system, such as hip dysplasia (HD) and elbow dysplasia (ED), as well as eye diseases (some of which result in blindness), and metabolic or cardiac diseases. Hereditary diseases can be curbed only by corresponding breeding programs that ensure mating only between animals that are certified to be healthy. Here, it is also important to consider the data for the animals' ancestors as well as for their descendents.

① Where to Learn about Breeders, *page 18*

▶ HUMAN CONTACT

Nonaggressive and basically friendly, confident behavior toward humans is one of the most important characteristics for a dog that lives in our society today. To ensure that humans represent something positive and completely normal for a dog, breeders must carefully select parents that possess these qualities and also provide enough positive human contact during the puppies' socialization phase.

① The Socialization Phase Begins, *page 25*

▶ HUNTING INSTINCT

This causes a beast of prey, such as a wolf or a dog, to use its nose, ears, and eyes to be on the lookout for prey and to stalk or pursue the quarry. The hunting instinct is closely linked with the ▶ PREY DRIVE (page 270). Humans avail themselves of the dog's hunting instinct for certain purposes and influence it through breeding. Guarding, for example, is nothing more than hunting without its final sequence—that is, without seizing and killing the prey. Pointers are a similar case: They detect the wild game, but once they get the scent they freeze in their tracks like a statue—they point to the quarry and thus indicate to the hunter: "Here it is," without pursuing and slaying it themselves.

⑦ Hunting, *page 243*

▶ HYPERACTIVITY

Some dogs are very active by nature, especially those that need a great deal of endurance and spirit for their original breed-specific task. But you also can unconsciously "ratchet up" your pet, for example, if someone in the household constantly is doing something with the dog and she never gets to calm down. Then she may be unable to cope with moments when nothing is going on. Deliberately deal very calmly with a very active or even nervous, frantic dog. Food that is too high in energy, such as a high-performance diet for a normal ▶ FAMILY DOG (page 263), can also result in hyperactivity and restlessness.

⑦ Causes of Bad Behavior, *page 229*

▶ HYPERSEXUALITY

This is an excessive interest in sexual activity. Hypersexuality is not uncommon in males and is caused by an elevated testosterone level. Such a male, once he reaches sexual maturity, is excessively interested in bitches of any type and often has an increased tendency to fight with other males, to neutralize competitors. Hypersexuality is stressful not only for the owner, but also for the dog. Because the inclination can be inherited, it makes no sense to breed such males. A lasting remedy is provided only by ⊙ NEUTERING (page 269), which should be performed before the dog is two years old.

⑤ Is It Really a Game? *page 170*

⊙ IMPRINTING-LIKE LEARNING

In the socialization phase, that is, during a restricted time period, dogs learn in a way that resembles imprinting. This means that all their experiences, however few or brief, are permanently recorded in their brain and have a lifelong effect. Learning deficits, too, have an equally decisive effect. This type of learning is not imprinting in the true sense, comparable to that described, for example, among gray geese by the behavioral researcher Konrad Lorenz. The geese follow the first moving object they see after hatching, and they irreversibly imprint on that object. Thus, goslings that imprint on a human, for example, see only him or her as a conspecific from that time on, rather than other geese. This is not the case in the imprinting-like learning process. Wolves or dogs raised by humans, for example, still recognize "real" conspecifics as such. The more highly developed an animal species, the less common true imprinting is, but the more common imprinting-like learning becomes.

① The Socialization Phase Begins, *page 25*

⊙ INADEQUATE EARLY SOCIALIZATION

This occurs when puppies grow up in a stall, kennel, or the like and have no opportunity to explore their surroundings and gather experience, or when they lack sufficient contact with humans. Inadequate early socialization almost always has a negative effect on the dog's development. This is magnified by the frequent failure of some breeding facilities to pay enough attention to the temperament of the parent dogs.

① The Socialization Phase Begins, *page 25*

⊙ INDIRECT ASSIGNMENT OF RANK

This helps the dog owner make clear, by means of behavior, his or her own social position relative to that of the dog without having to engage in any physical confrontation with the animal—which is inadvisable indeed. Examples are ignoring demands made by the dog, declaring privileged places such as the sofa or kitchen ⊙ TABOO ZONES (page 274) for the dog, being the first one through the door when leaving the house, and so forth. Especially with very self-confident dogs, or if the hierarchy is already disrupted, you should use these behaviors consistently.

① Indirect Assignment of Rank, *page 36*

⊙ INSTINCT

Instincts are inborn patterns of behavior that are elicited by specific stimuli, such as the ⊙ PREY DRIVE (page 270), ⊙ HUNTING INSTINCT (page 266), reproductive instinct, and brood-care (parental) instinct. They are basic programs of certain actions essential for survival. The higher the animal form, the more likely it is that learned behavior will prevail over instinctive behavior, which makes the animal more flexible in its adaptation to its environment.

⑤ Taking Your Dog Into Town, *page 162*

⊙ INSTINCT TO GUARD AND PROTECT

A certain guardian instinct—in the sense that she barks briefly when the doorbell rings—

is displayed by almost every dog. But the willingness to seriously defend her territory against "intruders" and protect her humans from threats (supposed and real)—if necessary, by using her teeth—is one of the desirable characteristics of the working-dog breeds in particular. The magnitude of the instinct to guard and protect, however, varies widely. A dog with a pronounced instinct to guard and protect requires responsible handling and must obey reliably, lest she become a danger. Good socialization from an early age is also important, so that the dog becomes familiar with a broad range of "normal" people and situations and thus is at least less likely to overreach later on.

The instinct to guard and protect can easily be unconsciously fostered if the natural tendency is already present—for example, you might additionally sensitize the dog by saying "Yes, go see who's at the door."

① What Breed Should I Choose? *page 20*

▶ MOOD

Your mood can be communicated to the dog, and she will react to it. The more sensitive a dog is, the more distinctly she will react to corresponding states of mind in her humans. In the interpretation of such mood transferences, however, the dog is frequently viewed in human terms. If she reacts to depression in her owner by low-spirited behavior, this has nothing to do with "wanting to console" in the human sense. The dog reacts to the unaccustomed mood in her human partner with uncertainty and makes contact with the person in a corresponding fashion. On the other hand, the dog's mood can also be transferred to the human. Owners of nervous dogs tend to become nervous themselves, which in turn increases the dog's nervousness.

⑦ Fear of Noises, *page 242*

▶ MOTIVATION

A dog basically does whatever seems worthwhile for him or her. It may be motivated by the action itself, as in the case of ▶ SELF-REWARDING BEHAVIORS (page 272), such as playing or chasing. Here, the playing or chasing on its own is sufficient motivation for doing it repeatedly. There is also positive motivation for a dog when a reward for a certain behavior is in the offing. For example, she or he may lie down in response to the audible signal "Down," and in return get some pats on the head, a treat, or words of praise. Motivation can also be negative, however. If the dog is taught the "Down" command by being dragged to the ground with a rough yank of the leash every time, after a certain time she or he will lie down just as quickly—to avoid the painful effect.

① Positive Motivation and Reinforcement, *page 26*

▶ MUZZLE GRIP

Grasping a pup's muzzle is a popular means of discipline among wolves and dogs. The older animal places its mouth around the puppy's muzzle—for example, if the youngster is being a pest or keeps trying to get at its mother's teats. Higher-ranking animals also use this behavior with lower-ranking pack members to emphasize their social status. Gentle grasping of the muzzle by a higher-ranking animal can also be an expression of a common bond, depending on the overall body language.

Humans can also clasp a dog's muzzle with one hand to give similar messages of reprimand or solidarity.

① Positive Reinforcement, *page 30*

NEGATIVE REINFORCEMENT

In contrast to ❍ POSITIVE REINFORCE-MENT (page 270), which acknowledges desirable behavior, negative reinforcement is used to arrest undesirable behavior. If you want the dog to get the point, the reinforcement must follow the behavior as quickly as a reward does. That is, the dog can properly interpret the correction only if the "punishment" follows the behavior by one or two seconds. All kinds of things can serve as negative reinforcement: a stern "No" or "Bad," a short tug on the leash, or the ❍ MUZZLE GRIP (page 268). The type of dog you have and the situation determine which kind of reinforcement works best in each case.

① Negative Impact, *page 28*

NEONATAL PHASE

"Neonatal" means "relating to or affecting newborns," and in dogs it refers to the period between birth and the time when the puppy consciously perceives its environment, using its eyes and ears—that is, the transition to the socialization phase. In the neonatal phase, a puppy is fairly helpless, but the instincts crucial for its survival are already functioning, including the ability to find its mother's teats and the warmth of its mother and littermates.

① The Neonatal Phase, *page 25*

❍ NEUTERING

When a male is neutered (castrated), both testicles are removed; in a female, neutering (spaying) involves removal of the ovaries and uterus. This renders the animals incapable of propagation, and they no longer produce significant amounts of sex hormones. For a male with pronounced ❍ HYPERSEXUALITY (page 266), neutering makes good sense. Bitches should be spayed if they develop pseudopregnancy after every ❍ HEAT (page 265) or if there is a predisposition to cancer of the mammary glands or metritis (inflammation of the uterus). Neutering affects only the processes and behaviors related to the reproductive instinct. It should not be used, for example, to make active dogs calmer, instead of providing them with more activity. Neutering of dogs being used as family pets is very much encouraged in the United States by the ASPCA and other organizations.

⑤ Solving Problems with Rowdy Dogs, *page 173*

❍ PACK

Wolves and other canids live in social units, so-called packs. A pack is headed by an alpha leader and wolf packs typically are headed by a mated pair. The domestic dog forms a pack with the humans with which she lives and expects an authoritative pack leader whom she can trust and look to for guidance. Anti-authoritarian training does not give a dog the stability she requires. Lacking that, all she can really do is whatever she thinks is right, and this behavior frequently is quickly described as ❍ DOMINANCE (page 262).

① The Question of Hierarchy, *page 36*

▶ PASSION FOR WORK

A dog with a passion for work has an inherently strong desire to "work" at something and dis-plays corresponding breed-specific characteristics. Thus, for sled dogs, "work" means an implicit desire to race, while for many hunting dogs it means untiringly searching for and flushing game or picking up scents. In a Border Collie, it entails pronounced herding behavior, and in protection-dog breeds, a corresponding willingness to guard and protect. There is no need to laboriously teach a dog with a passion for work what her or his tasks are; all that is necessary is to guide its existing tendencies in the right directions. If such a dog is permanently underchallenged, however—perhaps because it is kept as an "unemployed" ▶ FAMILY DOG (page 263) or is incorrectly trained—many problems can arise in everyday life.

⑦ Causes of Bad Behavior, *page 229*

▶ PEDIGREE

Dogs that come from a breed organization that is affiliated with the AKC should automatically receive a pedigree. This document lists various pieces of information, including the breeder's name and address, the kennel name, the dog's birth date and possibly microchip number and/or tattoo number, and in some cases the number and names of the dog's littermates. It also lists the names of the last four generations, along with the appropriate data, such as health information, trials, and show results. For breeds with service-dog tests, the breed type is also noted, that is, whether or not it is a performance breed, for example.

③ The Puppy Learns to Answer to Her Name, *page 76*

▶ PLAY INSTINCT

Playing is linked with curiosity and learning. When playing, dogs practice social behaviors and explore and try out all kinds of things. Puppies and young dogs play most intensely, but many dogs continue to play enthusiastically well into old age. Among wolves, adults are less apt to play and/or play in accordance with their condition in life. Play behavior varies widely among dogs. To some extent it is breed-dependent, but it also varies from one individual to another. Playing promotes bonding and also makes a good reward. For example, search-and-rescue dogs or dogs that search for drugs and the like are conditioned to a favorite toy during their training. If their work is successful, they can look forward to playing enthusiastically with this object.

⑥ Playing—What's Its Real Purpose? *page 183*

▶ POSITIVE REINFORCEMENT

Everything that rewards the dog and motivates her to exhibit a certain behavior again is described as positive reinforcement. It may be a friendly voice, as well as a treat, a toy, physical affection, or the clicker (→ page 192). For the reward to have the proper effect, it must come right on the heels (within one or two seconds) of the desirable behavior. In addition, the positive reinforcement must be so attractive to the dog that she is willing to make a real effort to obtain it.

① How Does a Dog Learn? *page 26*

▶ PREY DRIVE

This instinct is related to the ▶ HUNTING INSTINCT (page 266). It leads the dog, in response to a certain stimulus (such as movement), to seize the fleeing "prey," hold it firmly and, in the wild, ultimately to kill it. The prey drive is not equally pronounced in all dogs. But the stronger it is, the more easily it is triggered by an appropriate stimulus. A pronounced prey drive can also be linked with defending the prey. In training, this drive is put to use in different ways. For example, in a retriever, a balance between prey drive and retriever instinct is desirable, while in the training of protection dogs, emphasis is placed on having the dog fight for its prey.

⑤ Athletes, Watch Out! *page 157*

▶ PRIMARY REINFORCER

This term refers to everything that is inherently reinforcing for a dog. A typical primary reinforcer is food. For a thirsty dog, it can be water, for a water-loving dog, a swim in a stream or lake, and for a dog that loves to play, a ball or some other toy.

⑥ How Clicker Training Works, *page 192*

▶ PRIVILEGES

Alpha leaders lay claim to certain privileges, such as specified places to sleep. As these are taboo for the rest of the ▶ PACK (page 269), this is one way in which alpha leaders can make their social status clear to the other pack members. In terms of the human-dog relationship, using the sofa or bed of the human would be comparable, as would access to strategically important rooms such as the kitchen, the place where food is stored. Especially with self-confident dogs, or if problems have already arisen, you must be consistent in asserting your privileges where your pet is concerned.

① The Question of Hierarchy, *page 36*

▶ PUNISHMENT

A punishment is a penalty imposed for "wrong" behavior. The prerequisite for it, however, is that the dog must already have learned indisputably what the "right" behavior looks like. Otherwise, any action is completely incomprehensible for the dog. As "punishment" sounds quite negative; a better word might be "inhibition." We differentiate between positive punishment (something unpleasant is added, such as the ▶ MUZZLE GRIP (page 268), and negative punishment (something pleasant is taken away, such as a ball). Positive and negative refer here only to the adding and/or

taking away. A positive punishment would be used, for example, if the dog steals food from the table and at that moment a pot lid falls on the floor next to her, making a loud rattle. A negative punishment occurs, for example, when the dog is practicing fetching but makes a false start before a command is given, and a helper picks up the fetch object from the ground, so that the dog can't get it. Viewed in this way, there is no dog training without "punishment."

⑦ What to Do When Problems Arise?, *page 228*

▶ PUPPIES

Dogs less than about 16 weeks old are known as puppies. After that, the animal is a young dog until she or he is fully grown at the age of one to three years, depending on the breed.

① The Neonatal Phase, *Page 25*

▶ PUPPY LICENSE

Incorrectly, people still assume that where adult dogs are concerned, a puppy has the freedom to do whatever she wants until the age of six months. That is not true. In the wild, "puppy license" applies only to the

puppies in an adult animal's own pack. A wolf, for example, is unlikely ever to encounter puppies from another pack. Full-grown dogs behave in very different ways toward strange puppies. Some deal with them quite well, but others don't like puppies at all.

② 10 Questions about Dog Language, *page 68*

▶ RITUALISTIC FIGHTING

This type of fighting is quite common in the animal kingdom. These are ritualized fights between rivals of the same species, either to settle issues of rank or to chase away rivals during mating season. Their goal is to determine which animal is stronger, but without doing serious harm to the loser. Under unfavorable conditions, however, a ritualistic fight can escalate into a real brawl with intent to inflict harm. Then "serious" fighting begins, with the animals using their "weapons" —in the dog's case, the teeth.

⑤ The Cantankerous Dog, *page 172*

▶ SECONDARY REINFORCER

A secondary reinforcer is a stimulus that initially is neutral for the dog. Only when linked with a ▶ PRIMARY REINFORCER (page 271) does this stimulus also become a reinforcer. A typical example of a secondary positive reinforcer is the clicker (→ page 192). Its sound becomes a secondary reinforcer for the dog only when connected with food (the primary reinforcer). There are also negative secondary reinforcers, such as the rattling of the discs (→ page 226), which acquires its meaning through linkage to frustration (primary negative reinforcer).

⑥ How Clicker Training Works, *page 192*

▶ SELF-REWARDING BEHAVIORS

By engaging in self-rewarding behavior, the dog is not trying to achieve a real objective as a reward for her effort; rather, the action itself constitutes a "success" for the animal. Hunting is a good example; the pursuit itself is enjoyable for the dog—whether she captures any prey or not. Play, too, is self-rewarding, as is chewing on your valuable rug or your new shoes. Undesirable self-rewarding behavior can never be influenced by ignoring it.

① Ignoring, *page 31*

▶ SHARPNESS

In ▶ WORKING-DOG BREEDS (page 277), this refers to the dog's readiness to actively confront a threat (supposed or real). In contrast to fear-related aggressiveness, defensive aggressiveness is a desirable quality in many working-dog breeds, such as the Rottweiler and Doberman. In other breeds, however (such as the Labrador and Golden Retriever), both types of sharpness result in exclusion from breeding. A sharp dog must be handled very responsibly, since problems can easily arise in daily life, for example, if the dog feels she is being threatened.

⑤ The Cantankerous Dog, *page 172*

▶ SIGNAL

A signal is something that has acquired a very specific meaning for the dog through analogous training. It can be a verbal command, a whistle blow, a ▶ VISUAL SIGNAL (page 276), or a sound. In response to a certain signal, the dog exhibits a certain behavior; alternatively, she stops a certain behavior in response to a ▶ STOP COMMAND or signal (page 273).

② Give Clear Signals, *page 53*

▶ SIT FRONT

This refers to the dog sitting squarely in front of you after being recalled and is the best way to have your pet under control after the *come.*

Most dog trials require this behavior. It is important, however, that the dog not feel that the *sit* is being coerced or she might respond to the recall more slowly. Don't say "Sit" in a threatening way once the dog is there. Instead, make sure that she really comes quite close to you. Then she will sit almost automatically when she looks up at you, and all she needs then is a "normal" audible signal. Even a visual signal may be sufficient. Very well trained dogs that don't take off again after the *come* can also be told to assume the *heel* position right away, without an intervening *sit front*. At that point, however, every dog should *sit* at first.

③ The Command to *Come* and *Sit Front*, *page 111*

○ SNUGGLING

Snuggling promotes cohesion among pack members. It is very pronounced among puppies, for example, but pack leaders, too, like to lie pressed close together. Cuddling by dog and owner, therefore, is an important factor in bonding. Snuggling is best done after playing or a walk and in neutral territory— that is, not on the sofa or in the owner's bed.

② Communicating by Body Contact, *page 47*

○ SOCIALIZATION PHASE

It begins in the third week of life and lasts until about the sixteenth to eighteenth week. Only in this restricted period does the brain store experiences in an especially long-lasting way. Hence, it is quite important for your subsequent life together with the dog to consciously take advantage of this phase. Optimal socialization begins at the breeding facility. Socialization of the ○ FAMILY DOG (page 263) in this day and age means getting the animal used to different people and environmental stimuli, as well as laying the foundations for basic obedience and setting clear limits. Despite all socialization, however, the role of genetics must not be ignored.

Allegedly weak nerves or similar innate ○ TEMPERAMENT FLAWS (page 274) cannot be simply "socialized away." Later you can successfully build on the foundations laid in this phase by upbringing and training.

A dog retains the ability to learn all of her or his life. She or he just can't retain things as well as when she or he was a puppy.

① The Socialization Phase Begins, *page 25*

○ STOP COMMAND

A stop command tells the dog to immediately cease whatever she is doing at the moment. This is accomplished, for example, by using a ○ SIGNAL (page 272), to which the animal is conditioned by means of the startle reaction or frustration. Such a signal is given in an unemotional, businesslike manner, because it has acquired its meaning through being connected with frustration or a sudden surprise. On the other hand, you can also use other methods to convey to your four-legged friend that she must not do something: clearing your throat loudly, making growling sounds, saying "No" in a stern voice, or using some other audible signal, in combination with an appropriate look and corresponding body language.

⑦ Barking, *page 235*

○ STRONG-ARM METHODS

This term applies to training methods that use overt physical force or even pain to teach commands to a dog. They include, hitting, using prong collars, constantly yanking hard on the leash (possibly in combination with a choke collar), and dragging the dog into the *down* position by swiftly stepping on the loose leash. Strong-arm methods were fairly widespread at one time, and even today, unfortunately, are still in use at some dog training grounds.

① There's No One Way to Train a Dog, *page 15*

● TABOO ZONE

As a preventive measure, or if the dog has already established too many free spaces for itself, it is advisable to declare one area or another off limits, as a taboo zone. This might, for example, apply to the future nursery a few weeks before the baby is to be born, or to the kitchen in a household with a dog that is very aggressive in regard to food.

⑦ Upholding the First Dog's Rights, *page 216*

● TAIL

The tail is an important means of communication for our four-legged friends. It plays a role in almost every message, indicating whether the dog is alert, friendly, fearful, or trying to make an impression. In several countries (excluding the U.S.) docking the tail has been prohibited, with a few exceptions, for several years. Despite the widely held belief that a wagging tail is automatically a symbol of delight and friendliness, this gesture is primarily an indication of excitement. The rest of the dog's body language and the way in which she is wagging her tail determine the exact meaning of this behavior.

② How a Dog Shows Trust, *page 59*

● TEMPERAMENT

The temperament of a dog is determined by inherited characteristics as well as experiences. Which component accounts for what percentage, however, is debatable and probably will never be completely understood. The more strongly pronounced an inherited characteristic is, however, the less you will be able to influence it. If a puppy, for example, is very fearful and insecure in general from an early age, these qualities can't just be "socialized away." Similarly, a strong instinct to guard and protect can't be "prevented" by socialization. On the other hand, there definitely are dogs that approach everything new with an open mind and curiosity, despite ● INADEQUATE EARLY SOCIALIZATION (page 267). In any event, ensuring that the temperament of the parent animals is good is an important step. Nevertheless, the temperament of a genetically well-equipped dog can be completely ruined by mistakes in training.

① It Depends on the Breeder, *page 18*

● TEMPERAMENT FLAWS

Examples of temperament flaws are characteristics such as insecurity, fearfulness, gun-shyness, or pronounced mistrust. Here too, however, breed-specific aspects may play an additional role. For example, in ● HERD PROTECTION DOGS (page 265), mistrust is a desirable quality.

⑦ Causes of Bad Behavior, *page 229*

● TEMPERAMENT TEST

Temperament tests are given in some purebred breeders' associations of the ● AKC (page 258). For future breeding animals, passing a temperament test is mandatory in some cases. Its purpose is to determine which innate predispositions are exhibited by the dog being tested. An experienced judge of

temperament can tell what may have been deliberately instilled through training and what is "genuine." The test assesses, for example, how the dog behaves toward peaceable strangers, how well she voluntarily looks to her human partner for guidance, how she reacts in restricting or irksome situations (in tightly packed crowds of people, or lying on its back), how she acts in the presence of optical and acoustic stimuli, and how she reacts to sudden loud noises. The test also assesses whether and how the dog plays with her human partner (in some cases, also with unknown persons). In addition, certain breed-specific traits are tested, in accordance with the breed. Here, it is quite possible that characteristics that are explicitly desired in one breed will result in failure of the test by another breed.

① Where to Learn about Breeders, *page 18*

● TERRITORY

This is commonly interpreted as the area a dog regards as her sphere of interest. This normally includes the house or apartment or the land around the house or building in which the dog lives. Its boundaries are demarcated with urine marks. Depending on the strength of her territorial instinct, a dog defends her territory more or less vigorously. Some dogs also regard a certain space around them as their territory, even when they're away from home—including the car, a vacation apartment, or their immediate surroundings in an outdoor cafe or on a park bench. A pronounced territorial instinct can become problematic.

⑤ Solving Problems with Rowdy Dogs, *page 173*

● TIMING

Correct timing is extremely important in training dogs. Whether it is praise, criticism, or correction—everything must immediately follow (within a few seconds) the corresponding behavior. If not, the dog can't draw the right connection or will draw the wrong one. Dog owners frequently struggle to react quickly and accurately enough. For example, if you reward the dog with a treat for the *sit*, but you first have to dig through your pocket to find it and give it to your pet after she already is standing again and sniffing around, then you're rewarding her for the behavior that occurred last. If it rises from the *stay* and is already six feet away from the spot, and you wait until then to call her and take her back to the original site, all that takes too long. At the time she is preparing to stand up, she must hear a "No" or another familiar ● STOP COMMAND (page 273). Go quickly to her side and repeat the exercise.

① The Right Timing, *page 29*

● TRACKING

Tracking entails concentration and reliance on scent, and therefore it is a good activity for dogs. Tracking is used as a sport for working dogs and also in a hunting context. In the sport, the dog, on a long leash, does scent work. Depending on the performance category, the dogs follow trails of varying length (up to 6,000 feet) and age (up to three hours). "Age" refers to the time between the laying of the scent and the search. In a hunting context, using a check cord or long lead, the hunter's dog follows a short, straight, heavy blood trail of 10 to 20 feet with a treat at the end (any type of blood will do, whether from game or a meat processing plant). In this way the dog learns to accompany the hunter in searching, even in unfavorable conditions, for game that has been struck or wounded.

⑥ Skilled Trackers, *page 205*

⬤ TRAINING COURSES

⬤ DOG SCHOOLS (page 262) and dog clubs offer training courses from basic to advanced. The goal of these programs should be primarily to give the dog's owner a foundation for dealing correctly with the animal—not just to demonstrate how to teach the dog exercises like the *sit* or the *down* from a purely "technical" standpoint. Usually the two-legged partner has to learn much more than the dog.

③ Professional Training Courses, *page 125*

⬤ TRIALS AND TESTS

There are a great many trials that provide meaningful training opportunities for active canines. Some are tailored to the typical characteristics of a certain breed, such as sheepdog trials for Border Collies, so-called working tests for retrievers, or races for Greyhounds. In addition, there are field trials for dogs that are used in hunting. To undergo such training, a dog frequently must have a pedigree that is recognized by the ⬤ AKC (page 258). Generally, the offerings of dog sports clubs are open to all dogs, though tests must first determine what is suitable or not for each individual dog. This applies to protection service in particular.

① Where to Learn about Breeders, *page 18*

⬤ UNCONDITIONED STIMULUS

An unconditioned stimulus or "key" stimulus is one that triggers a certain reaction in a dog (or another living being) without special conditioning. Thus, it is an innate trigger mechanism. A typical example is salivation when the presence of food is perceived. Another example is the triggering of prey-capture behavior by movement.

① How Does a Dog Learn? *page 26*

⬤ VARIABLE REWARDS

When a dog learns new things by means of positive motivation with treats or some other attractive reward, this is species-appropriate, since a dog does only what benefits him or her. Frequent repetitions and systematically structured exercises help ensure that the dog reliably retains what it has learned. Next, you should stop rewarding the dog every time he or she does something correctly. Make the rewards variable, that is, occasional. Then your pet's level of expectation will remain high. Also, don't bring out the reward until the exercise has been performed. You don't want the dog to do something only if you're holding a treat in your hand—if that's the case the dog is conditioning you, rather than the other way around.

③ Cutting Back on Treats, *page 84*

⬤ VISUAL SIGNALS

Dogs communicate mainly through a sophisticated body language. Therefore, visual signals are useful in training dogs. Incomprehensibly, however, they usually are not permitted in companion and ⬤ WORKING-DOG TESTS (page 277) or trials. In other areas, including agility, shepherd dog trials, or hunting, they are commonly used and often essential. Visual signals are given with the hand and should make sense in terms of body language. That is, it would be hard for a dog to understand if the visual signal for the *down* was an upward movement of the hand instead of a downward movement toward the ground, as usual. Visual signals should be given very clearly and unambiguously, especially when a dog is first being trained.

③ How to Introduce Visual Signals, *page 102*

▶ WORKING-DOG BREEDS

Strictly speaking, working-dog breeds actually include all breeds that are developed or trained for a certain type of "useful work" (that is, for hunting, herding animals, pulling sleds, guarding property, and so forth). That is commonly interpreted to include breeds such as the German Shepherd, Rottweiler, Doberman, Giant Schnauzer, Hovawart, and others—that is, breeds that participate in the Versatility Test for Working Dogs (VPG).

① What Breed Should I Choose? *page 20*

▶ WORKING-DOG TESTS

In working and sporting dog clubs, certain tests are offered. They follow a strict pattern and focus more on athletic aspects than on everyday matters. They include the Companion Dog Test (BH) and the so-called Versatility Test for Working Dogs. It consists of three disciplines: tracking, obedience, and protection. In addition, there are special tracking and endurance tests.

⑥ Obedience, *page 202*

Index

Useful Addresses, Web Sites, and Literature

The American Kennel Club
260 Madison Avenue
New York, NY 10016
(212) 696-8200
www.akc.org

The Canadian Kennel Club
100-89 Skyway Avenue
Etobicoke, Ontario M9W6R4
Canada (416) 675-5511

United Kennel Club
100 E. Kilgore Road
Kalamazoo, MI 49002-5584
(296) 343-9020
www.ukcdogs.com

American College of Veterinary Behaviorists
Texas A&M University
College Station, TX 77843
www.veterinarybehaviorists.org

American Dog Breeders Association (ADBA)
P.O. Box 1771
Salt Lake City, UT 84110
(801) 936-7513

American Mixed Breed Obedience Registry
179 Niblick Road #113
Paso Robles, CA 93446
(805) 226-9275
www.amborusa.org

American Veterinary Society of Animal Behavior
Avsab@yahoo.com

Animal Behavior Society
Indiana University
2611 East 10th Street
Bloomington, IN 47408
(812) 856-5541
www.animalbehavior.org

Association of Pet Trainers
5096 San Road S.E.
Iowa City, IA 52240-8217
(800) PET-DOGS (738-3647)
www.apdt.com

National Association of Dog Obedience Instructors
PMB 369
729 Grapevine Highway
Hurst, TX 76054-2085
www.nadoi.org

AKC Canine Good Citizen Program
5580 Centerview Drive
Raleigh, NC 27526
(919) 816-3637
www.akc.org/love/cgclindex.cfm

American Temperament Test Society
P.O. Box 4093
St. Louis, MO 63136
(314) 869-6103
www.atts.org

Therapy Dogs International
88 Bartley Road
Flanders, NJ 07836
(973) 252-9800
www.tdi-dog.org

PERIODICALS

AKC Gazette
Subscriptions: 919-233-9767

Dog Fancy
P.O. Box 53264
Boulder, CO 80322-3264

Dog World
29 North Wacker Drive
Chicago, IL 60606

Ott-Lead
204 Lewis Street
Canastota, NY 13032
800-241-7619

BOOKS

American Kennel Club. *The Complete Dog Book.* New York: Howell Book House, 1992.

Ammen, Amy. *Training in No Time: An Expert's Approach to Effective Dog Training for Hectic Life Styles.* New York: Howell Book House, 1995.

Bailey, Gwen. *The Well Behaved Dog.* Hauppauge, New York: Barron's Educational Series, Inc. 1998.

Bauman, Diane. *Beyond Basic Dog Training.* New York: Howell Book House, 1991.

Davis, Kathy Diamond. *Responsible Dog Ownership.* New York: Howell Book House, 1994.

Dunbar, Ian. *How to Teach a New Dog Old Tricks,* 2nd Edition. Oakland, California: James and Kenneth Publishers, 1991.

Ludwig, Gerd. *Sit! Stay! Train Your Dog the Easy Way.* Hauppauge, New York: Barron's Educational Series, Inc., 2007.

Pryor, Karen. *Don't Shoot the Dog.* Waltham, Massachusetts: Sunshine Books, Inc., 1984.

Taunton, Stephanie J. and Cheryl S. Smith. *The Trick Is in the Training.* Hauppauge, New York: Barron's Educational Series, Inc., 1998.

Volhard, Jack and Wendi Volhard. *The Canine Good Citizen: Every Dog Can Be One,* 2nd Edition. New York: Howell Book House, 1997.

DOG LIABILITY INSURANCE

Almost all insurance companies also offer liability insurance policies for dogs.

Important Note

The guidelines provided in this manual apply to normally developed young animals from a good breeding facility, that is, to healthy animals of sound temperament. Anyone who acquires a full-grown dog must be aware that it already has been influenced in important ways by humans. The potential new owner must observe the dog very closely, including the way it behaves toward humans; he or she should also take a look at the previous owner. If the dog comes from a pet shelter, the facility may be able to provide information about the dog's origin and idiosyncrasies. There are dogs whose behavior exhibits obvious effects of bad experiences with humans; they may also have a tendency to bite. Even with well-trained dogs and carefully supervised dogs, there is a possibility that they will damage other people's property or even cause accidents. An insurance policy with adequate coverage is urgently recommended in any event.

The Author

Katharina Schlegl-Kofler is an experienced dog trainer and a recognized expert in matters of species-appropriate care and keeping of dogs. Her background includes many years of intense involvement with dogs and regular participation in workshops on the topics of dog training and behavioral research. For many years she has held successful puppy classes and training courses for dogs of all breeds, and these programs have met with enormous popular response. She is the author of several successful books on dogs.

The Photographer

Christine Steimer, a trained photographer and a dog owner herself, specializes in photographing domestic animals and pets. She works for international publishers, specialized journals, and advertising agencies. With the following exceptions, all the photos in this book were taken by Christine Steimer.

Conny Expose/Frank Aschermann: front cover
Oliver Giel: 65, 141, 151-1, 160-1, 160-2, 161, 196
Juniors/Steimer: 7 bottom
Tatjana Prawitz: 274
Reinhard-Tierfotos: 39
Ulrike Schanz: 30, 175, 191-3, 191-5
TBK-media: 42, 179 bottom, 207
Monika Wegler: 38, 126, 191-4, 221, 258, 266, 277

Acknowledgments

I am grateful to the firm Hunter Hunde- und Reitsportartikel GmbH in Leopoldshöhe for the Bucchi Bag hold-all and leash (page 128) that appears in the photograph.

First published in the United States and Canada in 2008 by Barron's Educational Series, Inc.

Published originally under the title *Das grosse GU Praxishandbuch Hunde-Erziehung*

© Copyright 2006 by Gräfe und Unzer Verlag GmbH, München.

English translation copyright © 2008 by Barron's Educational Series, Inc.

All inquiries should be addressed to:
Barron's Educational Series, Inc.
250 Wireless Boulevard
Hauppauge, NY 11788

Library of Congress Control Number: 2006940053

ISBN-13: 978-0-7641-6070-7
ISBN-10: 0-7641-6070-2

Printed in China
9 8 7

A Word about Pronouns

Many dog lovers feel that the pronoun "it" is not appropriate when referring to a pet that can be such a wonderful part of our lives. For this reason, we have used the pronouns "he" or "she" in alternating chapters to refer to a particular dog. However, for solely editorial reasons, we have used "it" in situations where the text refers to either a male *or* female. This was done simply to avoid the clumsiness of "he or she" in many places, and is in no way meant to lessen the value of animals in the world.

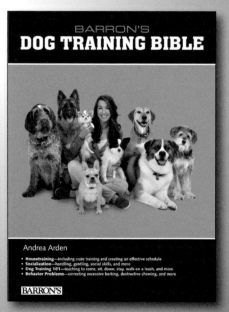